FOREX PRICE ACTION
SCALPING

an in-depth look into the field
of professional scalping

Bob Volman

LIGHT TOWER
PUBLISHING

Published by: Light Tower Publishing

ISBN 978-90-9026411-0

ProRealTime charts used with permission of ProRealTime.com

infoFPAS@gmail.com

Excerpts of the book can be downloaded from:

www.infoFPAS.wordpress.com

Disclaimer: This publication is solely designed for the purposes of information and education. Neither the publisher nor author shall be liable for any loss, claims or damage incurred by any person as a consequence of the use of, or reliance on, the contents herein.

Table of Contents

Preface

Ever since the days of old, the markets have suffered no shortage of volunteers ready to sacrifice themselves on the ever-growing battlefields of supply and demand. Fortune-hunters, plungers, gamblers, misfits, and a motley crew of optimists and adventurers, all have roamed, and will continue to roam, the marketplace in search for quick-and-easy gains. Yet no other venture has led to more carnage of capital, more broken dreams and shattered hopes, than the act of reckless speculation.

Strangely enough, despite the ill-boding facts and the painful fate of all those who perished before him, the typical trader still shows up on the scene wholly unprepared. And those who do take the trouble to build themselves a method, in most instances seem to only postpone their inevitable fall. On the slippery slope of the learning curve, things can get pretty unpleasant and many never recover from the tuition bills presented on the job. Not surprisingly, this has led to an endless debate on the actual feasibility of profitable trading, in which skeptics and romantics fight out a battle of their own.

To the skeptic, no doubt, the glorified image of a consistently profitable trader seems highly suspect. After all, the only ones who have always prospered in the trading field, at the expense of the ignorant, are brokers, vendors and clever marketeers. And if it is already hard to picture himself a proficient long-term investor surviving the odds, then, surely, the idea of a consistently profitable scalper must be bordering on the idiotic. To see the skeptic's point, one only needs to follow the route of common logic: in a line of business where so many traders have tried, and failed, to successfully trade the long-term charts, those venturing out on the miniature frames can only be setting themselves up for an even uglier fate, and a faster one at that.

And indeed, the shorter the time frame, the more erratic the moves on the chart; and with spreads and commissions cutting deep into a scalper's average trade, the odds seem stacked against the enterprise from the very onset. Success stories are few and far between and it's hard to not take note of the sobering statistics that appear to confirm all reservations, at least way more than defy them.

That being said, skeptics and statistics, of course, should never demoralize the dedicated. Scalping the charts profitably on a consistent basis is by no means an illusion. Nor does it have to take years to acquire the necessary skills. It is done every day again by many traders all over the markets, and it can be done by anyone who is determined to educate himself properly and diligently in all aspects of the field. The true issue is not the feasibility of profitable scalping but simply the quality of one's education.

Even so, scalping may not be for everyone. If nothing else, this book could be an excellent way to find out. Its sole objective is to show the reader all there is to know about the profession to effectively take on the job himself. Countless charts, setups and trade examples will be presented to fully ingrain the necessary techniques into the mind.

The contract of focus in all of the coming chapters will be the eur/usd currency pair. To a nimble scalper, this instrument is an absolute delight. It offers highly repetitive intraday characteristics, a low dealing spread and is accessible to even the smallest of traders; however, since price action principles are quite universal, not too many adjustments would have to be made to take the method to another market with similar volatility and attractive trading costs. In that respect, this guide may serve many non-Forex traders as well.

The benefits of scalping are plenty and speak for themselves. Just one single chart. No fancy indicators. One-click in and out. Everything preset. And opportunities abound in an almost repetitive loop.

Have a look at the example below. Figure P.1 is a snapshot impression of what a scalper's chart of the eur/usd can look like. The vertical axis shows the price of the instrument; the horizontal axis displays the passing of time and the curved line in the chart is an exponential moving average, the only indicator allowed. The boxes encapsulate some of the price action patterns that we will get to discuss later on.

Figure P.1 In just a little under an hour, the market offered an alert scalper numerous textbook trades.

To build a solid foundation beneath a scalping method, it will not suffice to merely deal with the technical side of trade selection. We have to examine all aspects of the profession from every possible angle so as to filter potentially disruptive elements completely out of the equation.

Each of the coming chapters will take on a part of the journey. We will delve into the specifics of chart selection, price behavior, pattern recognition, favorable and unfavorable markets, setups, entries and exits, targets and stops, traps and tricks, psychological issues, accounting matters—basically anything that comes to pass in the field of professional scalping.

Whether a beginning trader, a struggling one, or even a veteran in other fields of speculation, I sincerely hope this book will be enjoyed by all and that within its pages the necessary information is found to be able to scalp one's way through the market for many profitable years to come. This work will not insult the reader's intelligence by showing him all kinds of stuff that do not reflect the reality of trading. There is no plowing through endless chapters of meaningless babble and industry gobbledygook. *Forex Price Action Scalping* truly *is* about scalping. It is written by a trader at heart, and at all times with the aspiring trader in mind.

Free excerpts of the book can be downloaded from:

www.infoFPAS.wordpress.com

The Basics of Scalping

Chapter 1

Trading Currencies

Since the advent of high-speed electronic trading platforms, it has never been easier to set up an online account to join the daily tug-o-war in the foreign exchange. Little demand is made in terms of capital requirements and even less on the matter of proficiency. Pick a broker, wire some funds, set up a chart and one could be trading in less than an hour.

As straightforward as this may sound, behind the curtains of online currency trading hides an immensely complicated network of central banks, institutional organizations, investment corporations, hedge funds and global market operators, all doing business with each other in amounts that simply defy imagination.

The foreign exchange resembles in no way the average stock market or futures pit where all shares and contracts are traded orderly in one place; it is literally a melting pot of over a million participants, big and small, scattered all over the globe, trading in every time zone, and it is well beyond comprehension how all this activity is meticulously tracked, processed and ultimately transfigured into the dealing quotes on everybody's trading desk.

The Forex markets spring to life when the currencies are compared to one another. Hence the so-called *currency pairs*. Barring the occasional exception, most countries allow their national currencies to be freely traded against other currencies, which can result in some pretty exotic combinations. There is no point in trying to figure out the reason why the market at any given moment shows preference for one currency over another. It could be monetary obligations, fundamental prospects, interest rate decisions, fiscal policies, hedging purposes, ordinary tactics—basically anything could cause the flow of money to shift from one side to another.

As much as this may bear little relevance to the small independent scalper, he needs to understand that he will be up against some of the mightiest opponents in the business. To level the playing field to an acceptable degree, he has to operate under conditions that will not put him at an immediate disadvantage. That means he has to find himself a broker that deals him fair prices.

It is no secret that brokers are often regarded as a necessary evil and when it comes to choosing one, the options are just as plentiful as they are obscure. It is almost impossible to find a company with unblemished reputation. Freezing platforms, widened spreads, failed executions, terrible fills, requotes, hostile helpdesks, funds gone missing—these are but a handful of complaints that pop up left and right. And indeed, doing business with a shady company can be quite a roller coaster ride. It should be stated, though, that broker experience has improved considerably in recent years as more stringent rules and regulations have forced the industry to shape up.

There are basically two ways for brokers to go about their business. They either offer the pairs to be traded at their current value in the market and for this service demand a commission, or they waive that commission in favor of marking up the spread. This is the somewhat controversial practice of allowing both buyer and seller to trade through their system at a less favorable price than the actual quote of the underlying pair. The difference is pocketed by the broker.

Accepting the latter concept can be quite a tricky venture, not in the least since this mark-up tends to be subject to rather questionable flexibility. It is not uncommon for a broker to lure traders into opening an account by advertising acceptable dealing spreads, only to adjust these spreads disadvantageously in a live trading environment. Needless to say, this could severely compromise a trader's plan of attack, if not fully disrupt it. The scalper in particular will be seriously affected. After all, he is the one paying the dreaded spread many times a day.

Still, it is safe to assume that the vast majority of independent traders are signed up with this type of company, the so-called retail broker, and for good reason. Whereas the commission type broker targets the more professional (or more capitalized) trader, the retail broker, in general, entertains a policy that welcomes all kinds of customers and even provides them with cost-free and very user-friendly platforms to boot.

However, trading through these brokers does mean that one is not connected to the real volume of the market. Their platforms are essentially sophisticated copycats, mimicking the action created by the professional currency traders. This is not necessarily a bad way to trade, though, particularly when still operating on the smaller scale. When dealing with a reliable broker, it doesn't really matter whether the orders are sent to the market or not, as long as they are filled smoothly and correctly. Bear in mind, the Forex markets are not located on a centralized exchange, so, in a way, each and every order is a virtual one, true volume or not.

Since the spread, by far, puts a heavy toll on any scalper's daily business, the method in this book is designed around the one currency pair that should be able to meet all the necessary requirements of a tradable instrument: the immensely popular eur/usd contract. In terms of quotation, intraday opportunities and repetitive characteristics, this pair simply has no equal.

The aspiring scalper is advised, however, to only trade this instrument when dealt a spread of no more than 1 *pip* (price interest point) per round-turn. In the scalping business, it is a fine line between a winning strategy and a losing proposition, and that line may easily be crossed to the wrong side when the costs to participate surpass the 1 pip mark. If a broker cannot offer a scalper a bearable spread 99 percent of the time, it is best to look elsewhere. Even brokers advertising zero spreads in exchange for a commission should be carefully monitored. Reality has shown that one can still expect to pay half a pip in spread and another couple of pipettes (tenths of a pip) in commission. On some of the other pairs this may be the better deal but on the eur/

usd it usually boils down to about the same full pip spread per round-turn as with the no-commission model.

Despite the obvious need for caution when selecting a broker, there is no call for paranoia. The days of the scandalous companies residing on tax-friendly islands in the middle of the ocean are virtually gone. Nowadays, most funds are secured, platforms appear fast and stable and spreads are tightening more and more across the board. Almost every respectable broker will offer a 1 pip spread on the high and mighty eur/usd pair, or else they'd lose customers pretty fast. But do take time to select. Download as much demo platforms as your screens can handle, check the order type functions for ease of use and make sure they can be set to one-click mode. Above all, carefully scrutinize their spreads for at least a number of days. It's all part of the job.

Many readers, no doubt, will have already gone through this process, one way or another, but those new to Forex are strongly recommended to diligently check out the available options and not just fall for hype and flashy looking platforms. It is vital to understand that broker platforms not merely facilitate one's trading ventures, they literally form a lifeline between death and survival in the markets. In order to fully concentrate on the task of scalping there has got to be total trust in the speed and accuracy with which the orders are handled. Nothing can be so disruptive and detrimental to one's peace of mind as a low quality platform or a malevolent broker in the back.

Once a scalper has set up his account, wired over some funds and decided on his market to trade, he now has to craft himself a chart to trade from. In our next chapter, we will look into the matter of setting up this one special chart that should be able to serve a scalper's needs and wishes perfectly, all through the day. And everyday again.

Chapter 2

The Tick Chart

Anyone who has ever picked up a book on Forex will surely have come across the typical bombast of how the volume in the eur/usd pair dwarfs that of all other financial markets combined. The fact that this market is the most actively traded instrument on the face of the earth is often used as a sales pitch by clever marketeers in the brokerage industry. But sheer numbers alone should not inspire traders to venture out in the currency game.

A more crucial factor to consider, apart from the mandatory tight spread, is the way an instrument behaves price technically on the chart. Within his frame of choice, the scalper needs to see the typical characteristics of a tradable market: an acceptable number of intraday moves, repetition in behavioral patterns, buildup before breaks, pullbacks, breakouts, trends, ranges and the like. In other words, a very technical market that meets the demands of a technical trader. Not too many currency pairs will do. The eur/usd pair, however, does not fail to oblige. With an average daily range of close to a 150 pip, the intraday moves on the chart are highly exploitable from the long as well as the short side and there appear to be plenty of opportunities in almost any session.

Of course, there are many ways to go about one's trading and strategies and tactics are probably just as plentiful as there are traders around. Most any method, when sound, will have at least incorporated all the universal concepts of crowd behavior and price action principles, as well as a specified plan to take on the chart from a more personalized angle. It is important to understand, though, that trading in general, and scalping in particular, is not a hobby or a game that one can pick up by flipping through a couple of charts. Aspiring scalpers who look upon the profession of trading as a get-rich-quick scheme will soon come to realize the folly of it and not uncommonly after having wasted a large amount of their capital in the disheartening process of getting-poor-quicker. As any struggling trader may tell, developing a strategy on a technical chart is one thing, taking that strategy to the market is quite another. As we will soon discuss, there is a lot more to it than initially meets the eye and all aspects of it demand equal attention.

Indisputably, the beating heart of any scalping operation is the technical chart. All a scalper ever needs in terms of information can be found within a single graph. Since there is little sense in trading intraday movements on fundamental vision, an aspiring scalper has no option but to get acquainted with all the specifics of price action charting.

But what chart should he look at? The time frames to choose from are practically limitless and surely there are pros and cons to each and every one of them. In a way, deciding on the source of information is a fine balancing act between opting for a chart fast enough to deliver multiple opportunities throughout the day and one slow enough to still bear technical significance. Although all charts relentlessly monitor the everlasting battle between supply and demand, each frame will also have its own individual pulse. This can be measured by the length of the average moves, the buildup of pressures leading up to the breaks, the presence of tradable patterns and even by the way most classic tricks and traps will play themselves out. Once a trader decides on his chart, it is crucial to commit to it, to study it inside out, to learn how it breaths, moves and dances, to understand its beat.

A great chart to explore is the 70-tick. This is the sole chart we will be focusing on in all of the coming chapters and it is actually not a time frame in the usual sense. It forms a new bar after every 70 transactions (ticks) that take place among traders—regardless of volume—and on the eur/usd this should easily print a couple of thousand of bars in the course of a day. Sometimes this frame resembles a 30-second chart, but when volume picks up, it takes on a life of its own.

Note: Not all charting packages offer the adjustable tick chart setting (x-ticks), so it is recommended to check this out before subscribing to a provider. Furthermore, the actual tick count is dependent on the data feed connected to the chart. Since the decentralized nature of the foreign exchange does not allow for an absolute transaction count, volume data may differ from one provider to the next. The reader may have to experiment with the proper tick number in his personal graphics to produce a chart that approximates the setting of the ProRealTime charting package used in this book. This is no reason for worry, though. Close is close enough. In fact, if the tick count in all of our charts was set to something like 65 or 75, it really wouldn't have altered the patterns, nor their tradability, much. Within another package, however, the number may have to be set to something like 40 or even to a 100 or more. It all depends on how charting companies filter their incoming data. When comparing your bars to the ones is this book, look closely at the time scale below the chart and monitor also the average height of the bars. A calm market will show most of them in the range of 2 to 4 pip; a vivid trend may easily exceed that, but usually not for long. A good trick is to set the tick number to a level that resembles a regular 30-second time frame chart; if so, then you are very close. Bear in mind that Asian sessions (more or less from 02:00 to 10:00 in the examples presented) show substantially less bars per hour on a tick chart than do the European or American sessions; it is best to figure out the tick setting in the more active phases of the market.

Arguably, tick charts possess a distinctive advantage over time charts, primarily because the patterns in them are more compact in shape, which makes them somewhat easier to identify. When trading is slow, a tick chart will not print that many useless bars that flatten out the chart and take up unnecessary space; when trading is fast, it gives one all the more to work with.

This 70-tick setting is not a magical number, nor is it the best chart setting you will ever come across. Because such a setting simply does not exist. Choosing the source of information is a personal matter and depends very much on strategy particulars. Above all, we need a chart from which to time our trades with sniper precision. In that respect, the 70-tick mode captures the scalping beat of the eur/usd pair with remarkable accuracy. At times, following the bars on their march through the chart is like watching a brigade of colorful majorettes doing their routine. In many instances, these price moves may seem rather chaotic, complex or at least highly diverse, but to an observant eye the actual variables are quite limited. In the end, there are only so many moves choreographically possible before repetition sets in. It is this repetitive tendency of price behavior that we must try to anticipate in order to cleverly time our way into the market or to find our way out.

The 70-tick mode is a fast chart, but not so fast as to be completely disconnected from the more classic time frames used by plenty of others in the field. This is essential because we need those other players to come in after us to bring our trades to target. Basically, a clever scalper wants the majority of other traders to see the same thing, ride the same trends, catch the same pullbacks and trade the same breaks; he just wants to beat them to it.

This one single chart should be able to produce all the information necessary to make sound scalping decisions. Apart from a single moving average there will be no indicators messing up the screen. There is no need to know yesterday's high or low, whether the market is in an up or downtrend on a bigger frame, or if it is running into some kind of major support or resistance level from the day before. In fact, in most instances, it is totally irrelevant what happened a few hours back. A chart that shows about one and a half hour of price bars in one go should definitely suffice. The more information a scalper tries to cram into his chart, the more all this data will start to conflict. In order not to freeze up in the line of duty, it is best to not complicate the decision-making process, but rather to simplify it.

As for the technical side of our entries, there will only be seven individual setups to get acquainted with. These patterns form the core of the scalping method about to be presented. Each setup will be discussed in full detail, along with many examples taken from actual market activity. Entries and exits of trades will be pointed out precisely to the pip. All of these entry patterns will have both a bullish and a bearish version and serve to set up either a long or a short trade. Trend, countertrend, ranges, everything can be traded. When the objective is only a quick scalp, why discriminate. Allowing oneself the freedom to trade anything at anytime, that is the prerogative of scalping.

Chapter 3

Scalping as a Business

No matter how many years a trader has been active in the markets, the undeniable marvel of a price pattern coming to fruition will never cease to amaze the technical eye. One might think that the hundreds of books on crowd sentiment and technical analysis over the years would have fully destroyed the tradability of price action patterns, but nothing could be further from the truth. Just open up any chart, in any time frame, of any instrument, and before long the phenomenon unfolds.

These price moves are solely the result of traders with opposing opinions fighting it out in the marketplace. There are only two groups to distinguish: the *bulls*, thinking the market will go up, and the *bears*, thinking the market will go down. It is irrelevant whether they are in it for a short ride or a long ride, whether they are trapping other traders or showing true directional preference, whether they will fight till the end or betray their companions by joining the other team. The only thing that truly moves prices is their actual buying and selling of contracts at the present moment in time. If one group is more aggressive than the other, price will travel in favor of aggression.

It is widely believed that the activity in the chart is sending out clear signals as to who is currently toppling who in the market. There would be little point in technical trading if that was not the case. But that leaves us with a rather interesting question: If all these moves and patterns are so well-documented and their implications essentially unambiguous, why then is it so hard to succeed in the trading game? And even if the readability of the market was a false assumption and prices were completely random, rendering any strategy practically useless, why don't we see more traders break even instead of blowing their accounts with such laborious zeal.

We can safely state that at the core of a typical trader's misery lies a very simple fact that is often overlooked. The typical trader does not look upon his trading as a business. As a consequence, he approaches the market without a sound business plan. This is a classic and very common mistake that, strangely enough, somehow seems to come with the territory. In almost any other field, a sloppy attitude towards one's own profession will quickly stand corrected. Banks will not grant credit without seeing a proper business plan; partners will not hook up when confronted with a flaky organization; if one carries a flimsy product, customers will soon play judge and jury. Yet when it comes to trading, the freedom is overwhelming, the anonymity complete. A trader could simply decide not to take any responsibility at all, to hide himself completely in a make-believe world, to deviate at whim from whatever rules he laid out for himself and not give it a moment's thought. He has no customers to satisfy, no partners to answer to, no banks to please. As long as there are still funds left to trade, it is just so easy to entertain the illusion that things will turn around, that good times will come and that eventually the inevitable profits will come falling from the sky.

A trader should consider himself fortunate to recognize this absence of structure, and the self-foolery it brings about, before his funds run out. Interviews with top traders have discovered that even these widely acclaimed masters had to learn many of their valuable lessons the hard way and not having a proper plan was usually one of them.

But what exactly constitutes a proper plan in trading? Is it a bunch of rules that one should never break? Is it rigid formula to abide by? Is it a checklist to run before each and every trade?

Unfortunately, this is not so easy to answer. What works well for one trader may prove detrimental to another. Many professionals will surely have built themselves a method that leaves absolutely no room for freehand interpretation, whereas plenty of others would completely freeze up in such an inflexible environment. However, we can be certain that successful traders do share at least one common trait: they take their trading very seriously. We could say they have acquired the mindset of a regular business entrepreneur. It means they have invested in education, know their field well and do not indulge in unrealistic expectations. Since they understand the long-term aspect of their enterprise, they seldom get caught up in the heat of the moment. They are confident in what they are doing and as a result have no trouble putting capital at risk. They fully understand the cost of doing business and accept the losses that come with the job. They will not walk around with a checklist of dos and don'ts in their pockets, nor will they be constantly anxious about their capital at work or feel the need to check their bank accounts to see if they are up or down on the day. Even through times of adversity, they will remain calm and focused and always have the bigger scheme of things in mind. They operate from a structured frame. They are businessmen.

Although we may not be able to tell what exactly drives a trader to the markets, we can safely assume that very few will be attracted by the prospect of earning a living in yet another line of work. Many will have fled the monotonous drum of whatever they were previously engaged in, either discontented with their daily routine or with the wages earned. In search for a better life or income, many come to the markets accompanied by fantasies and dreams and, no doubt, a glorified vision of what it means to be a trader. Needless to say, the majority of them arrive totally unprepared. They may have picked up an introductory course on technical analyses and maybe got themselves all excited about the surprising simplicity of it all. Look at these patterns. Anybody can do this. Never mind the statistics. All the others must be fools. And with the fearless mind of the ignorant they burst upon the trading scene.

To avoid this very common route, or to escape it when already trapped, requires a totally different mentality. Without question, the single most important factor contributing to either success or failure in the markets is a trader's ability to distinguish fiction from reality. Much more than technical skill, mental health accounts for the decision-making process to run smoothly or not. But even people who have proven themselves fully competent and rational in other fields and vocations, when thrust into the markets, they are just as prone to emotional folly, false perception and irrational behavior as any ordinary fool. Such is the treacherous nature of speculation. In this line of work, one cannot depend on former achievements or powerful personal traits. When exposed to the markets, all previous images of the self can crumble in a very short space of time.

In a way, this process of self-destruction can be very beneficial. It is even argued that in order to ever reach the desired rationale of the master, a trader first has to pay the obligatory visit to the very depths of desperation and emotional despondency. If strong enough to survive and rise from the ashes of the self, he can then reinvent himself from scratch and emerge as a trader who looks upon the profession in a complete different light.

At some point in their careers, most traders, one way or another, will have to deal with this process and it may not be a pretty one, nor will it be pleasurable on the psyche. When dragged through this transitory stage, a disconcerted trader may deeply question all he knew about himself and even wonder if he is cut out for the job. It is all part and parcel of this wondrous business that can bring such generous rewards and misery alike.

It would be out of place for anyone not thoroughly trained in the psychological field to pretend expertise on the mysterious ways of the mind. All that can be offered within these pages is a personal take on these matters as seen through the eyes of someone who has traveled the rocky path himself. Even when dealing with the technical aspects, this guide serves no other purpose than that. Therefore, throughout this entire work, all relevant issues, whether technical or psychological, will be addressed from a very practical perspective.

But addressing just these two matters will not complete our journey into the realm of professional scalping. The viability of our method would be seriously compromised if we did not dig into the virtues of clever accounting as well. In a later stage of the book, we will take on this very crucial side of the business, in which the essentials of volume, risk-control and account buildup are extensively discussed. We will see how it is possible to substantially run up a small account, even when marginally profitable across the board. The aspiring scalper who is truly capable of looking upon his trading as a business will find this chapter most promising.

We will start out our journey by looking at the technical aspects first. The next chapter will take up the particulars of trade objective, damage control and order types. In a number of chapters after that we will run through all of the setups that form the basis of our technical approach. From then on, we will delve into the finesses of trade management, and further on into those of proper accounting.

Chapter 4

Target, Stop and Orders

Let us look realistically at the possibilities within a single scalping day. Many readers new to the ways of the faster chart will be anxious to know what kind of profits can be expected on a daily basis should one ever reach that pleasurable state of mastery. The answer to that is very straightforward. In trading, it is foolhardy to *expect* anything, so we best not go that route. Similarly, it would be silly to think one can simply switch on one's trading platform in the morning and start scalping away. At all times, the price action in the chart needs to align itself in a favorable way before we can even begin to think of trading a particular setup for profit. This holds up for any chart, regardless of time frame or instrument. On a scalping chart like the 70-tick, it may take minutes for something to set itself up, or it may take hours. To a smart scalper it is all the same, because he has no need for a trade. He will be able to idly watch the market from the sidelines, for hours on end if need be, and be totally okay with that. At other times, he will fire off his trades in quick succession, exploiting every possible opportunity a favorable market may present.

On balance, the 70-tick chart will offer numerous opportunities throughout the day. This tick frame is carefully chosen and it can serve a trader excellently in trending conditions as well as in slow and ranging ones. When planning a trade, however, it is of crucial significance to opt for a reasonable profit target that should be obtainable within the length of a typical move. Also, to not have the mandatory 1 pip spread weigh too heavily on our trades, we have to choose a minimum target that sufficiently offsets these costs without compromising the likelihood of it being reached. We also have to take our protective stop into consideration. Preferably, we will like to see it set as close to the entry as possible, but not so close as to run a risk of constantly getting hit before our position has time to prosper.

Obviously, these are matters to consider before delving into the heat of the market and they are best taken up as a rigid part of the method that is not to be tampered with. To neutralize the ever-present demons of fear and greed, it makes sense to prefer hard targets over adjustable ones. Many trading strategies are designed around the latter, though. The objective, no doubt, is to reap as much profit from a favorable market as possible. This may present a trader with the occasional huge winner, but more often than not, the market will turn sour on the trade and demand back a large part, if not more, of earlier profit. Naturally, there are ways to protect a profitable position with an adjustable stop. But that may cut short the proceeds prematurely. In the end, it is all a matter of choice and much of it depends on time frame and a trader's ability to cope with volatility and setbacks. It should be no surprise, though, that most *scalping* strategies are not geared towards catching that occasional huge winner but more towards reaping small profits from the market on a regularly basis throughout the day. In any case, our settings should not just reflect our personal desires; they have to comply with what is technically obtainable within the span of a typical price move on our 70-tick chart.

The following settings have proven their value over time and they are used in all of the examples discussed in this scalping method without exception. The target on each trade is a non-adjustable one and set to 10 pip of profit. Likewise, the stop is also set at a 10 pip distance from entry, but it is adjustable in the direction of the target only; either to close out a losing trade with minimal damage, or to close out a profitable trade that has lost its validity and needs to be scratched. Certainly, this will not prevent a scalper from getting fully stopped out on occasion, nor will it prevent him from exiting a trade that would have been a winner had he not hit the close-out button. Regardless of these outcomes, there is a fine technique that could be applied to help a trader decide on the proper course of action. In the section on Trade Management, we will deal with the subtleties of the so-called *tipping point of trade validity*. It is an exit technique that allows us to time our way out of a trade with the same precision as we plan to enter one.

Next to these price technical settings, we have to decide on the matter of volume per trade. This is where the currency market, more than any other, provides excellent possibilities. Whereas many stock or futures brokers demand a minimum commission to enter a position, making it rather expensive for the smaller trader, in currency trading the costs of stepping in are the same for both small and big participants in the sense that they are derived as a percentage of one's volume. A 1 pip spread on a full eur/usd contract of 100,000 units will equal $10; on a so-called mini contract of 10,000 units, it is simply a tenth of it, $1. This works out great because it allows a trader to start out as small as he likes without suffering an immediate disadvantage. Even most commission type brokers will only charge a trader a few pipettes based on his chosen volume, so that boils down to the same. It is a trader's personal choice to decide on his volume per trade. My advice would be to start out very conservatively until one slowly starts to come out ahead. In the section on Account Management, we will look into the matter of volume in more detail, and in particular on how to build up it up in stepwise fashion to effectively run up an account.

Note: The novice trader is always offered the opportunity to work himself through the learning curve on a papertrade account, trading virtual money; there are practical as well as psychological reasons why this may not be the best approach. It is recommended to at least apply a tiny amount of true capital, even on a micro scale of a 1,000 units, if need be. That way one stands to pick up the feel of actual trading more realistically and on top of that, the positions taken in the market represent true price levels and are based on actual broker fills. However, it could never hurt to explore a papertrade account for a number of days to get acquainted with all the particulars of order tickets and the such.

Being content with a relatively small and predefined profit target like

10 pip is arguably one of the better ways to scalp the eur/usd. All else equal, striving for very obtainable targets is a much more relaxed way of trading than aiming for extensive profits that may or may not be reached. And what's more, pocketing a 10 pip profit on a trade does not forfeit the right to nimbly re-enter and scalp another 10. Scalping 20 to 30, or even 40 pip out of a 60 pip swing is definitely not uncommon in a favorable market. Add to this the potential gains from a plethora of meaningless moves—that would most likely have produced zip profit on any of the bigger time or tick frames—and one may even start to appreciate all the senseless backing and filling of the market that could go on for days without direction, yet is still very likely to produce countless scalping opportunities.

Nowadays, almost any trading platform will provide a variety of ways to execute a trade. Next to the mandatory market and limit orders there may exist a whole array of esoteric order types that allow for a specific entry and exit techniques. Since scalping requires split second execution, we will keep things extremely simple and only use orders that will be executed either *automatically* by the platform or *manually* in one-click mode. This means we have to be able to set them beforehand to represent the right amount of volume and distance from entry. So, before choosing a broker and the platform that comes with it, a scalper has to make sure the following options are provided.

On the entry side of our method, we will only make use of the market order type. There is no fumbling around with limit orders in the scalping game. If we want in, we simply click the buy or sell button the moment the market hits our chosen level of entry.

Since we already decided on a 10 pip target and a 10 pip stop, it makes sense to have the platform send out these orders automatically the moment we take position in the market. This is referred to as the very popular *bracket order*. When engaged in a *long* position, anticipating higher prices, the target order pops up automatically 10 pip above our entry and the stop order 10 pip below it. Conversely, in a *short* trade, anticipating falling prices, the target order automatically shows up 10 pip below our entry and the stop 10 pip above it. If either of these orders are hit, whether for a profit or a loss, the order at the other side is automatically canceled. Hence the order also being referred to as an OCO, One-Cancels-the-Other.

If the bracket order is set properly, a trader, when in position, could basically leave his screen and come back a little later to either a 10 pip profit or a 10 pip loss. The target order, when hit, will be executed as a limit order, meaning it will be filled at precisely 10 pip from entry. The stop order at the other end is always a market order and once hit it will close out the trade either for a 10 pip loss or slightly worse than that. By the way, depending on the size of one's spread, on most platforms the stop order may have to be set at a distance of 10 pip minus the spread. For the purpose of simplicity, in all the coming chapters we will assume the 1 pip spread to be standard. Eventually, competition will force the spreads to go down even more. At the time of writing, the no-commission type 1 pip spread and its half-pip commission type counterpart seem pretty much industry standard.

It is the very nature of a market order to occasionally occur some *slippage*. Since it represents an order to be filled at any price the moment the market hits a particular level, there is the possibility of the market moving away from that price (after first hitting it) in the split second it takes the platform to work the order. In speedy market conditions, this may result in a less economical fill (occasionally, it may even work to one's benefit). On the good side, if a trader wants out or in, a market order will always be filled. A limit order, on the other hand, is set to be filled at a specified price, which brings with it the risk of either missing the trade (by not getting filled) or not being able to get out when its time to get out. For this reason, we will only use market orders to get into our trades and to exit them manually in case we need to bail out before the limit order of the target is reached.

Using the bracket order option and then let the market cast its verdict on the trade is a pretty relaxing way of managing an open position, but it may not represent the most effective approach. Arguably, a better way to go about it is to follow the price action attentively from the moment of entry and look for technical clues in the chart that could possibly negate a trade's validity status. Of course, this level to get out will be determined on technical grounds. This is where our tipping point technique comes in.

To close out a trade, we simply hit a market order in the opposite direction. For example, if a scalper fired off a market order to open a long position with, say, a full contract of a 100,000 units, a simple click on the sell button will flatten his position (close out) in an instant, because this order will send a 100,000 units the other way, bringing the position from open to flat. Depending on one's trading platform, this could also be done by hitting a close-out button. However, many less sophisticated platforms will not offer this option in one-click mode (after hitting the button, it may ask for confirmation to close out the trade, a setting that can not always be unchecked).

At all times, we should strive to send our orders in one-click fashion. In doing so, inexperienced traders may occasionally slip up by hitting an order to exit not in the opposite direction but accidentally in that of the original position. Instead of flattening out, that will leave them with a double open position. It happens. If a one-click close-out button is not offered and the opposite order technique provokes anxiety, then a way to go around it is to immediately hit the close-out button the moment an entry is taken. That will pop up the confirmation ticket, which can then be activated with a click of the mouse when it is time to exit the trade.

An excellent way to set up one's order tickets is to show the buy and sell buttons in a small window on top of the chart. To do this without having them ever disappear behind the chart, a platform should provide the option of showing the tickets *always-on-top*. That way, they will always remain visible, even if the chart is touched with the mouse.

In this fashion, a trader has only one screen to look at. It will show him the technical chart and allows him to enter and exit with a simple click of the mouse. Another reason why the single screen setup is preferable is because it hides all other information from view. Once in position, all we have to monitor is how the market responds after our entry. We have no need to know the status of our account, nor the current loss or profit on the running trade. That kind of information is not only useless, it may affect the decision-making process in a non-desirable manner (fear or greed may kick in). It is vital to realize that mental stability, more than technical skill, is the most important ingredient in the process of doing what needs to be done. The more we create ourselves an environment that protects us from harmful distraction, the more we will be able to focus on the chart and diligently execute our plan.

Chapter 5

The Probability Principle

Readers already familiar with technical analysis should understand that this particular scalping method takes a very minimalistic approach to chart reading and shies away from anything that might clutter up the screen and distract a trader from concentrating on the sole thing that truly matters, which, of course, is price. In fact, apart from a single moving average, the 20ema, there is nothing on the screen but price.

Eager technicians who have already been experimenting with every possible tool in their charting package may feel strangely bereft not having any indicators, trendlines, boomerang bands, retracement levels, stochastics and parabolic curves all over the chart. May it be suggested to give up that fight. It is a losing proposition and it will only add confusion and doubt to one's trading. What's more, depending on indicators might keep a scalper out of perfectly healthy trades or even suck him into the market at precisely the wrong time. When it gets to pulling the trigger, no algorithm code could ever compete with sound observation.

The best way to look at a live price chart is as if it were a non-moving snapshot. Forget the next coming candles for a moment and look at what is already there. What does it tell us? Do we see higher bottoms appear, lower tops? Are levels being defended, attacked? Are prices contained in a narrow range, are they swinging wildly? It is not that hard to do, really. Barring the occasional erratic mishmash, the market, one way or another, usually tips its hand quite transparently. But it will not hold up a sign saying when to buy or sell. That is why we have to scrape all available pieces of information together before we can even begin to think of taking a trade.

Strangely enough, most amateur traders tend to do exactly the opposite. They appear to have little regard for the overall picture and seem to concentrate mainly on their beloved setups. And it shows up in the chart. We may never be able to tell what drives other traders to do what they do at any given moment, but it is obvious just by looking at the terrible spots that get traded every day that plenty of traders have very little clue themselves.

The point to grasp is that we have to have a very good reason to step into the market and put capital at risk. We can't just go around firing off trades and hope for the best. In order to really feel confident about what we are doing, we have to find an *edge* in our trading, a tiny technical advantage that puts the odds in favor of our trades.

There is no denying that this magical edge, by far, is the most sought after element in the game of clever speculation. We could say it is a trader's equivalent of the philosopher's stone. Possess the edge in the market and one could turn lead into gold. And quite like our ancient alchemists, in an almost universal desperation to find it, most traders are looking for it in all the wrong places. Try as they may, they won't find their edge in a box full of indicators. All the money in the world could not buy it on the internet. A trader will not stumble upon it in a stroke of good fortune. Simply because the edge is not a *thing* that can surface by itself. It can only be obtained through the blood, sweat and tears of committing oneself to countless hours of studying markets, patterns, setups and price action principles.

Bear in mind, though, that no edge will ever make a trader beat the market. For the market is not a beatable object. A trader can only strive to beat those in it less proficient than himself. Hence the value of proper education. The true edge in the market, it is safe to say, is simply one's ability to recognize and exploit the incompetence of others.

Even so, it is important to understand that trading is very much a probability play. It is not a game of win or lose. The objective is not to score a winning trade or to beat another trader. In fact, throughout the whole process of trading, the outcome of any one trade is totally irrel-evant. At all times, the clever scalper should have the bigger scheme of things in mind.

Detaching oneself from the need to reap profits from each and every trade has enormous benefits. For example, if one truly understands the principle of a probability play there can be no agony in temporary adversity. If a trader executes his method correctly and consistently, all results, good and bad, only reflect the typical variance to be expected in a random distribution of outcomes.

The good part is that even a marginal edge will eventually prove its value. Or it wouldn't be an edge. This is an essential concept to grasp. Here's another way to look at it: If you were to engage in a game of dice, with the numbers 1 through 7 representing profit and the numbers 8 through 12 representing loss, would you be upset if 11 came up? And then 9 and then 11 again? Surely, with a statistical edge of 7:5, you would be very happy to roll these dice again. Because things will cer-tainly look up after about a hundred of individual throws, let alone a thousand. This is no different in scalping with an edge. It also shows us the folly of being upset after a losing trade. And of euphoria after a winning one, for that matter.

So, more than aiming for profit, the objective should be to do what needs to be done. If so, then the edge in one's play will take care of the rest. Diligently executing a particular method is the only way to fully exploit probability in the market. Accepting whatever outcome the mar-ket has in store is all part of it.

It is quite amazing, actually, how little this approach is practiced, even by those more experienced. Trying to predict direction, for instance, is a very common way to look at the market. After all, traders love to be right. But there really is no point in that. Who is looking anyway? Those that strive for glory in their trading are simply deluding themselves. And what's more, they stand a solid chance of producing the exact oppo-site of what they set out to find: a hurt ego, a lot of anger, a sense of betrayal, fear and frustration, and most probably a lot of losing trades.

A clever scalper is an observer more than a participant. Regardless of circumstance, he will remain neutral and observant, paying equal attention to the forces that oppose his potential trade as to those in favor of it. He will show no preference for direction, nor will he try to predict the next coming move. At times, he may take a conservative stance; at other times, he will show more aggression. It is all up to the scalper. But whatever he does, he will make sure it is in accordance with his personal method or else he will not put his capital at risk.

A tiny little edge can go a long way; it could even run up the smallest account to any desirable height. But it will only serve those who understand to concept of probability and the long-term aspect of it.

Now let's find out how all this relates to a 70-tick intraday chart of the eur/usd currency pair. It is time to let the charts do the talking.

Trade Entries

Chapter 6

The Setups

Scalping a market profitably requires a very disciplined mindset and a carefully chosen array of trade setups that allow for a minimum of freehand interpretation. Even the novice trader will quickly come to understand that simply shooting from the hip is the fastest way to blow up an account. The problem lies in the misleading assumption that a trading plan is in place when in fact there is no such thing as a solid plan at all. This can be a painful basis to trade from and it is not uncommon for even the promising trader to be fully unaware of it. Especially when there are some successes along the way, a trader may be led to believe that he is doing everything right, even though his results keep lagging far behind the potential of the strategy at hand. More often than not, this will bring all sorts of negative emotions into play, such as frustration, anger, agony, vengeance, fear—ultimately pushing the baffled trader only further downhill. When it comes to trading, misinterpretation of the notorious rut is not exactly atypical and often leads to an erroneous revision of the original plan, if not a total distrust towards the setups used. And so the dire quest for the holy grail can start all over again.

Fortunately, there are ways to avoid this very predictable route and it starts with looking at the plan from an analyst's perspective. Strip that trading plan to the core and analyze it as if it were somebody else's. Put this plan to the stand and let it defend itself. This is no time to be gentle on it. See how this plan holds up under severe cross examination and find out if it is guilty of either vagaries or deceit. If this is the plan that will accompany a trader in battle, better make sure it will not crumble apart under enemy fire.

A number of questions need to be thoroughly addressed before any trading plan could ever pass the viability test. Are the setups well defined? What are the conditions to trade them in? What are the conditions to stay out of the market? What target objective accompanies what setup? When is a running trade no longer valid? How to exit an invalid trade? What is the maximum stop-loss level on the trade at hand? When it looks like a setup but differs slightly, can it be traded? How to handle missed entries? How to handle slippage? When to scratch a valid trade? How to handle a new setup when already in position? And probably much more of this.

And these questions are just addressing the technical mechanics of the plan. We haven't even touched upon the psychological pitfalls that await any unprepared trader for sure.

As already stated, a trading plan, by itself, is not a checklist of dos and don'ts. That kind of rigidity will only serve to stifle a trader in a field of work where he may need to be flexible more than stiff-minded and apply logic more than rules. For the market itself is never rigid and no situation will ever present itself exactly as it has done in the past.

Arguably, the best way to obtain an understanding of what scalping is about is to dive into the waters and learn to swim with the sharks. Yet very few will survive the audition. Fortunately, there is a much healthier way that is almost just as effective, which is to rehearse every imaginable situation beforehand by studying countless examples of setups, trades, half-trades, missed trades, re-entered trades, and basically anything that might occur in the line of duty. The coming chapters of this book will have that mission in mind and hopefully provide most of the answers to the questions above.

This second section is dedicated specifically to identify the seven setups that make up the technical core of this scalping method. But it is important to understand that the setups by themselves have very little meaning. They are just tools to get us into the market. Our first aim is to assess the overall price action in terms of possible future direction. Only when the current forces in play put pressure on prices more one way than another can we begin to consider deploying our entry techniques. In a later stage of our technical journey, we will discuss when and why to forgo even the best looking setups on account of unfavorable conditions.

Every setup has its own set of characteristics although some of them can appear rather similar in structure. It is not uncommon for one setup, at a particular moment in time, to contain all the makings of another. Some setups perform extremely well in trending price action, while others set themselves up to exploit the many ranging phases of the market. Most of the setups will appear several times during the day, yet the conditions under which to trade them may not always be optimal. Furthermore, not every taken trade will lead to the desired 10 pip profit—far from it—but overall these patterns should provide the disciplined scalper with enough opportunities to come out ahead in virtually any session, although that should never be an objective by itself.

To identify the particular setups, all of them are named according to their main characteristic and each will have a chapter of its own to study its specifics in detail.

The setups are:

1. DD. Double Doji Break

2. FB. First Break

3. SB. Second Break

4. BB. Block Break

5. RB. Range Break

6. IRB. Inside Range Break

7. ARB. Advanced Range Break.

All of these setups, one way or another, revolve around the 20-bar exponential moving average, the *20ema*. This widely followed indicator plots the average closing price of the last 20 candles (bars) with a slight tweak in calculation (the exponential), giving the present closing prices somewhat more weight than the earlier ones. Some traders may prefer an 18ema or 21ema, but that doesn't really alter much. Any number of bars between approximately 15 and 25, either exponentially plotted or as a simple moving average (sma), will usually give the short-term trader a dependable guideline as to whether the market is currently trending or merely drifting sideways. Is the average sloping up, most traders will be operating on the buy side (go long); is the average sloping down, traders will look for entries on the sell side (go short).

The average can also be used to anticipate a shift in price direction when it is going from sloping to flat or from flat to sloping, and in many cases it can almost literally push prices out of a sideways pattern. When the average is not trending but more waving sideways, with prices not staying on one side of the average but alternating above and below it, it acts as a warning sign to be more selective in picking trades. The market apparently has entered a very indecisive phase that needs to be cleared up first.

Faster averages, like 15 and below, track price even closer but have the tendency to be constantly breached by individual bars without the trend really changing; the slower averages, like 30 and up, tend to point out the trend rather well, but, to a scalper's fine taste, may be lagging behind too much or simply produce too little setups.

Bear in mind that this 20ema should always act as a guide, not a law. Sometimes a trader may even have to discard it. Frankly, it is perfectly possible to trade the markets without it, but overall its visual value will be proven in almost any trade setup and since it doesn't clutter up the screen, it is a great average to have in the chart.

In a bullish trending market, with the average sloping up and most of the candles traveling above it, the safest trades are to the long side and so a trader should be on the lookout for setups to go long, preferably in the vicinity of the 20ema.

In a bearish trending market, with the average sloping down and most candles traveling below it, the safest trades are to the downside, so a trader should be on the lookout for setups to go short, preferably in the vicinity of the 20ema.

In topping markets or heavy chart resistance, when prices cannot seem to make further advances, a trader should look to go short but still have an open mind towards going long.

In bottoming markets or strong support, when prices cannot seem to make new lows, a trader should look to go long, but still have an open mind towards going short.

The Double Doji (DD), the First Break (FB) and the Second Break (SB) are typical *with-trend* setups, meaning that they deliver their best results when originating from a *pullback* situation in a strong visible trend. A pullback is a number of bars that travel in the opposite direction of the trend. One could say that the trend is temporarily taking a breather by allowing prices to go against it. It is also referred to as *countertrend* traders countering the trend. The general assumption, however, is that the pullback in a trend is ultimately short-lived and that a true trend will soon pick itself up. With-trend traders, using their with-trend setups, try to capitalize on that continuation, and, thanks to the pullback, at more favorable prices to boot.

The Block Break (BB) is seen in all markets, trending and ranging, topping and bottoming. The Range Break (RB), Inside Range Break (IRB) and Advanced Range Break (ARB) are setups that appear in sideways markets and topping and bottoming markets. Range formations could also appear in trending markets, but since these consolidations, by nature, are somewhat extended, it is best to look at them as standalone patterns and trade them without too much regard for the current trend.

When it comes to the difference between a pattern and a setup, both terms can be used interchangeably, for a setup is always a pattern, even if it contains only one bar. But technically, the term *pattern* is mostly used for a somewhat larger formation or a number of bars in which a smaller formation, the *setup*, can appear. This setup formation will then be used to trade the break of the bigger pattern.

Despite the sometimes confusing terminology, trading, of course, is first and foremost a visual endeavor. However, getting oneself acquainted with the names appointed to each individual setup may actually serve a structural purpose as well. On the brink of taking a trade, identifying a particular setup, by naming it, will lessen the tendency to shoot from the hip. The names by themselves are not significant. Let's start by examining the DD setup first.

Chapter 7

Double Doji Break

The Double Doji Break (DD) is the most straightforward setup in the method and is just as easy to identify as it is to trade. For those readers not familiar with the basics of candlestick charting, a doji is a price bar (candle) with more or less the same opening price as closing price. Prices may travel up or down within the duration of the bar, forming bar extremes (tails), yet if they return to the area of the opening level upon the closing of the bar, then we are dealing with a doji. In any bar, the area between the opening price and the closing price is called the body. The price levels outside the body are called the tails of the bar. In case of a doji, the body is almost non-existent since the opening and closing price are more or less the same. These bars are essentially a sign of market indecision. When the chart prints another doji next to the first, the temporary indecision obviously builds up. In most instances, however, a brief stalling of prices bears little significance; but when two or more dojis appear in what might be the end of a pullback to a nice trend, somewhere in the 20ema zone, a trader better place his finger on the trigger and get ready to trade.

Once prices have retraced about 40 to 60 percent of the most recent swing (due to the activity of countertrend traders), the original trend stands a good chance to resume. It is fair to imagine that a large number of traders who missed out on the move will not let this opportunity escape. Grateful for the more attractive levels to trade from, they will fire their orders with-trend the moment they sense the pullback to peter out. This is a well-trodden strategy, and a clever one at that. After all, more attractive levels not only reduce the potential loss on a trade, a trader also stands to reap more profit from the trend should it indeed continue on its march. Still, it can be a tricky proposition to decide when exactly to step in.

In the scenario of a waning pullback, countertrend traders face an important decision of their own: either book their profits and get out of the way, or hold on still, in anticipation of more countertrend activity, or, who knows, even a complete failure of the trend.

It is impossible to predict whether a pullback is just a harmless little countertrend, or the beginning of a new trend in the opposite direction. But that is essentially irrelevant. In a probability play, we have no need for guarantees. We just trade probability. And trading a pullback situation in the area of the 20ema is simply one of the better ways to enter the market with-trend on any chart. However, we do have to assess the validity of the trend itself.

A firm trend on a 70-tick chart is characterized by having the majority of bars close in the trend's direction, while at the same time these bars, on average, are a few pip taller than the overall bar in a non-trending market phase. We could say that trending bars look somewhat more aggressive than non-trending ones. In our charts, a bearish trend will print mostly black bodied bars (closing price lower than opening price); a bullish trend will print mostly white bodied bars (closing price higher than opening price). Logically, in the pullbacks the coloring will mostly be reversed. Therefore, a nice white bodied uptrend, for example, will show a smaller black bodied pullback. Assigning colors to the bodies is just to aid the visual process of recognizing price action. Many traders have no need for it and they may have their charts set up in one-color fashion.

In all its simplicity, the DD setup is a powerful tool to capitalize on a continuation of a trend and in most instances it is best acted on without second thoughts. The trend itself does not necessarily have to be overly explicit for this setup to prove its value; in fact, it could even be a new-born trend—in essence, a fresh move that just broke out of a sideways consolidation phase. An important requirement, though, is that prices, from the moment of entry, have to have a clear path ahead of them, at least on the chart at hand (we will never know what looms in the dark). Therefore, the DD trade should only be taken in the absence of immediate *chart resistance*, meaning the path to the 10 pip target should not be blocked by visible clustering price action not far to the left of the setup.

Not uncommonly, it is the pullback itself that obstructs the path to target. The pullback, when deemed harmless, is ideally running diagonally against the trend and pretty much one-directional. When it presents itself as a block of clustering and sideways trailing price bars, it could seriously cut short a future advance or decline. Some examples will clarify this for sure.

The dojis in this setup do not have to be dojis in the absolute sense. Small candles, usually no more than 3 pip in length, are best considered to express similar indecision as any regular doji and therefore can also serve as valid candles in this particular pattern. The more compressed the doji bars are compared to the overall price action, and in particular to that of the trend, the better the market's current indecision is displayed within the DD setup. In contrast, the smaller the average bar in the trend, the less the DD setup, with similar small bars, will stand out among the rest. It is not uncommon, in these cases, for the market to show a rather subdued reaction to the break of the DD pattern (if at all).

In all instances, a trader has to call on his personal experience to determine whether the current technical conditions are supportive enough to engage in a particular setup play. In other words, due to circumstance, he may have to skip what appears to be a solid setup on its own. In Chapter 15 on Unfavorable Conditions, we will look into this more closely. For now, it is best not to worry too much about the subtleties of skipping or taking trades. In general, most setups will show up under conditions that will not put much strain on the decision-making process. We either trade the setup or we just skip it.

Note: Although we should basically *strive* to scalp the chart like we would in the safety of a solid backtest, obtaining similar results in the actual market will be extremely difficult, if not completely impossible to achieve. Therefore, as much as even a thin edge theoretically should hold up over time, it may not do so when taken into account all the situations that could affect its potential. This is the main reason why so many strategies that show excellent performance records derived from historical testing simply fail to deliver when taken to the real market. Because they do not incorporate the disruptive effect of the human hand. The solution: refraining from strategies that show a marginal edge under ideal circumstances. It is not the strategy itself that should be distrusted, though, just the crippling effect of those at helm of it (ourselves included).

Ideally, all bars in a DD setup show equal extremes on the trend-side (the side from which the break is to be traded), but more often than not that is just not the case. For this reason, the most important candle to watch in the DD setup is the one with the highest high—for possible long trades—or the one with the lowest low—for possible shorts. The position of this bar in the doji group is irrelevant; its extreme on the trend-side, on the other hand, is crucial. This bar is called the *signal bar*. When dealing with a setup in the making, the signal bar is the one to watch most attentively. The moment its trend-side extreme gets taken out by another bar, we've got ourselves a signal to trade. The bar that takes out the high or low of this signal bar is called the *entry bar*. Obviously, this is the bar in which to take position. This terminology holds up in all of our other setups as well.

One more distinction can be made regarding the tradability of the pattern. When the setup is currently showing two dojis that have their trend-side extremes more than one pip apart, the pattern has to be judged in relation to the trend before it to see if it is still eligible as a tradable event. In case of a rather weak trend, for instance, it may be wise to skip the DD trade altogether when the extremes are more than one, but certainly more than two pip apart. In a very strong trend, on the other hand, it may pay off to be less conservative and just trade the pattern on a break of the extreme. All this will be clarified in the upcoming examples.

Before we get to the charts, let us walk through a DD setup example and see how it is best approached in the situation of a possible upside break: Once the uptrend has been identified, either well on its way or just starting out, it is simply a matter of waiting for a pullback to emerge. The 20ema should now be sloping up with most bars traveling above it. At some point, the trend may lose a bit of steam and a number of bars will start to travel in the opposite direction, towards the average that is. Not long after, average and price may collide. Since the trend is up, this pullback is widely considered to be a temporary event and so a lot of scalpers will be watching the possible low of it attentively. It would be silly just to fire a long order on account of prices reaching the 20ema. It is better to watch out for some sort of sign that prices may be about to reverse. Watching a bar pierce the average to the downside, for instance, only to see it quickly close above it again, is a pretty good starting point. In case the current bottom of the pullback is represented by two or more neighboring dojis, more or less resting on the 20ema (their tails preferably dipping below it), a scalper calmly waits for a new bar to take out the highest high of the doji group. By definition, the high of any signal bar is taken out when the current price bar in the chart goes exactly one pip above it. Upon seeing the signal bar being taken out by another bar (the entry bar), the scalper immediately enters long at the market.

In the event of a downtrend and a potential short position, all of the above is simply reversed: once the inevitable pullback emerges and prices arrive at the now down-sloping 20ema, the alert scalper will start to monitor the price action with close scrutiny, comfortably knowing that a number of setups are at his disposal to trade this market from the short side. Once he spots two or more dojis colliding with the average, and then another bar that takes out the lowest low of the pack, he knows he is dealing with a DD break and he will fire an order to sell an already predefined number of units at that spot. This sell order, when set properly, will be instantly bracketed by a 10 pip stop above the entry price and a 10 pip target below it.

It is important to understand, though, that the highly regarded 20ema is just a tweaked moving average of the last 20 closing prices and does not in any way offer support or resistance to the market on account of its presence. It does point out a dynamic visual level of where prices *tend* to stall when countering a particular trend. But that, most probably, has more to do with the seesaw characteristics of the market than with the average itself. Quite similar to the two-step-forward-one-step-back principle. This 20ema just so happens to catch the bulk of the pullbacks quite well. On any chart. Hence its practical usefulness. Admittedly, there may be a strong self-fulfilling prophecy aspect attached to this average, but then again, that basically holds up for price action in general. A clever scalper will not concern himself with the actual reasons behind the moves in his chart. For there is no point in speculating over other traders' motives. All he has to go by is what takes place in the chart on a recurring basis. And his task should be to exploit repetition.

Now let us see how the DD setup, the first in a line-up of seven, is effectively traded in the real-world environment on a 70-tick chart.

Figure 7.1 This first chart shows us a classic DD break example. In this case, no less than four dojis had formed into the 20ema zone (1). One of them broke the average briefly to the upside, but all four of them shared equal lows below it. True, the pullback was more a thin horizontal string of price bars than a diagonal move against the trend; as a result, it did not really bring prices any closer to those players on the

sidelines. But that is not necessarily a requirement. The very fact that prices are unable to travel against a trend often betrays a lack of countertrend interest. This could very well be interpreted as a with-trend play incentive. Not uncommonly, sideliners harboring with-trend views on the market only need to see a tiny break in the direction of the earlier trend to deploy new with-trend positions at the speed of light. One price bar taking out another bar's high or low by a pip can already trigger a waterfall of with-trend orders cascading into the market. This activity could leave a serious trail of countertrend sorrow in its wake. In many instances, the degree of with-trend aggression *after* a pullback mimics the strength of the trend *before* it. In this chart, for instance, the follow-up action between 00:40 and 01:00 is very similar to the pre-pullback action from 23:58 to 00:10. This *trend-equals-trend* principle is only a rule of thumb, so by no means a rule, but it is handy to keep in mind when contemplating the likelihood of a possible 10 pip ride. The weaker the trend before the pullback, the more any potential chart resistance after it might play an obstructing role. In general, the most dependable DD setups are the ones occurring at the end of a one-directional, diagonal pullback in a very strong trend.

Each of the four dojis here could pass as a signal bar, because they all share equal lows. The arrow in the chart points towards the first bar that took out these lows, and this bar is therefore called the entry bar. A scalper does not wait for this entry bar to finish. The moment it takes out the signal bar's low, by traveling exactly one pip below it, a market order is fired and the short trade is on.

Note: It should be stressed that no matter what charting software the scalper holds preference to, the bars in it should have a price scale in increments of one full pip. The trading platform may show prices in increments of pipettes (tenths of a pip), but that will not do for the chart. If this is neglected, a series of price bars with otherwise equal extremes will most probably show a jagged edge of fluctuating extremes, making it seriously harder, if not impossible, to determine a proper break level to base an entry on. If this could already pose a problem in the event of a simple DD setup, then it will certainly do so when it comes to the more streamlined setups that we get to discuss later on.

Furthermore, it is strongly recommended *not* to use the chart on the trading platform as the source of information, even if it offers the tick chart setting and is set to 1 pip intervals. Get yourself a decent stand-alone package solely for charting purposes and leave the trading platform completely running in the back. Do make sure, though, that the price in the chart corresponds with the bid-ask spread on the trading platform. Monitor this carefully. Sometimes the *bid* will resemble the price in the chart, at other times the *ask* is more close. It may differ a few pipettes here and there, which is only natural; but if either one is constantly off by more than a pip, then something is not right. Logically, the tighter the spread, the more chart and platform will align. If it doesn't look right, either change broker or charting provider until you get them both to align.

Figure 7.2 Look how small the two little dojis are (1) compared to most of the other candles in the trend. This exhibits the compressed indecision a scalper likes to see. Any trend, no matter how strong, will have pullbacks in it. That is just the nature of the markets where so many opposing ideas are traded up and down. A trader may not like it while in a trade, but when seen from a sideline perspective, the pullback brings

great opportunities about. For instance, to trade a nice little DD in the 20ema, like the first setup in the chart above.

The second DD setup (2) broke eight minutes later. There is nothing wrong with this particular trade. The setup is slightly inferior to the first since the doji highs are not equal but two pip apart. Still, there is no technical reason not to take the trade. The trend is clear and so is the pullback. Fact is, though, that this trade would have had to be scratched for what looks like a 7 pip loss when price dipped below the setup lows (don't worry about the exits yet). It shows us actually a very good example of how important it is to immediately accept any loss as just a cost of doing business and to remain on the alert for another setup in the same direction. Not from a vindictive stance towards the market, but simply because the chart may still be eligible to be traded in the same direction of the earlier trade. Any proper setup will do. In this situation, the market printed another DD pattern just a few minutes later (3). Have a look at the four little dojis, all with equal highs pushing against the 20ema. The moment this tiny block of price action was broken to the upside, with-trend players quickly stepped in. And equally fast, countertrend traders ran for cover.

Note: By definition, when a countertrend trader bails out of his position, he can only do so by firing a with-trend order, turning himself into a with-trend trader, whether he likes it or not. When enough countertrend traders are forced to bail out (to protect themselves) and at the same time enough with-trend traders step in, the chart is likely to show a continuation of the trend because of *double pressure* in the trend's direction. And vice versa for with-trend traders who are forced to bail out due to strong countertrend activity. That will turn a with-trend trader in a countertrend one the moment he bails out. The principle of double pressure is a crucial concept to grasp; in fact, it forms the core of our edge in the market. If we cannot picture double pressure to kick in, we simply do not put capital at risk.

Figure 7.3 Here the downtrend was unmistakably strong. Just look at the many tall black bars in it and compare them to the smaller white bars in most of the pullbacks. Still, that does not mean that all bears are on board. It just shows a temporary lack of bullish enthusiasm. In fact, it is fair to assume that the sharp downswing in the first half of the chart caught many bears by surprise. As a result, there will always be a large number of traders on the sidelines with only one thing in mind: to find a tradable pullback to get in on the party, and sooner rather than later.

It can be a painful sight to see an obvious trend take off and not be in it, but patience and discipline need to be practiced. The pullback will come. If it does not set up a proper trade, then so be it. In this chart a very tradable DD setup emerged once prices finally reached the 20ema (3).

As far as the DD setup is concerned, basically three things can happen when a pullback approaches the 20ema. Let us look at it from the perspective of a downtrend. 1: The highs of the dojis barely touch or not even touch the average before prices turn south again and break the low of the DD. This could be traded in a very clear trend but every now and then it may suck a scalper into the market a bit too early, meaning the pullback may not be quite finished yet and is likely to have another go at the average. It is not uncommon for this kind of price action to activate the exit strategy. It should be noted that countertrend traders, the ones causing the pullback to happen, can be very persistent. But how can we blame them. They just want to make a profit and show guts in their attempts. Should they manage to take control of the 20ema and keep prices above it, the first part of their job is accomplished, for they have turned the trend from down to sideways (at least temporarily). 2: The dojis (or just one of them) pierce the average, but are immediately pushed back and close below it again. This is arguably the most favorable way to trade a DD. A good example of it is the first DD setup in this chart. 3: The dojis pierce the average but are not pushed back so easily. This is the somewhat riskier version because it shows conviction in the pullback. Still, it can be very tradable, provided the trend is very strong and the break of the low of the DD is not occurring too long after the average was taken back. Once a number of bars start to rest on the average, using it as support (relatively speaking), turning it sideways or even lifting it up, the market may be dealing with a trend change. In these situations, it may be wise to wait for a more distinctive setup like a SB or BB (see Second Break and Block Break, Chapters 9 and 10).

The second DD setup in this chart (5), although less attractive, is still very tradable. The first doji in the setup is the one that pierced the average. The two neighboring doji bars remained below it. This setup is slightly inferior to the first on account of the distance between the highest low and the lowest low. It is two pip apart. Preferably, we like to see the extremes just one pip apart, or better yet, have equal lows. However, with a downtrend still very much in tanking mode and the pullback being very orderly and diagonal, this setup is good enough to trade.

It may be interesting to compare for a moment the first DD setup at (3) to the situation at the end of the chart, at (8). Here we can see why the latter setup, a triple doji pattern in the 20ema zone (technically a DD), is best skipped on account of its inferior quality. There are a couple of reasons why that is the case. First of all, the pullback leading up to the three dojis it is not an orderly, one-directional countermove against the trend. In it, we can spot a higher low (7), which is technically a sign of bullish strength. It means that countertrend traders bravely aborted a trend continuation. It is a higher low because the bottom of it sits higher than the low of the previous bottom of (6). If we also bring the earlier low of (4) into the equation, then we can count three lows in the area (4-6-7). To a classic technical trader that spells a well-known bottoming pattern, also known as a *reversed-head-and-shoulders* formation (far from picture perfect, though). It is not necessary at all to be acquainted with these rather esoteric patterns that will surely warm the heart of the typical technical analyst. Applying a bit of logic to our chart reading may just as well do the trick. In its most basic form, technical trading is no more than (a) reading the overall pressure of the market, (b) opting for a trade that corresponds with that reading and (c) to assess whether the path to the target is paved with chart resistance or relatively safe to venture out on.

Looking at the first DD setup, for instance, it is not hard to see that it is showing up in an unmistakable downtrend. Not even the little *double bottom* pattern from ten minutes before (another technical marvel) could challenge that fact (1-2). In more subdued markets this pattern may have given off a clear warning sign, but compared to the power of the trend at hand it is best perceived as a countertrend attempt that is most likely to fail (in terms of probability). In fact, had the three dojis from the skipped setup at the end of the chart (8) shown up in the area of the first setup (3), similarly a bit above the average, then trading a break of them to the downside should have been administered without hesitation. So, in other words, the reason for skipping the DD short trade is not necessarily the fact that the doji bars display themselves on top of the average, but more that they do so in combination with a couple of other hints that could be interpreted as warning signs that the current downtrend may be coming to a (temporary) hold.

Figure 7.4 Things are not always so evident in the market as displayed in the wonderful chart above. All the more reason to fully exploit the opportunities when they are offered on the proverbial silver platter. Both setups here are quite self-explanatory.

How could a scalper not grab his chance when confronted with a perfect DD setup in what looks to be the end of a pullback in the 20ema (1). Four tiny dojis, gently nestling in the average, three of them with equal highs—if that doesn't spell a great opportunity, then what does.

The second pattern (2), though much higher up in the trend, still provides an excellent opportunity to reap some more profits from this generous market. The fact that the trend was already 50 pip underway does not in any way diminish its longevity prospect. At least not from a technical perspective. Only when the pullbacks start to be more persistent, maybe forming double tops or double bottoms or clustering blocks of horizontal price action, should a scalper be more careful in picking his next with-trend trade. With no signs whatsoever even remotely suggesting that the market is about to give up on its trending inclination, a scalper is best advised to just bite the bullet and pull the trigger on any next trade that comes along. If that trade does not work out, then that is okay. What would not be okay, is a scalper being affected by it.

Figure 7.5 Although the market at the point of entry is hardly trending, this DD break (1) can be safely traded because the little pullback leading up to it is actually not only a pullback in the 20ema, but also a *test* of the range breakout zone from about 10 minutes before (the 1.2890 area). When prices reside above a horizontal level (a support zone) and then finally break through it by a number of pip, the market has a strong tendency to climb back up to that former support level to touch it from below. This is technically called *testing the breakout zone*, and it is very likely to be welcomed by traders on the sidelines, for these higher prices now give them more favorable odds to start shorting the market. This principle is equally capitalized on if it is not a level of support that cracks to the downside but a horizontal level of resistance that cracks to the upside and is then tested back. In fact, one could say that all the market ever does is cracking and testing support and resistance, even on the tiniest of scales. Pullbacks, for instance, quite often have their bottoms or tops acting as a test of some former resistance or support level. So, as much as we think the 20ema is stopping the pullback in its tracks, in many cases it is the former price action a bit to the left that is either offering support or showing resistance.

And just like the pullback in a very strong trend is likely to be short-lived, so is the typical pullback to a broken horizontal zone. Countertrend traders, by nature, anticipate the break to be false and they will buy it back up or short it back down. In most instances, it won't take long for them to see the folly of it because no matter how you look at it, they present their opponents, those that did not trade the initial break for whatever reason, with more favorable levels to trade from. Of course, either party could win in any kind of battle, but it in the long run it will pay off to not trade against a trend, nor against a proper horizontal break, for that matter.

Take a look at the two bars in the 20ema zone at the end of the chart (2). They provide a good example of when to ignore a setup that under other circumstances may have been tradable. First of all, the second bar, the black bodied one, is not really a doji, but still it is attractively bearish (price closed in the lower region of the bar) and not overly tall. So, seeing this two-bar pattern appear in the 20ema, we could basically regard it as a proper DD short setup. On top of that, the trend is point- ing down and the pullback rather straightforward; why would it be wise to skip this DD? Because the DD bars, compared to the overall length of the price bars preceding them, in both trend and pullback, are not compressed at all. In fact, they both are about the biggest bars in the neighborhood. One could argue, and rightly so, that a break of the DD did not materialize until two new, and this time *little* dojis underneath the average were broken by a third candle a few minutes later (3). Even so, with the entry on this trade almost equaling the low of the pullback and the overall price action quite slow and subdued, it is recommended to not engage in a short at this point in time.

Note: It may be interesting to contemplate for a moment the reason why any trader would want to buy or sell something at any moment in time. After all, even if the value of the underlying instrument was to be accurately estimated, it is highly unimaginable, if not plainly impossible, for anyone to be able to put an absolute price tag on it. At the end of the day, value is nothing more than a perception in the eye of the beholder. And price a mere reflection of consensual appraisal of many. The real world shows us that both are very brittle items with a rather short life- span. The more obscure and unfathomable the underlying instrument, the crazier the notion that the average trader would be qualified to make a proper call on the price/value relationship. Trading currencies by the trillions just about tops the list of daily irrational behaviors, for there is no way a mere mortal would be able to make sense of the many global Powers That Be on a fundamental basis. With that in mind, how is it possible that a trader would be able to trade anything at all, and walk away with consistent profits to boot? The answer to that is simply that the smart trader does not trade the underlying instrument, he trades other traders. And more so, he trades their pain and incompetence. He trades the fact that they have to react to their many mistakes to protect themselves. He exploits predicament and agony, all of it highly visible on a technical chart. To exploit others more than being exploited himself should be the ultimate satisfaction of any trader who is not in this business out of philanthropic idealism or to indulge in masochistic tendencies.

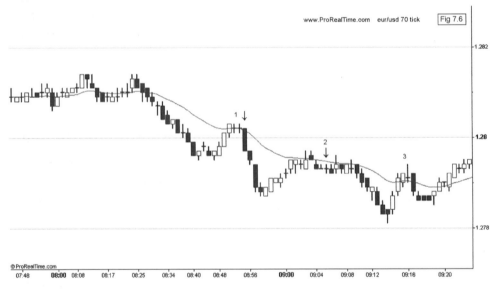

Figure 7.6 The sideways action in the beginning of the chart was broken to the downside by a series of distinctive bearish candles. Then formed a classic pullback eating back about 40 percent of the move, stalling into the 20ema (1). Two nice little dojis, both no more than 2 pip tall and with identical lows, presented a patient scalper with a safe opportunity to enter the market short once the lows were broken.

Note: Since a trader has to be very alert and immediately act on a break of a candle's extreme, it is handy to check the box of the *tick counter* in the charting software should this option be provided. This tick counter will appear on the vertical axis of the price chart and counts down the number of ticks per bar (in these charts from 70 to zero), and then starts all over again in a new bar. Why is this handy? Quite often, a signal bar will show a closing price at one of its extremes; should a trade have to be entered on a break of this bar, chances are that this trigger may be presented right on the first tick of the next bar in case this entry bar opens with a one pip *gap*. A gap is the difference between the closing price of one bar and the opening price of the next. Although most new bars will show an opening price equal to the previous close, gaps do occur quite frequently, and particularly in setup situations, where the price action could be a bit jumpy. A scalper, not alert enough to act on an entry bar that takes out a signal bar, runs a risk of missing his trade. Surprises are not uncommon, even to the focused, which is why it is good to keep track of the signal bar's lifespan. Hence the very handy tick counter. It also works the other way around, by helping a trader to relax a bit when there are still quite a number of ticks to go in a particular bar of interest.

The second DD setup broke about fifteen minutes later (2). With both trend and pullback of very fine, almost harmonious quality (trend bars all bearish, pullback bars all bullish), it was safe to anticipate the market to fall further still. The five-bar doji formation in the top of the pullback, four of them sharing equal lows, presented the scalper with a great *signal line* (a series of equal trend-side extremes) to trade a downward break from. A small discomfort had to be weathered when, two bars after the break, prices briefly pierced the average a bit. That's all part and parcel of trading. A trader cannot expect the market to not put up a fight. As long as that fight remains within the boundaries of his risk profile (as will be discussed later on), the scalper has no option but to stand pat and see what happens. In any case, it's only a trade.

The third DD setup in this chart (3) presents us with a bit of a judgment call. Trade or skip? Technically, it is a DD pattern in the 20ema at the possible end of a diagonal pullback. However, it has three things going against it that would make me want to skip this offer: first, the pullback, though diagonal and one-directional, retraces not just a part of the with-trend move before it, but all of it, implying growing bullish enthusiasm in the area; second, the pullback bars are taller than those in the with-trend move it is countering, which may be another sign of countertrend strength; third, the setup stands rather tall, which would make a possible scratch rather expensive (we will get to that later as well). Prices did halt nicely, though, in the resistance of the previous DD setup's signal line. Still, a conservative scalper would probably decline this offer. But we couldn't really argue with a more aggressive individual having a go at it.

Figure 7.7 It is important not to *jump the gun* when it comes to taking trades. Always wait for the proper setup to be broken before entering, no matter how much you can already picture prices to move a certain way. Expectation and bias are terrible companions to put faith in.

When presented with a group of four or five neighboring dojis, like setups (1) and (2), all with equal extremes, it can be tempting to already fire an order to the trend-side of the market without waiting for the setup to be actually broken. Such can be the anxiety of anticipation (or greed). But not being able to wait for a true break to materialize is a serious shortcoming that is best addressed as soon as possible in a scalper's career. Quite ironically, the impatient trader, after pulling the trigger, is prone to not only find himself caught up in a market that somehow does not want to break as anticipated, his very patience may now stand to be tested with a lot more venom to it. Of course, from an educational viewpoint that is an excellent reprimand. Another thing that might help to avoid this kind of behavior, is to ask oneself what exactly is gained by front-running a break. In case the anticipated continuation of the trend indeed emerges, then, in the event of a profitable trade, the standard entry would have probably delivered the same 10 pip profit. So little gain there. In case the trade did not set itself up as a tradable event, because the break never materialized, the scalper actually loses out due to his own impatience, maybe so much as by having to close out this non-trade for a 5 pip loss (a *scratch*). The gain that may come out of this is when a valid trade, too, would have had to be scratched; now his more economical entry (probably no more than a pip to his advantage) will provide the front-running scalper with a more economical exit compared to the patient trader who entered on the actual break. Is it worth it, one may ponder.

The first DD setup (1) consisted of no less than four neighboring dojis, all sharing equal highs. Patiently waiting for the break of the highs is always the proper thing to do.

Note: Next to the trend being obvious here, alert traders could also anticipate further price advance by keeping track of the *round number zone* of 1.2700. The currency chart is full of round numbers (the last two digits ending at 00, 10, 20, 30 etc) but two zones in particular stand out on any currency pair as being the most relevant: the 50-level and the 00-level round number zones (the half cent and full cent levels). It means that these zones have a tendency to represent—either visible or hidden—chart support or resistance, making it rather difficult for prices to proceed straight through them without some hesitation at best, if not a serious bull/bear clash. Bear in mind, these are zones, not actual pip levels, so when they get breached, even by a fair amount of pip, they could still hold up as support or resistance (we will take on this phenomenon in more detail in the Range Break chapters). Big banks, institutions and the like, are the players actually taking prices up or down in the currency game, not the average independent trader trading from his home. These big guys usually do not fret over a couple of meaningless pip in the middle of nowhere, but they do tend to attack and defend the round number levels rather vigorously. Trading can be rather thin when prices approach these zones, meaning that a lot of traders prefer to stay on the sidelines to await how the market handles these major levels. This can show a very peculiar side-effect of prices being literally drawn towards these round number levels, simply because there are not too many traders standing in the path of them. What will happen when these round numbers are hit is impossible to tell, but before impact has taken place, prices tend to be sucked straight towards them. We will refer to it as the *vacuum effect*.

In case of a proven trend, it is not necessary to be intimidated by these round numbers. They are easily breached enough for a trade to still finish profitably. What's more, it is fair to assume that a number of stop-loss orders will reside beyond these obvious levels and once hit they may even help a trade along. Still, when it comes to the DD setup, it may pay off to be a bit more conservative when contemplating a possible trade straight into a round number level. Since the DD setup antici-pates an immediate continuation of the trend, we need a large number of players to think the same thing (double pressure). And participation in the round number zones may just be too thin to call a break of the DD setup a high probability trade. Some of the other setups are better suited to take on these situations, because they really build themselves up. The DD setup, often representing just a tiny two-bar buildup at the end of a pullback, is always best acted on when there is nothing stand-ing in the way of the direction of the trade, not even a round number that, chart technically, appears to be quite harmless. For example, the second DD setup at (2) is of inferior quality when compared to the first (1). Not only is the round number zone of 1.27 directly hovering above it, to the left of the setup some *clustering price action* has formed, no doubt as a result of that same round number resistance. Any cluster of price bars nearby on a level higher than a long entry, or on a level lower than a short entry, is likely to represent resistance. It would depend on the chart at hand whether that resistance is perceived too big to overcome to grant a trade permission. So, it would be best to see if there are some other signs pointing either in favor of the trade or against it. Quite often, determining whether to step in or not, weighing the pros and cons, can be a delicate proposition. For example, some might argue that the price action preceding the first DD setup is also of the clustering kind. Still, I would not hesitate one moment to fire off that trade. Sometimes it is hard to explain, because the differences seem so subtle; but I would not go so far as to suggest that gut feel has anything to do with it. At all times, the decisions should be based on technical grounds. On balance, when the trend is not overly explicit and things look a bit shady in terms of possible resistance, it is best to stay out in DD situations.

The third DD setup (3) is even worse than the skipped second. The entry price may be more economical, since it is lower in the chart, but way more important than that is what lies above it on the path to target. The clustering price action below that round number is clearly blocking the path, so it is best to not risk capital on this trade. Prices actually ran through it without any trouble, but that is totally irrelevant. Scalping is all about probability, not about outcomes.

Figure 7.8 Another nice DD break in the 20ema (1). How hard is it to trade these sort of setups? Not hard at all, one would think. As a nice

bonus, we can clearly spot the *trend-equals-trend* possibility on this trade. The more distinctive the trend before the pullback, the more the one after it is likely to mirror the first. This is not a perpetual phenomenon, though; it works best on a strong first move, followed by either a first pullback or a sideways progression from which the second move is built up.

How about the DD setup about twelve minutes later (3)? Had the pullback preceding it been more straightforward and more diagonal, like the one leading up to the first DD, then this setup, too, would have been quite tradable. In this situation, however, the pullback is presenting itself more as a block of prices (2) than as an angular pullback into the 20ema. Shorting a break of the DD pattern from the perspective of the overall pressure is essentially the proper thing to do, if not for the fact that prices now face the troublesome task of having to pave their way through *chart resistance,* as any horizontal cluster of bars blocking the way can be looked upon. That is not to say that the current downtrend is perceived to be over, not in the least, but just that the likelihood of reaching a 10 pip target without being forced to scratch the trade first has now clearly diminished. If it has diminished up to the point of resembling a mere coin flip or worse, a scalper is better off at the sidelines than inside the market.

At this point of the journey, telling the subtle difference between a proper setup and its questionable counterpart could appear to be quite challenging; if so, it should be comforting to know that everything will fall into place soon enough. Well before a trader has earned his full degree of proficiency, he will have seen just about any trick the market might pull. After all, patterns, ranges, trends, minor ripples, shock waves, traps, even the freak oddity—if the seasoned trader has seen them all a thousand times before, then so too will the dedicated novice once he gets the hang of these price action principles.

Chapter 8

First Break (FB)

The First Break setup (FB) provides an alternative way to pick up the trend in the event of a stalling pullback. Whereas the DD setup needs a minimum of two neighboring bars to locate a possible turning point, the FB setup, under the right circumstances, is perceived to be such a powerful signal that no further confirmation is needed to trade a break of it. The signal bar to the break is simply the *first* bar in a substantial pullback that gets taken out in the direction of the trend. Once that break is set, a scalper enters with-trend to capitalize on a quick resumption of the market's original intent.

There are some requirements to be met, though, before the FB pattern can be considered a valid trade setup. In fact, in the majority of cases, a scalper may be better off skipping the trade altogether. Despite its discretionary nature, this setup is certainly worth studying because in the right environment it produces excellent odds.

The first condition concerns the trend itself. In ideal situations (in terms of FB acceptance), the trend is formed by a very determined one-directional surge of price action, preferably shooting out of a sideways consolidation. The price bars in it should ideally be longer in length than the overall price action before it and also be printed in rapid succession. At times, these moves can appear out of nothing, but they are most likely to show up when the market has already been slowly building up pressure to set a significant break. Once that break becomes a fact, the market may see a sudden burst of activity that logically traps a lot of traders on the wrong side of the field. In a downward surge we will see the chart spit out a number of black bars closing on their lows; in an upward surge, a number of white bars closing on their highs. By the looks of these sudden moves, or *spikes* as they are often called, it can safely be derived that the current action is not just a reflection of tiny scalpers stepping in and out but that the bigger time frame participants are also involved in them.

The second condition deals with the shape of the pullback that tries to counter this flurry of one-directional activity. Nothing ever climbs or falls in a straight line, so even an aggressive move sooner or later will find the notorious countertrend traders on its path. Logically, seeing these new players come in against the trend, a number of with-trend players will quickly start to pocket some profits. This double pressure will accelerate the speed of the pullback and chances are we may easily see a retracement of 40 to 60 percent of the trending move before it.

When opting to accept the FB setup, we indeed want to see this pullback materialize in full-fledged fashion. Not necessarily equally strong as the move it is trying to counter, but definitely not as a weak attempt either. Preferably, the candles in the pullback are also one-directional in their closes, meaning that if the trend was down, printing black bodied candles, this pullback will have mostly white bodied candles in it. And it should not stop or falter in its run before the area of the 20ema is reached. Take heed of the word *area*, because when the trend is formed by only a few very tall bars that broke free from a consolidation zone, the moving average may be lagging behind and thus be out of reach, even to a substantial pullback. At other times, the pullback itself is so violent that it might easily perforate the average more than it normally would before calming down. So the 20ema is a guide, not a barrier.

When both required conditions are met—a strong trending surge and a firm straight pullback in it—the chart will show a very visible fishhook pattern. Most of the time, the pullback (hook) will not exceed the halfway mark of the trend, although it is not exceptional to see a retracement even further than that.

The third and last condition to grant the FB setup validity is that the pullback is the *first* to go against the trend. The first pullback in any newborn trend is highly prone to be slammed back itself by with-trend traders the very moment it stalls. Later pullbacks, on average, tend to put up more of a fight in the 20ema zone before giving in to the with-trend traders (if at all).

By now a very legitimate question may have arisen among readers trying to figure out the logic behind some of the price action principles already discussed: what is it with these countertrend traders, what makes them so persistent in their need to constantly swim against the tide? Are they self-indulgent masochists, suicidal maniacs, utterly mad? Can't they tell when a trend is on and don't they know the odds are technically in favor of the trend to continue?

To answer these questions we may have to ask another. What is a trend to begin with? *We* may perceive our trend to be so obvious that even a novice could spot it a mile off, but still the move itself may only be a minor ripple in the trend on a bigger time frame. And this other trend, in turn, may simply be a pullback in an even bigger trend. This pattern of hierarchy could even go on until we're looking at the monthly charts and beyond. So who is actually countering who at any given moment in time? There is no feasible answer to this riddle. It all depends on perspective and opinion. That is why trading is such a fascinating clash of opposing ideas and insights. It is this perpetual disagreement on price and value that causes the market to provide endless liquidity to all participants involved. And luckily so, or there wouldn't be any trading done. Just imagine a market where everybody would agree. Who would be so generous to sell us a contract should we want to go long, or buy our contract should we want to go short? Nobody would. Therefore, a trader should be very happy knowing that he can buy and sell his contracts at any moment in time.

Despite the multitude of strategies bombarding the marketplace, for the scalper there is only one world to consider and that is his own particular chart of choice. Everything else is irrelevant. That one chart is the frame in which to decide whether the market is trending, ranging or pulling back, and any decision to enter or exit the market should be based on the setups and the candles in that chart alone.

Now let's have a look at this FB setup and see if it is easy to identify. Keep the three required conditions in mind: a bursting move, a straight pullback, the first pullback to the move. The moment a bar in the (substantial) pullback gets taken out by its neighbor in the direction of the trend, we have our signal to enter the market with-trend for a quick 10 pip scalp.

Figure 8.1 This chart shows a perfect example of the FB trade (1). Although not necessary, it can be a nice bonus to see the candle that needs to be broken (the signal bar) turn out to be a full-grown doji, with its closing price very close to the side of the break. Despite the fact that such a bar closes more or less at the same level as it opened, it shows visible evidence of the bull/bear fight within it. When it closes back on its lows in a downtrend, it hands us a strong signal that the trend may be about to resume. But basically any candle in this setup will do. They should not be any taller than 7 pip, though, in order for us to still be able to wrap a 10 pip stop around them (7 pip for the candle, 2 pip for the break on either side, and 1 pip to account for the spread. More on this in Section 3 on Trade Management).

Note how most of the bars in the downswing are firm black bodied candles, whereas those in the pullback are all smaller in size, yet nonetheless white bodied and non-hesitant, aiming for the 20ema or beyond. Not even one bar in the pullback got broken to the downside until the signal bar in the 20ema appeared. It is also the first pullback to materialize. One couldn't ask for a better FB setup.

Technically, this particular FB is also a DD setup. After all, there are two dojis—with equal lows—appearing in the 20ema. That would render the necessity of the pullback to be the *first* a non-issue, because now a scalper could simply trade a DD setup, which does not have that kind of restriction.

As we march through all of our setups in this book, we will most likely see many more examples of situations in which one setup is part of, or equal to another. The reader should not let himself be confused as to what to call it. The names of all patterns are essentially irrelevant.

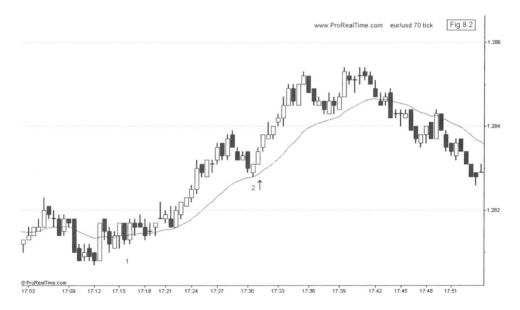

Figure 8.2 In the beginning of this chart there is a nice ten minute build-up to break the 1.2820 zone (1). The tops of most of the bars remain capped at a horizontal level, but the lows are slowly progressing upward. That is a clear sign of tension building up towards an upside break. The reader is prompted to always check the chart for any kind of clustering price action in it. Whatever is compressed will eventually unwind, simi-

lar to a spring jumping free. It is referred to as *pre-breakout tension*. The later to be discussed BB setup (see Block Break, Chapter 10) is solely designed around this principle. But all throughout the chart, setup or not, we can expect tension to build up, one way or another.

Once a break is convincingly set and the move jumping out of it sufficiently strong and one-directional (no mini pullbacks in it), it is a matter of waiting for the shape of the inevitable pullback to assess whether the situation will present us with a legitimate FB. Pullbacks that retrace about 40 to 60 percent of the trend and simultaneously collide with the 20ema provide excellent opportunities for a with-trend scalp. Whether it is a DD, FB, SB or BB that sets itself up, a scalper welcomes them all. In this chart, it turned out to be a proper FB setup (2). However, when compared to the previous chart, Figure 8.1, the bars in both trend and pullback are not so outspokenly one-sided. The trend has some black bars in it, the pullback some white ones. On close inspection, though, we can see that no bar in the trend had its bottom broken to the downside until the last one in the top; in the pullback, no bar was broken to the upside until the signal bar appeared in the 20ema. All in all, that makes for a tradable FB. A long order can be fired the moment the signal bar gets broken to the upside.

This setup provides a good example of how a tick counter can help to indicate when a signal bar is about to end and a possible entry bar about to begin. When prices travel in the top range of a potential signal bar (for an upside break), or in the bottom range (for a downward break), it is smart to keep track of the tick count in it. There is always the possibility that the entry bar will open with a one pip *gap*, which will be an immediate break of the signal bar on the first tick, and thus a valid reason to fire an order. Hesitating in that spot may result in a worse entry price or even lead to missing the trade altogether.

When using market orders instead of limit orders, it is unavoidable to occasionally incur some *slippage* when entering on a trade. Since a market order aims to grab the price of the moment, but has no specific price attached to it, it could be filled disadvantageously in the event of the market moving away. There are basically two reasons that could cause this to happen. The first is a technical one, meaning the market

moved away from the entry price in the split second the order was surf-
ing the internet to get filled. That happens even on the best of platforms.
The second reason is self-inflicted, as a result of acting too slow.

The technical reason, obviously, cannot be avoided. We will certainly
not be using any limit orders and see half of our trades move away from
us without being filled. Even if we were to operate a high-tech platform
that allowed us to put in limit orders at the speed of light, that would
not eliminate the risk of not getting filled. Therefore, if we want in, we
hit the market order button.

The self-inflicted slippage as a result of hesitating at the moment of
entry is more common than one might think. Balancing on the brink of
a trade can trigger a lot of anxiety within a trader's mind. As a result,
some will act prematurely without waiting for a proper break; others
simply act too slow and some may not act at all. These things happen
and they are only natural. It may take many months for a trader to
routinely fire off his trades without the slightest sense of discomfort. A
thing to strive for, of course, is to act when action is required, whether
that still provokes anxiety or not. Eventually all these feelings will wear
off.

Should a trade be entered with somewhat larger slippage, like a pip
and a half or so, just remain calm and manage the trade as if it was executed properly. Most winning trades surpass the 10 pip target without
too much trouble, so even being filled uneconomically, and thus having
a target objective a little further out (by the same amount the entry got
slipped by), should not make that much difference. It may cause the
damage control to be more expensive, though—so be it. But on occasion, it does happen that purely due to slippage, a trade never makes it
to the target and eventually has to be scratched, maybe even for a loss.
Still, that is no reason to get upset. Nothing in the market ever is.

Should a trade be missed, for whatever reason, it is important not to
whine over it but to quickly adapt and see if the situation can still be
saved. Just as often as the market tends to shoot off and not look back,
it shows a tendency to stall right after the break. And even if it spikes
away without us in it, in many instances, just a few bars later, price
will quickly pull back to revisit the breakout level. Both situations pro-

vide us with an excellent opportunity to step in after all. We may even be dealt the exact same price as the original missed entry. However, in case a trade is truly missed and does not pull back, it is essential to not chase price up or down, no matter how much a scalper wants in. That is very poor trading and reeks of amateurism. If the moment is really gone, it's gone and a scalper moves on.

Figure 8.3 The speed of that spiky trend around 16:15 says it all. Price action like this is very often caused by traders responding to a news release. The fact that it also broke a technical pattern (1-2, a so-called *bull flag*, don't worry about it) and cracked a round number zone (1.41), no doubt caused this sudden burst of one-directional activity to be even more violent. Whenever a trader sees something like this happen on his chart, he should immediately think: FB! For that is the fastest entry into a new trend after a pullback (4).

Notice how the 20ema could not keep up with the strength of this move, in spite of the reasonable pullback that ate back about 40 percent of it. This is typical for sharp moves that contain only a few very long bars. The average may have an exponential calculation to it, which puts more weight to the most recent closing prices, it is still an average made up of the closing prices of *the last 20 bars*, and at the end of the pullback about half of them had their closes way lower in the market (below the average). This is why the 20ema can only act as a visual aid and not as a definitive level that needs to be touched first.

A handy trick to determine whether a FB entry may be imminent in situations like this is to watch out for an opposite colored bar to get printed in the pullback (could also be a doji without a colored body). In this example the pullback is bearish, with the candle bodies being black; the moment a white bodied candle appears, the scalper may be dealing with a possible signal bar. But only once the high of that bar gets taken out does it signal an entry to go long. This is only a handy aid, though, because by itself the color of the signal bar is irrelevant. Any bar in this setup that gets broken in the direction of the trend should be considered a valid signal bar.

The time scale below this chart gives the reader a good impression of the occasional huge difference between a tick frame and a time frame chart. The action between 16:15 and 16:18, just three minutes, printed about the same amount of bars as in the 40 minutes before that. That is about 13 times as fast. Shock effects, like news releases, can be extremely volatile and fast paced, but with a bit of luck, an alert scalper may still reap some profits from them before they wear off. It is not uncommon for a target to be reached within a matter of seconds. To the downside, it should be noted, there is the possibility of being stopped out equally fast. Under calm conditions, it is quite rare for a full stop of 10 pip to be hit, yet it is a market like the second half of Figure 8.3 that makes for an excellent candidate to produce this feat. The mere speed of it could make it impossible to scratch an invalid trade at a better level. Therefore, accepting a FB trade in super fast conditions is synonymous to accepting the risk of a larger stop than normal. But since these trades come with nice odds, getting stopped out on occasion is just part of the normal distribution of outcomes in a probability play.

In this chart, the market, within a minute or so, almost printed an exact copy of the earlier situation that led up to the first FB trade. Both trend and pullback are almost identical. It is a bit of a judgment call to decide whether or not to trade the break of the second pullback (5) in similar fashion as the first. The pros to this trade are the facts that the market's pressure is still pointing very much in the direction of the current trend and that the bottom of the second pullback neatly tested the top of the earlier upswing (5 tests 3). And, of course, that a signal bar got taken out to the upside. On the other hand, the pullback is not the first to the trend, which basically renders the option of a FB invalid, due to strategy restrictions. It is not for nothing that a FB trade is often skipped in favor of a better setup under relatively normal conditions. But these are not exactly normal conditions. So the judgment call is purely a result of the exceptional quality of the market. Does it matter what a trader decides to do, skip or trade? Probably not. It would only matter if these situations occur almost every day, for then they need to be implemented into the strategy and not be looked upon as an oddity anymore. For what it is worth, skipping the trade here is probably the best thing to do, because, after all, we are dealing with a second pull-back. Taking the trade anyway and getting stopped out could harm the not yet confident scalper, for he may be prone to the negative illusion of being reprimanded for strategy deviation. Should the trade work out, then he may start to foolishly entertain the idea that he is allowed to deviate from his strategy at will on account of his excellent insights. The proficient scalper, on the other hand, will just look upon any trade as just another trade. It either delivered on its potential or it did not.

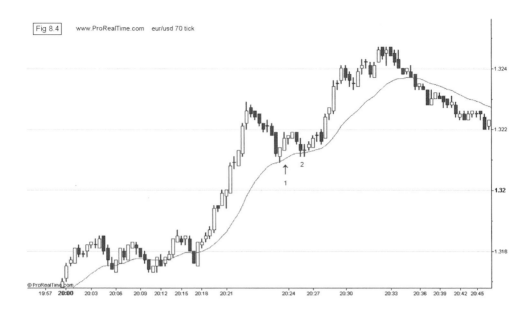

Figure 8.4 The first twenty minutes of this chart show what is referred to as a sideways consolidation, also called a *range*. It actually appeared after an already extensive run-up of the market (not visible on the chart). Still, it makes sense to regard a trending move that shoots out of a sideways consolidation as a *new* event. And so we can look upon that huge move here as a newborn one; therefore, the pullback in it should count as a first. In scalping, it will pay off to keep things very simple and not scroll too far back in time to search for more information, and in particular for information to either validate or reject a trade. On average, about one and a half hours of price action on a 70-tick scalping chart will show more than enough bars to assess the current forces in play in proper light; and so it is best to just act upon a valid signal without too much second thoughts. In hindsight, sometimes a trader may regret not having scrolled a little further back in time to spot the huge resistance that caused a particular trade to lose. But then he should also consider the possibility of not having traded a large number of his winners on account of similar perceived resistance further back in the chart.

In the faster paced markets, it is not uncommon to be filled with some slippage. Being aware of a terrible fill and at the same time seeing the trade not want to take off can be quite a mental challenge. Just imagine to be filled at about three pip above the close of the signal bar (1). That would have taken the trade about 6 pip in the minus at the low of that tiny pullback a few minutes later (2). Technically, though, all the market did was pull back a couple of pip. Despite the discomfort of being so many pip in the minus, it is vital to stay calm and composed throughout any trade and only resort to bailing out when the technical conditions warrant such action (see Chapter 14 on Tipping Point Technique). And never because the current loss becomes mentally unbearable. What point is there in setting a 10 pip stop to anticipate an extraordinary condition, only to reject that measure when such a condition finally arrives.

It is crucial to understand, and accept, that a large number of trades at some point before the target is reached will see at least some, if not all of the paper profits being eaten away; and a great many more will simply have to endure the initial hesitation before finally taking off. It is just the way the markets work and in essence also the very mechanism that makes pullback trading possible in the first place. It would be very selective reasoning to welcome a pullback when looking to trade, yet to despise one while in position. When in the market, a trader, at all times, should keep his eyes on the chart and not on the mesmerizing fluctuations of his profit and loss window. If the traded break is picked with care, it most probably will defend its very existence and send these countertrend traders packing. The uncertainty of whether a trade will work out or not, and the fear of having capital at risk, can trigger all sorts of unhealthy emotions that will hardly contribute to managing the open position in proper manner. It may help to ask yourself what exactly there is to be uncertain about? Since we all know that certainty is nothing but an illusion in the marketplace, how could *un*certainty really be an issue? Many times, though, a trader's discomfort is not caused by the possibility of a losing trade, but more by the disturbing uncertainty of whether it was the right thing to do to take the trade in the first place. This immediately shows us the necessity of proper education. Whereas a trader can never be certain about the market's response, he has got to be certain about his method! All a trader can go by is the likelihood of his edge to comply with probability over a longer term. Therefore, he has got to trust his setups and take every valid trade. It is pointless trying to imagine oneself being able to predict just these situations where probability will not work in favor of a trade. At times, it can be very tempting, though. But it is crucial not to give in to this treacherous temptation. Prediction and hunches are like the ever-present hecklers who thrive on confusing the performer. Since they cannot be denied a ticket to the show, it is best to ignore them and just do what you have to do, even if it hurts.

Figure 8.5 Seeing a number of textbook FB setups appear in a row may give the impression that this sort of price action happens all the time. It does not. And when it finally does, maybe once or twice a week, it may not necessarily present itself in tradable fashion. In the unfortunate event a trader is signed up with one of these shameless brokers that outrageously mark up the spread in wild markets, or prior to, and in the wake of, a news release, any trading venture will be reduced to a foolish act of gambling. Even on the eur/usd pair, spreads are known to go up as high as 10 pip. Under these conditions, a scalper is strongly advised not to step into the market anyway, no matter how tempting the chart. That would be a clear demonstration of poor judgment. According to sound probability, every trade should be looked upon in the same man-

ner and regarded as equal in terms of probable outcome. They either work or they don't. Accepting a trade under terrible conditions—which would be considered wholly untradable under other circumstances—is the same as saying: I can afford this because I *know* what's going to happen next. Delusions of grandeur are not uncommon amongst those traders not yet ready to grasp the probability principle.

Figure 8.6 Another very straightforward example of a quick trend shooting out of a sideways pattern and a pullback taking back about 50 percent of the move. The pullback candles neatly follow one another to the 20ema zone without the with-trend traders trying to take over yet. It is also the first pullback in the (new) trend, so this action makes for a great FB setup (1). What is different, compared to the FB examples seen so far, is the shape of the signal bar leading up to the first break. That one could not be more tiny, yet is a very valid signal nonetheless. Small as it is, there are just as many transactions done in it as in any of the other bars (not necessarily the same volume, though; tick bars do not the count the number of contracts changing hands, they only indicate the number of transactions taking place). The fact that price is stalling in it does not make it any less a signal bar. On the contrary. Sellers and buyers are apparently in complete harmony with each other, at

least for the duration of that one bar. When that happens at the possible end of a pullback, an alert scalper should get very ready to trade.
Every time prices stall in the area of the 20ema, countertrend traders
will be extremely quick to exit their positions once the chart starts to
move in the opposite direction again—especially so when the pullback
was countering a very strong move. A scalper should capitalize on these
countertrend traders running for cover and fire his order as quick as he
can in the direction of the trend once a signal bar gets taken out. If all
goes well, then in just a matter of seconds new with-trend traders will
pick up on the action and jump in themselves, helping the trade along.
Note: To produce the 1 pip signal bar, for educational purposes, I actually cheated on this particular chart by setting it not to 70 but 69 tick.
Compare this chart to Figure P.1 in the Preface pages. They are essentially the same, if not for the tiny difference in tick setting. As you can
see, adjusting the tick number by a mere tick can already alter the way
most bars are displayed. Yet both charts are equally tradable.

The situation above does present us with a technical issue regarding
proper trade management. In concerns the matter of stop placement.
Although we will delve into this in a later section in more detail, this
chart shows a rarity that we might as well address straightaway. In
a normal FB situation, a stop will be placed a pip below or above the
signal bar that gets taken out at the other end. But there are circumstances under which the stop is best placed a little further out to give
the trade a little *wiggle room*. When signal bars are extremely tiny, as is
the case in this chart, it may be wise to apply this; but it should never
be applied indiscriminately. Usually a technical point of resistance or
support will be taken into account to derive the maximum amount of
this extra leeway. In the section on Trade Management, we will look into
this more closely. Note that the opening of the entry bar (on top of the
arrow) coincided with the level of the high of the signal bar. By looking
at the bar alone, it is not possible to tell whether this trade would have
been entered before prices briefly dipped below the signal bar or after.
Such is the limitation of hindsight.

Here the 20ema is not supporting the trend literally, but that is not
necessarily an issue in these sort of trades. Come to think of it, it can

even be a plus to see prices pierce the 20ema and close below it. The deeper the pullback, the lesser the chance of the market trying to test an even deeper level in the trend, which makes for a reasonable safe trade. On the other hand, if the pullback is dipping so deep that it retraces about 70 percent or more of the with-trend move, then, despite the lower levels, sideline players may get a little bit more cautious, which may cause the trade to fail. Regardless, when it comes to taking a *valid* trade, a scalper should not make distinctions between deep and not so deep, or safe and not so safe. A setup is a setup and a trade is a trade. And a 20ema is just a 20ema that may be lagging behind or even be too fast. Still, it cannot not be denied that some trades just look a lot better than others. But as long as the setup meets the requirements of validity, the trade should be taken. After all, any setup that stands a better chance than 50 percent to work out, no matter how shady its appearance, is a tradable event. Such is the nature of long-term *positive expectancy*.

Note: A trade that stands a better chance than 50 percent to work out does not necessarily imply that in more than half of the occasions the target will be reached. Since a winning trade results in 10 pip of profit and a losing one in about 6 pip of loss on average, the target only needs to be reached in about 40 percent of the occasions for our trades to be profitable in the long run (though marginally). In a random play, like a game of dice, a bigger profit on a smaller chance of winning would offset the smaller loss on a bigger chance of losing. Eventually both players would statistically break even. But not so in the markets. If we truly have an edge, we can tip the scale of fortune to our benefit by playing only these situations that deliver favorable odds. That is a major advantage. In fact, it even allows us to throw in the spread and still come out ahead. Naturally, stating to have an edge in the market is a daring assumption, and one that is often scorned. But those that educate themselves diligently and in proper manner will find it. And the best place to look for it is in the disability of other traders to educate themselves in similar fashion.

Figure 8.7 This chart should not leave any doubt behind as to whether that pullback in the right-hand corner was a valid pullback in terms of price action. Nothing but white colored bodies, and not one candle in it broke the bottom of another until the very last bar at the top (1). A point of discussion could be the origin of the trend leading up to it. Should we consider the trend to have started at the top of the chart around 14:00, then this very nice pullback is technically not the first. But how can we ignore such an harmonious pullback to such a lovely trend? Even despite the fact that it broke the 20ema to the upside, it is just begging to be shorted on first break. Granted, allowing oneself the freedom to deviate from an original plan of attack could be a tricky proposition. But every now and then it may be wise to let logic prevail over rigidity. With time and experience, this will become second nature; however, it should only be applied sparsely and certainly not as a means to jump the gun on a trade. As to the situation in the chart at hand: imagine this kind of a pullback to surface, say, fifty times in the course of a year's trading, and every one of these situations would have been traded on first break. Chances are extremely high that, on balance, these trades would have rendered themselves profitable. That is what *positive expectancy* means in trading. And why a trader cannot go around cherry-picking his *valid* trades. He has to take them all.

Chapter 9

Second Break (SB)

Next to the DD and FB setups, which are very straightforward stand-alone reversal patterns, the Second Break (SB) is one more chart formation that sets itself up to reverse a pullback in the area of the 20ema. But this time it requires a little more chart action to determine the exact spot to step into the market. It is a pattern that could be seen as two FBs following each other in relatively quick succession.

As was explained in the previous chapter, a reliable FB trade is a rare occurrence. It was recommended to wait for certain exceptional circumstances to take advantage of this particular setup. That leaves it fair to deduct that, under normal conditions, the first break is considered an inferior proposition. If we cannot expect a particular setup to return a healthy profit over the long haul, then the only sound thing to do is to skip such a setup.

The good news is that skipping a first break does not mean the potential for a trade in the direction of the trend has fully blown over. On the contrary. The first break, if it indeed fails, can actually play an important role in the development of a much better trade setup, the so-called *Second Break*. If the chart sets itself up favorably, a scalper may have an excellent trade on his hands to capitalize on the resumption of the trend after all.

Let us see how this SB setup is ideally constructed. Since it is a pullback trade, we first need to see a trend to begin with. This does not have to be a very outspoken trend, but we do need to see the overall market pressure point in favor of the trend's direction. The pullback should be very orderly and preferably somewhat diagonal. In all cases, a potential trade should not have to crack a lot of chart resistance in order to get to target. We could say that the conditions that favor this setup very much resemble those of the earlier discussed DD setup. And as is the case with most with-trend plays, no matter how inviting the trend in the chart at hand, ultimately it is the shape of the pullback that has the biggest say on the matter of participation.

If you think of it, there exists a strange symbioses between with-trend traders and countertrend traders, for either party needs the activity of the other. Since trends sooner continue than reverse, it is not hard to imagine who is losing out the most in this fragile cooperation. That is not to say that a consistently profitable contrarian is merely an illusion. When equipped with great technical insight and a magical sense of timing, a clever countertrend scalper can really live it up, even in the best of trends. But the trick is not to overstay the hospitality of the market. This can be a delicate balancing act between pushing for profit and running for cover. Fortunately, it is not our task to defy the countertrend professionals. We will just let them be and even thank them for bringing prices to more favorable levels. Our tactical aim is to cleverly exploit the predicaments of less skilful players who have little concept of what they are doing and who will find themselves repeatedly trapped on the wrong side of the market.

Let us walk through a hypothetical short example in a downtrend to see how this could play itself out. After having witnessed the bullish pullback from the sidelines, with-trend traders, at a certain moment, will start to re-enter the market somewhat more aggressively. Many will try to pick a spot in the vicinity of the 20ema to deploy new short positions. This renewed with-trend enthusiasm will put pressure on the pullback and force a lot of contrarians to quickly bail out. As a result, prices may stall and slowly turn around in the direction of the trend again. If this is done aggressively enough to take out a signal bar's low, then a first break is a fact. As has already been stated, under normal circumstances this break is not acted upon in our method. Still, the market has given off a clear signal that the pullback party may be coming to an end. Naturally, not all market participants will pick up on the hint or deem it trustworthy. In fact, sideline contrarians may look upon the with-trend bounce as a welcome opportunity to now counter the market at more economical levels. If so, they will put pressure on the trend again and as a result prices may once again be lifted up towards the 20ema.

From our sideline perspective, things are now getting very interesting; at this point, we like to see a second with-trend attempt to topple the pullback, and preferably executed with a little more aggression. But as clever scalpers will not do the dirty work ourselves. We will remain on the sidelines and simply sit back to watch how the situation unfolds. We should be on high alert, though, and ready to fire off our shorts in one-click fashion. After all, since the overall trend is still down, the chart may soon present a major with-trend opportunity to put these obnoxious and resilient contrarians where they belong: out of the market. A second with-trend attack will most likely do the trick. If it indeed materializes, our task is to hop on the bandwagon as soon as we can. The moment a *second* signal bar gets broken in the direction of the trend, we will enter the market short and hope to enjoy a nice ride of pullback implosion.

So, why not trade that first break to begin with? After all, should the market immediately take off, then we are already on board; and if not, then at least we would be nicely positioned for that possible SB later on?

That is a very fair question, but sincc we haven't yet touched upon the various exit techniques regarding the faltering trade, it may prove a little difficult to provide a satisfying answer just yet. For the moment, it should suffice to explain that a failed first break is often looked upon as a countertrend signal to push new life in the pullback; and thus an incentive to once more attack the trend. Although this second thrust runs a solid chance to be countered itself, it may just be strong enough to activate our exit strategy, meaning the FB trade has to be closed out for a small loss in order to protect the account. Remember that the maximum stop of a full 10 pip is solely a worst-case scenario measure. That means our average stop will be much closer than that. To avoid the risk of getting ourselves stopped out prematurely, it is best to forgo the FB trade in anticipation of a superior setup. This approach, it is fair to say, does contain the occasional drawback of seeing prices take off and never look back.

Let us recap what we have gathered so far on the hypothetical short and then dig in a little deeper. First there was a firm swing down (the trend), then a minor swing up (the pullback to the 20ema), then a tiny move down (the FB), and then a tiny move back up (second thrust in the pullback, defying the with-trend bounce).

Having fenced off the first with-trend attack, countertrend traders now face the critical task of having to crack the high of the pullback from just moments ago. That would be a technical feat of significance. The general premise may very well be that upon cracking that high, even by as little as 1 pip, a least a respectable number of with-trend traders will start to get cold feet. No doubt, a big part of their paper profit has already been eaten away during the pullback and at a certain point they have to protect what's left of it. If scared enough, they may very well bail out on a break of that earlier high, and in doing so become countertrend traders themselves. After all, one can only close out a position by taking an opposite position, such is the nature of the game. And while these with-trend traders are bailing out to protect themselves, new contrarians, smelling predicament, will quickly try to capitalize on the situation by taking fresh countertrend positions, challenging the trend even more. Brilliant as the plan may be improvised, there is one little oversight that might just spoil the fun: it is a plan against the trend.

Therefore, despite this countertrend persistence, it is safe to assume that in most instances with-trend traders will not let themselves be intimidated that easily. They know they have the trend on *their* side, and the stronger it is before the pullback, the more they will look upon that very pullback as a great opportunity to short the market at very economical levels. If so, then for a second time in the same area countertrend traders will take a beating. Should it turn out that they have exhausted themselves in their two attempts to turn the trend, and now lack the courage or the funds to cook up a third, the chart, at some point, will print a bearish candle that takes out the low of a previous candle. This is the second break (SB) a sideline scalper has been waiting for. He will short the market the moment the break becomes visible on his screen.

Hopefully the point is taken that the smart scalper does not recklessly join in because he *expects* the countertrend attack to fail. He waits patiently for his fellow with-trend traders to start pushing their weight first.

With a bit of imagination, one can picture in a downtrend a M-pattern at the top end of the bullish pullback, usually in the area of the 20ema (resistance). In case of an uptrending market, the pullback will be bearish and in the bottom end of it one might see a W-pattern in the 20ema (support). Both are extremely dependable stepping stones for a continuation of the trend. Technical traders may recognize the very common double top and double bottom reversal patterns. Here they are called reversal patterns because they reverse the pullback (not the trend).

Since the SB setup is made up of two individual breaks that very much appear on their own terms, its formation comes in many shapes and forms. The most visual variations deal with the number of bars between the first break and the second. In similar examples as the one described above, the second break will occur not long after the first, maybe within one to four bars. This will keep both breaks rather close together, making the pattern quite compact in shape and easy to identify (the M- or W-pattern). Quite frequently, however, the number of bars between the first and second break will surpass that of only a handful, turning the SB pattern in a more elongated, wave-like formation. Still, this does not compromise the high probability factor in any way. The exact same forces and principles are at work, it just takes the market a little more effort to get the message across.

Now let us see how some of these SB setups present themselves on a real-time chart. There is no need to memorize any of the particular bar sequences because in practice the market may come up with an infinite amount of variations. If one understands the idea behind the setup, recognizing it in the market will soon become second nature. The concept by itself is rather simple to grasp: countertrend traders try something twice, fail on both occasions and then, either demoralized or panic-stricken, give up on their plan by quickly bailing out.

This simultaneous activity of with-trend traders entering and countertrend traders exiting creates a temporary hiatus of countertrend interest, which reinforces the trend with every newly conquered pip until it simply wears off.

Needless to say that somewhere down the line, countertrend traders will come out on top or else the markets would indefinitely rise or fall. It is crucial, though, to not let ourselves be scared out of perfectly healthy trades just because we are afraid to get trapped in what might be the exact turning point of the trend. As long as the market is trending and not running into obvious resistance, we should consider *every* orderly pullback a temporary event and use it to our advantage by trading our setups at every possible turning point. Once we start denying ourselves trades because we think the market has gone too far, we enter the realm of the paranoid amateur who lives in a fantasy world of being able to predict what is going to happen next. Essentially, there are only two reasons to skip a valid trade: obvious chart resistance and unfavorable trading conditions. In all other instances, probability traders should just trade probability. And there is arguably no higher probability of a winning trade in the markets than to take that trade with-trend after a pullback peters out.

Figure 9.1 Classic SB setup with only one bar between both breaks. From a technical viewpoint, it would have been defensible to regard that first break (1) as a regular FB setup and trade it as such. After all, the market did crack a nice level of support earlier on (the 1.3315 zone), to which prices were definitely responding to the downside. However, both trend and the two-bar pullback somehow lack the distinctiveness and fervor necessary to allow for that kind of aggression. But sometimes this hinges on personal preference more than on chart technicals. My favorite FB should ideally come out of a strong pullback that ate back at least 40 percent of an even stronger move, with the market showing obvious signs of shock or turmoil. If that is not the case, my bet will be on the occurrence of a second break. In practice, though, the market will hand the trader a lot of borderline situations that balance on the brink of being either this or that. Aggressive scalpers may trade these borderline cases with similar enthusiasm as they do the textbook setups, whereas more conservative individuals may opt to wait for a superior trade. It will take hundreds of trades to determine which of the two is the more profitable approach. In the end, the differences may very well be negligible. From a psychological point of view, however, being consistent in the approach may prove to be more relevant than the actual strategy itself. If nothing else, it will bring peace and harmony to the table, and

leave doubt and regret out the door.

One look at the chart above and you can see why it is so important to not lose track of the bars in the area of the 20ema, and particularly once the FB is set. It took the market just two candles after the first break to print a second break (2), and off it went again. The trend may be our friend, as goes the saying, but it will not exactly ask us out on a date. As scalpers we have to be assertive and grab whatever opportunity is offered.

By the way, did you see the M-like pattern unfold in the 20ema? As already explained, we can also look upon the SB short setup as being a double top at the end of a pullback. As any technical trader will acknowledge, a single top is perceived much less a tell-tale sign than a double or even triple top. Hence the SB being superior over the FB.

Figure 9.2 This chart seems a little rough at first glance, but if one follows the forces in play, it is actually quite a decent chart price technically. It needs no further clarification why skipping that FB (first arrow) is the logical thing to do. At that point, the market may have been showing a preference for the upside (printing higher bottoms as it goes along), but it is way too early for a trader to display FB aggression.

If you look closely at the price scale on the vertical axis, you can see that the 1.2850 round number level is playing a major role in this chart. When breached for the first time (2), it must have made a lot of counter-trend traders very happy, for these important levels are best not broken in an overly eager one-directional move. A better way to go about it, is to do it in a stepwise fashion.

As is often the case after an extensive run-up, once prices start to stall and then break down (3), clever countertrend traders aggressively step in. In this chart, they managed to force back the bulls quite significantly. Prices did not stop to drop until they found support in the chart (4 tests 1). That pretty much evened the score. However, it did not take long for the bulls to try their luck again. Not encountering too much resistance on their path, they quickly brought prices back up to challenge the round number zone once more (5). A pip below the previous top, countertrend traders typically deployed a fresh wave of shorts, forcing prices back again, but with a little less zeal. This time the pullback neatly halted in the 20ema (6).

When this signal bar to the FB cracked to the upside, so did the round number and prices now even surpassed the former top to the left by a pip or so (7). And then were forced back down *again*.

This is the point where a sideline scalper has got to be on high alert. There is only one pressing question that needs to be answered by the market and chances are it won't take long for that answer to arrive. Is that round number zone going to hold up as resistance or will it give in to the bullish forces that are attacking it? In the space of just a few minutes, the market has seen three breaches of it, all three of them cut short. Something's got to give. Either the bulls will give up on their attempts, or the bears will succumb to the upward pressure.

At the point of the second touch on the 20ema (8), obviously by a very bearish looking candle at the moment of impact, there is still no telling which side of the market is the more dominant party. Prices could bounce up once more, stall completely, or drop like a rock and never look back. Still, in these situations, it would be wise to already place the cursor on the buy button and anticipate a bullish breakout. Not because of preference but simply because only a bullish breakout will require immediate action, which is to enter long at the market after a second signal bar gets broken to the upside (9); a victory of the bears, on the other hand, will most probably not generate a short setup for at least a fair amount of bars.

Let's look at this SB situation more closely. It is safe to assume that at this particular moment in time, little scalpers are not the only ones ready to trade that upside break. All sorts of traders, big and small, active on a variety of time frames, will be sitting up straight, either dreading or hoping for the market to pop. Although the cracking of a round number zone regularly passes as a total non-event, this particular chart shows the level being strongly defended as well as attacked. It isn't hard to imagine a large number of stop-loss orders floating above it (of traders currently short); should the number crack, the market could show a mean reaction that could even be the start of a major rally. Big players love to take these orders out when given the chance. They thrive on other traders' paranoia and take pleasure in testing these resistance zones multiple times, just to see how the defenders react to either pinpricks or more aggressive attacks. Bear in mind, though, that big players cannot have their way with the market completely unchallenged. It would be incorrect to assume that they are only opposing the smaller participants. On their path, they will encounter loads of other big players for sure. And each of these opponents will also have great technical insight and no doubt a bunch of allies to join forces with; together they just may possess the power to swing the market in another direction. And each party will feel no shame revising its strategy in a flick of a moment. To the tiny scalper, the trick, of course, is to not get trampled in this parade of dancing elephants, but to cleverly ride their backs.

Note: In hindsight everything is easy and the chart, like the one above, may show perfect looking bullish dojis in the 20ema that make for excellent signal bars to a possible break (bars 6 and 8). But try to imagine that in real-time these candles looked very bearish *the moment* the average got hit. So, when it comes to reading candles, do not let first impressions deceive you, but stay alert and expect any bar to fully change shape when there are still ticks to go in it. What's more, very bullish or bearish candles with a perfect hindsight hit on the 20ema (no piercing), in real-time may not even have touched the average at all up until the very last tick that closed the bar. Exponential averages, after all, put more weight to current prices than older ones, which explains a possible sudden lift or drop of the average in case the current candle is very strong and ends on its high or low. Keep this in mind when looking for a signal bar to set up a possible trade. Although we do not actually need visual confirmation in the shape of a tell-tale bar (we trade breaks, not bars), it is always nice to see some distinctiveness in a particular signal bar.

Let's compare this SB setup to the one in the previous chart, Figure 9.1. Apart from the fact that the first chart is bearish and the second one bullish, are these patterns really that different? Visually, sure. But technically, the same unmistakable forces are in play. A trend (or strong move), a pullback, a failed continuation of the trend, another pullback, a continuation of trend. The bearish chart shows the M-pattern, the bullish one the W. In any case, both reactions to each second break literally speak volumes.

Figure 9.3 It is a great technical plus to see a trend present itself with indisputable clarity. The 70-tick chart may be a speedy one and set

to serve a scalper's short-term strategy, it is not so tiny a chart that it is completely disconnected from the somewhat slower tick or time frames. That means that a nice solid trend on our chart is very likely to be picked up by a great number of other participants as well. Maybe all the way up to traders trading a 10-minute chart. The more clear the trend, the tougher the job to counter it. Although countertrend traders can be rather persistent and courageous in their attempts to fight the market's direction—and at times quite successful—it would suit them to make a clear distinction of when and when not to undertake these tricky ventures. Those that entertain the folly of trying to obstruct a very determined trend will simply find themselves tossing pebbles at a giant. There are just too many with-trend traders around hoping to treat themselves to a piece of the pie, and they will welcome any countertrend attempt with open arms.

The first SB pattern in the chart above has a FB in it that is rightfully skipped (4). The pullback leading up to it does not have the makings of a standard one-directional countertrend move, nor is it the first to counter the trend. It is best to wait and see how the situation unfolds.

On close inspection, we can see that the signal bar that led up to that first break actually first cracked a series of highs to the upside (3). In combination with the little double bottom pattern from a few minutes before (1-2), this must have looked very promising from a contrarian perspective. And it must have inspired at least a number of with-trend traders to start dumping their profitable positions out of fear of seeing their paper profits being fully eaten away. And still the market didn't budge. That spells short with a capital S.

When searching for a with-trend setup, and then be presented with one, a novice trader is still very prone to make a rather classic mistake. And that is to be intimidated by the very activity that brings prices towards him. False perceptions show the nasty habit of emerging right before having to take a trade. Fight them and trade (6).

In a way, it is highly understandable for a trader to become at least a little paranoid in a line of business where every move simply revolves around trapping and trampling, or luring and betraying the fellow businessman. But let's face it, this is what it is, and a trader is best advised to come to terms with the treacherous nature of his profession as soon as possible. If it is any consolation, even the seasoned trader gets trapped. Everyday again. No trader will ever have control over the market. But it is important to not let the market control the trader, either. In other words, you cannot go around predicting when your setup will *not* work. If it is a *valid* setup, you have to take it. In a later section, we will look into those situations where an otherwise valid setup loses its validity on account of the current conditions being unfavorable to the trade. For now, that is not relevant.

The second SB pattern is a beauty, and quite of the textbook variety. First there was a strong one-directional pullback leading up to a first break that could be legitimately skipped at that point in time (8). But look at these white bodied candles, not even a black body in it; it means that every candle closed higher than it opened, which is a strong display of bullish sentiment. Should such a move scare a trader out of the idea to still go short on a possible second break? Not in this chart. Moves like this, in the opposite direction of a strong trend, are extremely prone to exhaust themselves; it's like running up a hill without a break. Running downhill without a break is a lot easier, hence the principle of the trend being a friend.

The little doji at the top of the pullback is the signal bar to the first break (7). A scalper can rightfully skip the FB (8), but he should not lose sight of the activity in the 20ema zone. The market now resides at a crucial spot. Will the next coming candles manage to stay above the average, or will prices continue their decline? The odds strongly favor the latter. Firstly, because the trend is down to begin with. Secondly, because that pullback is running into the technical resistance of the previous pullback from 20 minutes ago, no doubt making a lot of traders want to short it; remember how pullbacks tend to *test* earlier broken levels, and then bounce back. Here that pullback tested the level from where the first SB setup broke down (7 tests 5). Thirdly, because in a strong downtrend new highs as well as new lows are very likely to get shorted. New highs, because they provide more favorable prices to short from. New lows, because they break in the trend's direction. Look what happened when a second signal bar low was cracked and the SB setup completed (10): the market dropped like a stone, just like it did 10 minutes ago.

Traders that can appreciate a nice touch of pattern repetition should have a close look at both of the SB setups here, and particularly at the three-bar price action leading up to each second break (the bars above 5 and 9). Both situations, though minute in shape, provide excellent examples of how the psychological warfare among traders can be displayed in a small number of crucial bars. We *could* simply see a doji, a bullish bar and a bearish bar. Or we could read: countertrend doubt, countertrend hope and countertrend fear. And one only needs to look at the ensuing price action to see what happens when fear turns into its uglier variant: panic.

Looking at all of the setups so far, the impression may have arisen that in the majority of winning trades prices will make a one-directional, dedicated dash for the profit target from the moment the break is set. What a wonderful world that would be. It may be a bit disheartening to realize that this will simply not be the case in a vast number of our trades. Understanding this principle is one thing, accepting it is quite another. Staying calm after entry and not being tricked into prematurely bailing out of still very valid trades (although slightly in the minus) is what separates the professional from the amateur. The reader, by now, may have become a bit anxious to learn about the specific exit techniques attached to this scalping method, but it is really deemed preferable to go through all of the setups first and not front-run any of our future lessons. For now, it should suffice to say that, as a rule of thumb, most running trades will simply keep their validity as long as prices travel in the target's direction, and if not, as long as they do not take out any specific highs or lows, particularly those of a setup.

Figure 9.4 Irrespective of strategy and bail out technique, let's contemplate a hypothetical situation in which a trader acted upon that first break in the chart above (2). It shows the typical predicament of having to decide whether to stay in and still believe in the trade, or bail out to prevent further damage. Technically, this trader did the right thing by trading a very trending chart from the long side. Should his strategy allow him to trade any first break in a respectable pullback, then he did not slip up in that department either. Still, his trade is about 6 to 7 pip in the minus at the lows of the pullback (3), with no certainty of that being the end of the agony. What to do?

It is irrelevant what this particular trader would do. What is important, is to realize that getting trapped in a tough spot is not merely the privilege of traders acting before their turn. Situations like this will most certainly present themselves in almost any session, no matter what set-up is involved or what strategy is used.

Trades do show the tendency to stumble and falter *in relation to the entry price* probably more often than not. Chart technically, however, the market may only be exhibiting its typical hesitation before making another swing in the direction of the trend (and the trade). If we look at the chart in question, for instance, and imagine ourselves to be in that first break trade, then being so many pip in the minus is hardly a comforting prospect for a winning trade. The market, on the other hand, is completely oblivious to a trader's hopes and fears. All it did here is what it usually does before moving on, and that is to test, very technically, a former level of support or resistance. Here it tested, to the exact pip, the low of the first little pullback from about seven minutes before (3 tests 1).

Still, this is where a trader, quite unwillingly but forceful nonetheless, may get swept into an emotional battle with the market should the latter force him to take a loss, only to treacherously turn around and provide the anticipated swing after all. Unfortunately, this is a very common and often painful experience, and even more so to those not alert enough to recognize the trap and immediately re-enter (4).

First of all, not being able to re-enter as a result of having faced a little loss just moments ago is a clear case of burnt-finger anxiety. Apparently, a recent loss has negatively affected the decision-making process—at least long enough to miss the next trade—which is a sign that the trader is no longer thinking in probabilities. Having one's emotional balance rock up and down as a function of the outcomes of one's trades is a surefire way to burn out sooner or later. Whether a trader freezes up after a loss or prematurely re-enters to vindicate himself, both equally common, his decisions are no longer based on exploiting a technical edge but find their footing in emotional instability. Needless to say, things can quickly go from bad to worse.

But let us also examine a common psychological knot even a more stable scalper might find himself wrapped up in. Seeing his stop getting hit for, say, a 6 pip loss, but alert enough to re-enter (technically) and obtain the 10 pip winner after all, this trader may still experience very uncomfortable feelings of being trapped, tricked and even bereft by the very market that just allowed him to make a 4 pip profit on balance. Why would that be? Most probably, because even a lot of experienced traders cannot shake the idea of having to prove themselves right in *every* trade—to justify the risk they take with each position in the market. They are not thinking in probabilities either. They may survive on technical proficiency, but inside they are a psychological mess. Imagine for a moment that the market had neither presented the first nor the second trade and no position had therefore been taken. Our trader would probably feel alright, calm and open minded towards the market. But now that he got his 4 pip profit, he feels bad and bereft! And it is very logical why he would feel that way; after all, since he was right on the direction of the market, he feels the market *owes* him these 10 pip, but he only got a measly 4.

Really, all this agony—the inner battles, the compulsive desire to prove oneself, the irritation when contradicted by the market—will simply pass once a trader fully accepts the risks, the losses and any outcome the market may come up with. In other words: once he starts to think in probabilities. It is the only road to relaxed trading and ultimately to consistent, profitable results. No individual trade, not even a nasty string of losers, should be able to disrupt a trader's confidence in his abilities or in the method used. As long as a particular strategy is not proven counterproductive—which is to be assessed by analyzing many hundreds of trades over a specified period of time—a trader should just trade his setups, and thus probability. There is no point in counting pip on a trade per trade basis. Count them at the end of a session or over the weekend. Inside a session it is simply trading time.

Let's get back to the chart; although not every first break trade will falter like this, this case serves to show how dangerously these FBs can be challenged; and it also shows us how well a second break in the pullback is likely to be picked up by with-trend traders awaiting their chance (4). The signal bars to the SB trade (two dojis with equal highs) also function as a regular DD setup in this chart (3).

Note: If the entry on the SB (in the bar taking out the two dojis) was somehow missed, it does not have to mean the opportunity is lost. The market, quite frequently, will offer a trader a second chance to get in, usually within the first couple of bars after a break. After all, there exists a strong tendency of prices to revisit (test) the level they just broke out of. This phenomenon, if it indeed presents itself, may even allow a trader to get in on his missed trade at no extra cost. It may depend on the situation to determine the point where trying to get in is best forgone. This is more a matter of bars than it is of price. On average, it is fair to say that in calm markets a trade can still be entered within the next couple of bars. If one is lucky, it may even result in a slightly better entry price. But that should never be a reason to deliberately miss an entry! Thousands of good trades, no doubt, are missed out on each day because of traders trying to outsmart the market by waiting for a more economical level that never shows up.

If you look closely, in the strict sense of the setup there was another SB about 12 minutes later (the FB at 5 and the SB at 6), but it is not hard to see why this market situation is definitely of inferior quality. Let me explain: in a bull trend, for instance, the low of the pullback leading up to the first break counts as a standard measure to be tested later on should the market not immediately want to proceed (the first low in the W-pattern). If it is tested and holds up (the second low in the W-pattern), the trend is often perceived to be technically sound and thus prices could very well live up to their upward projection. The idea of the second break being such a high probability trade is based on the premise that this low is indeed tested, even if it is not exactly to the pip. But having to enter a second break about 7 pip above the entry of the first, without having seen a proper test of the earlier low or even the 20ema, just does not make for a high probability trade anymore.

Admittedly, in this chart the distinction between the proper SB trade and its ugly counterpart was not exactly subtle. In many situations, however, there will run a much finer line between taking and skipping a trade. That may put the trader a little more to the test. In the end, a trader can only make do with his current state of proficiency and hope to grow with each new day in the market.

Note: When studying a questionable situation in hindsight, it is always essential to evaluate the case with an open mind. That way one stands to learn and benefit the most from whatever happened in the past. Skipped trades, for instance, that turn out a winners, and accepted trades that turn out a losers, may only represent outcomes in the normal variance of a probability play and should not necessarily be interpreted as a reason to act differently next time.

Figure 9.5 Although not technically identical, these two setups are very similar in price action, but there are some subtle differences that may be interesting to point out. In the first setup, the skipped FB (3) resulted in a short resumption of the trend before countertrend traders brought the market once again up to the 20ema (4). The thrust of this second leg of buying activity, however, never made it past the earlier high of (2). Apparently, not even the comforting thought of having the round number level of 1.40 right below the current prices (as support) could inspire new countertrend traders to finish what their companions had started. That may be an indication of underlying weakness. Still, things in the market are never fully evident and not seldom it takes only a couple of bars to change an outlook completely.

Nevertheless, when prices could not muster the strength to lift themselves any higher, the situation got nasty quite rapidly for the bulls. An alert scalper would surely have recognized a very promising M-pattern develop below the 20ema and not much later a textbook SB entry (5). In situations like this there is no need to postpone entering on the SB out of fear of that round number support (as resistance to a short). Waiting for the round number to crack first, as if to have weakness confirmed, is certainly not advisable. Not only does it deliver a terrible entry (in relation to the stop), the same danger of the level holding up is still luring. Because the possible resilience of a round number is more a zone than it is an exact level. In other words, for the sake of a more healthy scratch, it is better to be short a pip above a round number than one below it.

There is arguably no notion more highly regarded among technical traders than the popular wisdom of cracked support becoming resistance and cracked resistance becoming support. This is indeed a wondrous phenomenon that relentlessly shows up in any time frame, in any market. A fine example can be seen in the chart above when the first pullback to the second setup touched the 1.40 level from below (6). Why any scalper would want to buy straight into a *first test* of cracked support (now resistance) simply baffles the smart trader's mind, for it must be about the lowest probability trade in the field. Put yourself in the position of a bull for a moment and imagine your buy order being filled right there in the 20ema at 1.40. What do prices need to do for this trade to render itself profitable? They would have to dig their way through the very visible resistance of the clustering activity directly to the left (the M-pattern of the first setup). And not only that—they would have to do that after already having climbed up about 10 pip against the trend without pausing. These conditions provide a bull with terrible odds. Needless to say that a clever bear will welcome any bull with open arms, for such foolish bravery provides his own setup with the near power of foresight. After all, if going long at a particular spot makes for a terrible low odds trade, then taking the other side of that contract should basically be a formality.

Of course, it is not any of our business to judge whoever is doing what at any given moment in the marketplace. It is just information. In that light, we would simply see prices stall in the 20ema after a nice pullback. That makes it interesting for us. If two tiny dojis would set themselves up, then maybe we've got ourselves a nice DD trade in the making. If a first bar gets broken to the downside and prices travel up again, then a very dependable SB may still set itself up. All the more reason to stay focused and alert.

This particular setup shows a fine example of why it is wise to skip most first breaks in favor of a possible second break. The reaction to the first break (7) was simply non-existent. No doubt some countertrend traders will look upon this as a sign that the bears were a bit reluctant to push on. And with-trend reluctance equals countertrend hope: if somehow prices could be brought back up above 1.40, cracking the high of the earlier attempt in the process, maybe that would scare a number of with-trend traders out of their shorts, trigger some stops and convince new buyers to join the countertrend attack.

The reason for being so elaborative on this four-bar setup, is to explain the buildup to yet another technical marvel that in the hierarchy of tradable patterns may rank among the top of them all: the notorious *false break*.

Take a close look at that fine doji (8) that becomes the signal bar to the second break just moments later (9). For a brief moment, at least within the space of 70 ticks, that bar must have looked very bullish, white bodied and leading the countertrend parade. But the moment it stuck its head above the previous high (and simultaneously above the round number), with-trend traders ruthlessly slammed back the countertrend attack, warning every potential buyer on the sidelines to either back off or perish. Seeing a strong bullish candle transpose into a very bearish looking doji is the perfect deterrent to anyone still entertaining countertrend affinity. Particularly so, when that candle also represents a very classic false break (it falsely broke the earlier highs of bar 6 and 7). By definition, a false break traps any trader trading it as a true break, so these unfortunates are the first to feel the pain and they will have to act almost immediately to stop it. Of course, they can only do so by closing out their trades in the opposite direction, enhancing the falseness in the process.

What makes the false break more dangerous than most other market traps or tricks (from the perspective of those trapped in it) is its visual clarity. Especially when it tried to break the trend. The more traders see the same thing, the less chance for countertrend folly. Up to a certain point, of course. But usually long enough for us to scalp another 10 pip out of the market.

Just looking at these two SB setups shows us clearly the path of least resistance in the market. Why go against it, when you can go with it?

Note: This chart also provides a nice example of why being biased on the direction of the market could prove to be a terrible guide in scalping. At the left side of the chart, just 10 minutes before the first SB setup, the market looked to be trading in an uptrend (prices well above the 20ema). We cannot derive from this chart whether the 1.4020 zone represented chart resistance further to the left, but let us assume for a moment it did not. Then the chart presented a scalper with a textbook DD setup in the 20ema (1). The trade that came out of it, obviously, never got anywhere. Clever bulls will immediately switch into neutral, accept the loss and move on. A biased scalper, on the other hand, after being stopped out, would probably feel slightly uncomfortable with this little mishap. Since he pictured the market to travel higher, seeing it travel lower instead just doesn't feel right. How could the market be so wrong? The point is: would this scalper be able to reset his mind from bullish to neutral to bearish in time to take that first SB short entry just a few minutes later? A good question.

Figure 9.6 The first SB entry (4) in this slowly trending chart broke a cluster of no less than five dojis, all sharing equal highs. Notice how nicely the lows of the dojis (3) tested the earlier low of the signal bar

leading up to the first break (2), which in turn was a test of the 50-level that had been broken a few minutes before (1, resistance becoming support). **Note:** A test of a level does not necessarily have to occur in opposite direction. In this chart, the lows of (3) test the low of (2); the low of (2) tests the earlier high of (1).

By now, the observant reader will surely have noticed the remarkable tendency of prices to move in an orderly, stepwise fashion when traveling from one level to the next. Our 70-tick chart provides us with a wondrous view on these technical dynamics. With amazing clarity, it portrays, often to the very pip, the way most levels get attacked, defended, conquered, tested and abandoned. And that is not all. Technical chartists could have a field day just counting the many popular *chart patterns* that keep on reappearing in this excellent chart. Bull flags, bear flags, triangles, channels, double tops, pennants, head-and-shoulders, cup-and-handles, triple bottoms—it's a nonstop parade of technical phenomena.

So, if that is the case, are we not missing something here, and in all of the examples shown so far? Why aren't there any trendlines or pattern boundaries drawn on these charts?

The answer to that is even simpler than the question itself: there is no need to. All you ever need is already within your grasp. It is easy, effective and very, very profitable. Why look for more?

Surrendering to simplicity, it is fair to say, does not come natural to the human mind. Even when the desire is very much present. In fact, it can be a daunting struggle, almost like a ritual event, a rite of passage of some sort. And it is a journey that must be traveled alone, in the solitude of one's own perception. One might even call it a leap of faith. But believe me, once a trader makes it through that gate, he will experience a sense of freedom that seemed unreachable just days before.

The second SB setup in the chart could not be more tiny a pattern, yet it has all the makings of a perfect W-formation, comfortably supported by the gentle slope of the 20ema. You can almost visualize how the average is holding up its palm to cup the price bars in it, providing just enough push to help them through the current 1.4060 resistance.

But this situation does present us with a classic dilemma that sooner or later will surface on any trader's screen: what to do with a new setup (5) while already in position?

Since the appearance of a second trade is by no means a rarity, we have to reflect on it for a moment to see how it is best resolved. In trading there can exist some interesting conflicts among what is statistically justified, practically preferred or logically demanded.

Let us first examine some of the typical options that come to mind when presented with that second trade while already caught up in a first. 1: Ignore the new trade. 2: Take the new trade as a stand-alone event and manage both trades individually. 3: Skip the new trade but adjust the stop and profit levels of the current trade to those of the new trade, had it been taken.

And one could even opt to add some subtleties like pocketing the current profits on the first trade right before the break of the next, and then re-enter again when this second trade comes into effect; that doesn't sound so bad, if not for spread and slippage.

If we look at the options from a mere statistical viewpoint, then it leaves us little room for discussion as to what the proper action should be: take any trade that provides an edge.

But that may not be enough to go ahead with the trade. To evaluate our options wisely, we have to take into account every possible factor—physical, mental, technical and financial—that could theoretically compromise our play.

When opting for the adjustable target model, for instance, having to juggle two trades simultaneously may turn out to be a challenging task, even to the experienced trader. Adjusting stop and target levels correctly with only seconds to spare will be virtually impossible in any market, let alone in one that is moving fast. Even worse, manual scratches may accidentally cause unwanted open positions. Why? Because many traders are used to exit their positions by clicking on the opposite order ticket. For instance, when in a long trade, instead of hitting a close out button (on many platforms, a multiple mouse-click process), they just click on the sell ticket. This one-click exit usually works fine, because the majority of trades get scratched well before the market has time to activate the automated bracket-stop. But if one starts to hastily adjust the bracket levels, due to a second position overlapping a first, a trader may lose valuable seconds to act appropriately and he may find himself exiting his position just as the platform beat him to it. The result: a freshly taken, yet uncalled-for position.

Even in a calm market with no intention to adjust anything, taking the second trade may prove to be too heavy a burden on either the account or on the trader's comfort zone.

In other words, things can go from very orderly to very messy in just a small space of time. The culprit: blindly following a statistical edge and disrespecting practical circumstances.

Am I painting too negative a picture here, or just being realistic? That may depend on the trader in question, the sophistication of the platform used, the amount in the account, the experience in the market, or what have you.

My personal preference, as you may have already guessed, goes out to sticking to the original trade and letting everything else pass by until that trade is over. Firstly, with so many possibilities to scalp the market in a relaxed state of mind, I do not see the need to complicate matters for the sake of a few extra pip. But there is another reason I would have to pass up on that second trade, and one that easily outmatches the mere freedom of skipping trades for the sake of simplicity. It is called maximum risk per trade.

Although we will delve into this in more detail in a later section on Account Management, let us look into some of the particulars briefly to clear up some common misunderstandings regarding this matter. First of all, there is the issue of margin requirements. Margin, in general, is the minimum amount of capital in the account required to trade a certain amount of volume (units) with. This differs per company, but Forex brokers, on average, allow a trader a huge leverage to play with, going from as low as a 20:1 up to a whopping 400:1, or even higher than that. A leverage of a 100:1 simply means that a trader can trade a $100,000 worth of units, but only needs a $1,000 in the account as margin. What does this have to do with not being able to trade a double position, the reader may wonder; would a consistently profitable trader, especially with the huge leverage offered to him, not have enough funds in his account to trade that second position? The answer to this is that it may not be an issue of funds.

There are a few things to address here that may be of importance to a trader unfamiliar with proper account management. First there is the common mistake of confusing broker margin with allowable risk. As much as a 1000:1 leverage may represent an ideal circumstance for trading, to actually use that kind of leverage would border on the suicidal. It is not a broker's call to decide on the matter of risk. The smart trader puts no more than a certain percentage of his capital at risk on any one trade; he will then simply adjust his volume to match his risk model. For instance, should he want to use a 10 pip stop on a trade, his volume will be twice as large in comparison with another of his strategies that requires a 20 pip stop. But his risk per trade will be the same. This is an important concept to grasp. Even traders who have proven themselves to be consistently profitable over time are highly unlikely to go overboard on allowable risk per trade. Chances are, they would not have reached their state of consistency in the first place had they not respected the universal law of account protection: Anything can and will happen, even to the best of traders, so rule number one, at all times, is to protect the account. Many experienced traders do not risk more than 2 percent of capital on a single trade. Overall, that is a fair percentage and it would probably suit the consistently profitable scalper in similar fashion. But the key issue here is consistency. Any scalper not yet proficient enough to reap profits from the market on a regularly basis (many weeks on end) is best advised to approach the market with a lot more prudence, preferably risking no more than 1 percent of capital per trade. But regardless of the percentage chosen, once a trader has agreed on his maximum risk per trade, he should exploit his granted leverage to the fullest and assign the maximum volume possible to his position without violating his choice of risk. That simply means that there will be no trading a second position while already caught up in a first, because the maximum amount of units are already at work. Doubling up would seriously violate the risk per trade rule, with no less than 100 percent. Of course, one could argue that the second position is a trade on its own and therefore is entitled the same amount of volume as the first position, but that doesn't really hold up, if you think of it. Trading two positions simultaneously in the same market and in the same direction is essentially one position entered in two instances. There is much more to be said on the relationship between volume, leverage and risk and all of it will be discussed in Chapter 16 in the section on Account Management.

Figure 9.7 The first SB setup here looks a bit messy at first glance, but on close inspection it meets all the demands to qualify for a perfect W-pattern in support (2 and 4 test 1). The average, clearly, had a hard time keeping up with the sudden burst of activity: first a bullish buying frenzy that came out of nowhere (long line of white bodied candles around 20:00) and then that sharp, three candle decline (tall black bodies) that ate back almost 50 percent of the earlier swing. But look where that pullback came to a halt; straight into the earlier resistance (now support) of the 1.3860 zone.

That sharp sudden upswing could have led to an excellent FB setup (3), if not for the pullback failing the requirements (it showed a two-step decline, basically a double top). No reason for disappointment, because a scalper can always switch to plan B, which is to patiently wait for a superior break to appear (6).

Interesting how that very bearish black bar (4)—that tested the earlier low of (2) to the exact pip, forming the second bottom in the W-pattern— was immediately countered by an equally bullish bar that managed to close back just above the 20ema (5). Such can be the power of support. If you don't know what to make of a strong bearish bar countered by a similar strong bullish bar, whether that is neutral or bullish (relatively speaking), then try to imagine them as one, meaning as if the chart printed not 70, but 140 ticks per bar. Then you get a bar that opens on its high, runs all the way down, looking very black and bearish, only to close back on its high again. The result: a perfect looking bullish doji— just like the signal bar leading up to the first break. Two dojis in the bottom of a pullback in technical support: that spells W-pattern!

Note how the technical buildup to the second SB entry (11) is quite similar to the first. In the first setup the lows of (2) and (4) made up the bottom of the W-pattern. In the second setup, the lows of (8) and (10) do the same. Now that the market calmed down, the 20ema is once again typically running below the lows of the setup. Even more technically, these lows find support in the highs of the previous setup (the highs of the first W-pattern). All in all, this represents very stepwise price action and things look quite good from a bullish perspective.

A nice bullish doji (10) became the signal bar to the ensuing break. However, as discussed in the text below Figure 9.6, this second SB trade is skipped when already in position on the earlier SB. If still on the sidelines, for whatever reason, it provides a nice opportunity to get into the market after all. That being said, chances are a sideline trader may feel a bit uncomfortable getting in on that second SB trade knowing that he missed a more economical entry just moments before. All very logical, in a way, but remember that entering a trade is never an issue of price. It is just a matter of probability.

Let us go back to that first SB setup for a moment. If we follow the path of this trade from the point of entry (6), we can see that it flourished for about 8 consecutive pip, only to see the market take a sudden turn and demand back all of the paper profits in its trip back to the 20ema (8). Very few traders remain completely unaffected by this drastic change in prospect. Seeing a trade almost hit target and then crumble apart like a house of cards is often perceived as a personal attack, a mean and vindictive act of the market, just to spite a hard working trader aching for profit. Needless to say that this perception sneakily triggers all sorts of unhealthy emotions, with feelings of bereavement, unjustness and deception ranking among the top.

This personal fight with the market, looking upon it as if it is an entity, a living, breathing organism, a mighty opponent, is a typical trader's illusion, and not only on the part of the novice. As usual, the enemy here is obviously not the market but the demon within. If you find yourself being able to look at the market technically, analytically and above all in a calmly manner when *not* in position, only to see yourself lose all objectivity and emotional serenity when stuck in a trade, particularly one that appears to be faltering, then you have no option but to embark on some serious soul-searching. What is it that you want out of this trading business? What do you *expect* the market to offer you? What do you expect yourself to accomplish? What makes you want to obstruct your own path to success, time and time again, by warping your sense of reality every time you are exposed to either losses or gains? Why can't you look at the market from a statistical viewpoint? Or better yet: why *can* you think in probabilities in hindsight, but *fail* to do so in the reality of a running trade?

Maybe there is one single question that encapsulates all queries more than any other: what is it that you are afraid of?

The answer to this will undoubtedly differ from trader to trader and one could probably take his pick from an almost infinite supply. Just to name a few: Fear of being ridiculed. Fear of being wrong. Fear of losing capital. Fear of getting trapped. Fear of missing out. Fear of commitment. Fear of boredom. Fear of pressure. Fear of failure. And, who knows, even fear of success.

Unfortunately, there is no ready-made solution on how to distance oneself from the many perceptions that obstruct clear and analytical thinking when under pressure. A trader could be told a hundred times over to think in probabilities, but when the mind is not yet ready for structural change, it will simply ignore even the most sound advice. Just like it is pointless to tell somebody grieving over a shattered dream, for instance, to just get over it. It's a process.

And therein lies also the good news. We know it can be done. Eventually, a trader will come to realize that he has no alternative but to start detaching himself emotionally from all his actions in the market. Only then can he begin to look upon his trading as merely exercising a carefully crafted business plan. This thought-process may take its time to surface—weeks, months, sometimes even years. In many cases, this transition comes about so gradually that the trader may not even be aware of it; other times, it may occur rather unexpectedly; who knows, one might even hear the proverbial *click*.

Chapter 10

Block Break (BB)

If all setups were to qualify in one of three categories, the options being either with-trend, non-trend or countertrend, then the patterns we have discussed so far—DD, FB and SB—are unmistakably with-trend ventures. They not only acknowledge the presence of a trend, they try to capitalize on its continuation as well. And that makes sense, if you think of it. Although opinions on its definition may differ widely across the board, the love for the trend in general is quite universal. Almost any trading method will incorporate at least a couple of clever with-trend plays to hop on or ride out a good move.

Unfortunately, as any chartist will surely admit, things seldom materialize in the most desirable way. Many times there is a lot of pulling and pushing and backing and filling, even in a very visible trend, and this often ruins the possibility of using the classic with-trend setups to get ourselves in position. It is all part and parcel of the trading game. However, in many such instances, the opportunities are not necessarily lost and with a little luck and patience we may just be able to pull a nice trump card from our sleeve: the multipurpose Block Break setup (BB).

This setup comes in many shapes and forms and we would probably not do it justice if we were to casually generalize on its appearance. A most simplistic description would be to characterize the pattern as a cluster of price bars tightly grouped together in a narrow vertical span. Preferably, the barriers of this block of bars are made up of several touches each, meaning that the top and bottom side of the pattern clearly represent resistance and support. On occasion, depending on the speed of the market, this group of bars could appear and be broken in a matter of seconds, but the formation itself could best be seen as a miniature trading range.

If we were to draw a rectangular box around all the bars that make up this pattern, what should emerge is a distinctive block of price action in which a relatively large amount of contracts changed hands without price being really affected. But the tension within should almost be tangible, like that of a coil being suppressed by a weakening force that is bound to give in. If prices eventually break free in the direction of the path of least resistance, we immediately enter the market on a break of the box. This makes the broken horizontal barrier the *signal line* to our entry point. Should prices break out at the less favorable side, then no action is taken just yet.

When encountering this cluster of bars at the possible end of a pullback in the area of the 20ema, a trendside breakout would require similar action as would a break of a regular DD or SB setup. In fact, if we would also wrap a box around a group of dojis that make up a typical DD, we would basically create a miniature BB setup. The same goes for the SB pattern as a whole, though be it that the entry in this setup usually shows up *before* the highs or lows of the complete pattern are taken out.

But make no mistake, when it comes to the BB setup, we are not just dealing here with another trick to take a with-trend trade at the end of a pullback, although that is one of its functions. What gives this pattern its unique quality and personal character is its multipurpose application. This setup could essentially show up anywhere in the chart, while still conforming to the requirements of a tradable event. Its abundant presence makes it one of the better weapons to tackle almost any market, trending or not.

There are some factors to assess, though, before we can start to regard this pattern as a valid setup. We cannot simply trade any odd block break and expect the market to take off for at least a 10 pip run. As is the case with any other setup, the block break, too, should be seen as just an *aid* to get in on a market that has already been identified as favorable; it would be a painful mistake to use it as a pet setup with little or no regard for underlying conditions.

But what exactly is a favorable market?

As we have already observed, a pullback in a trend, for one, leaves little room for discussion on that part. But how about a sideways market that just printed a nice double bottom and a higher bottom in support? How about a market that broke so violently that countertrend traders cannot even force a noteworthy pullback in it? How about an uptrending market that shows clear signs of resistance, like double tops and lower tops? And what about a market that seems chaotic in any respect, apart from the fact that it successfully slammed back all attempts to break a round number zone?

The situations above, just randomly chosen, may be as different from each other as night and day, but they do have one particular characteristic in common: not so much that they paint a very vivid picture of the perpetual clash between the bulls and bears, but more that they show us who is currently winning. The market may put up a fight, as it tends to do, but in the end, prices simply have no choice but to succumb to whoever is pushing the hardest. Just when and how, that is for a trader to find out. But maybe it is nice to know that the point of surrender is often preceded by a suppressed block of candles ready to pop.

Since there are just too many variations of the BB setup, it is best to get to the charts and see them in the flesh. Before we do that, let us first point out the most likely places for this setup to show up. In essence there are only three. 1: As a block of bars in the end of a pullback. In case this pullback is quite extended, the setup may at times show the characteristics of a countertrend trade. 2: As a horizontal pullback in a strong trend. This block usually shows up in a very brisk move that just cannot seem to pull back. Whereas a typical pullback seems to move somewhat diagonally against the trend, this one merely travels sideways, forms a block, and then breaks out in the direction of the trend. 3: As a block of bars in a non-trending market. This block can be found in topping or bottoming price action and even in the midst of a sideways consolidation. It can be played with-trend as well as countertrend.

As we will see in the next three chapters on Range Breaks, the BB setup can also be involved in the breakout of a bigger pattern, the range, but we best take on that correlation once we have familiarized ourselves with the more individual block breaks first.

In the coming charts we will see all of the BBs encapsulated by a rectangular box, aiding the visual process of identifying the highs and lows within each block. Although it is not necessary to draw these boxes when engaged in a live session, it does come in handy to at least plot the signal line in the chart. That way we can keep a real good eye on the exact break, because the highs or lows that make up the signal line may be several bars apart.

Note: When looking at the chart, it is quite tempting to focus mainly on the moving price action and on the possible development of a tradable setup. Yet the status of the overall picture deserves the most attention. Whatever price bar is currently being formed, it can only derive value from its relation to the bigger picture. It is this wider view on the price action that ultimately determines our setups to be valid or not. On average, an hour and a half of price action will usually do just fine. To stay sharp and not lose focus, repeatedly force yourself to judge the price action in its present light. Do you see higher bottoms, lower tops, horizontal breakouts, round number fights? Is the market trending, running in resistance, testing support? Keeping track of the 20ema is just one way of assessing the current pressure in the market, and an excellent one at that. But the whole array of actual tops and bottoms in the chart determines the overall pressure. More distinctive higher bottoms than lower tops: the pressure is currently up. More distinctive lower tops than higher bottoms: the pressure is currently down. Alternating tops and bottoms: the current pressure is evenly distributed.

Figure 10.1 You may not think much of it at first glance, but honestly, you can hardly get any closer to a free ride in the market than by trading patterns like this to the upside on a break of the box. First of all, looking at the left half of this chart, we can clearly see that this market is in an uptrend. Maybe an alert scalper already took some profits home. Maybe he had to give some back when prices finally dipped below the 20ema a little before 06:00. It is irrelevant. What *is* important, though, is to keep the radar scanning for trades to the long side; with a market looking like this, it is way too early to entertain bearish fantasies. It is not so much the pip gain that defines this market as bullish, but more the calmly manner in which it trails higher, finding hardly any obstacles on its path (the path of least resistance). Even below the 20ema, countertrend traders kept their activities to a minimum. That is a very bullish tell-tale sign. But with prices currently below the 20ema, how do we prepare ourselves for a possible continuation of the bullish pressure?

This is where a block break pattern could supply a simple solution. Let's examine why the box is drawn like it is. For starters, in a bullish setup, the exact bottom barrier of the box is not a crucial element; after all, since we have identified the overall pressure to be up, we are not going to trade a break to the downside, at least not for a while. Still, by curbing both sides of the pattern with horizontal lines (or wrapping a box around it), a trader does obtain clarity as to what is going on within the boundaries of the setup: it shows him the most prominent level of resistance as well as that of support.

It should take little technical insight to see why the top barrier here—the potential signal line—is drawn as depicted. The first top it is resting on (4) is the first high after a little bottom was set in at (3). Of course, we can only identify this high once prices have retraced from it relatively strong. At this stage, the market is not talking BB yet, but at least we now have a low and a high to monitor.

A few bars down the line, the market manages to test both the low and high to the exact pip (5 and 6), which is excellent—the test of the high in particular. A successful test of the low, although not essential, is always a welcome sight to anyone contemplating a long position. The test of the high, on the other hand, is crucial. If our first high is tested to the very pip and not broken, then we've got ourselves an equal high—and thus a valid reference point to draw our top barrier from. Every new candle that manages to touch this top barrier without breaking it is only confirming its significance. The premise involved is a simple one: the longer the barrier holds, the sharper the reaction when it finally succumbs.

Although the price action within the box has an amplitude of a mere five pip, the battle between the bulls and bears could not be more technically displayed. The highs run into the resistance of earlier support (2). The lows of the box find support created by the earlier highs of a little bull flag pattern (1). After the lows of the box are put in (four equal touches of the bottom barrier), the market gives us another major tell-tale sign: a higher bottom in the box (7); yes, by a mere pip, but in scalping that is vital information nonetheless.

Granted, the initial reaction to the break (8) in this particular example is not exactly brutal; we might even say it is quite hesitant (9). Although many block breaks can be sharp and brisk, the hesitant version is certainly not uncommon. Who is to say what traders are thinking when price cracks the box—false break or not? Especially in a quiet market, prices tend to take their time. When this happens while in position, it is important to remain calm, even when the bars crawl back inside the box. It is all part of trading breaks.

It may offer peace of mind to keep a good eye on the 20ema while in position. Despite the fact that the average may be traveling sideways for the biggest part of a developing block, once the box break is set, it often jumps into trending mode and shows a strong tendency to guide prices along. And you may be surprised how often it will play a role in the actual breakout, too. In fact, the most reliable breakouts are those where the average literally pushes the bars out of the box. To see how this works, have a look at the next chart below, which shows us a stunning example of this phenomenon.

Figure 10.2 Painted by the magical hand of the market in the space of just twenty minutes, the BB setup in the chart above looks treacherously non-descriptive. However, this one little pattern may very well represent the near perfect box, should there exist such a thing as perfection in the tricky nature of the market.

Let us see how exactly this pattern earned its credentials. Earlier on, the bullish character of the market was somewhat curbed by the resistance of the 1.3480 level (1). After a little *backing and filling*, as aimless price action is often referred to, the market drifted lower in the next 30 minutes of trading and then established its most distinctive low so far (2). Of course, we can only identify this low once the bulls start to buy themselves into the market again and take prices back up. Since it is our primary intention to trade this particular chart to the upside, we have to wait patiently for some sort of resistance to come in. This resistance can then later be cracked. The first sign of it was portrayed by the first distinctive top of (3) that followed the low of (2). That gives a scalper a potential level to put his signal line on.

Now that we have a high and a low to go by, it is just a matter of following the price action until anything tradable develops. Preferably, we like to see a number of equal highs hitting the potential signal line, but the market is not always so kind as to serve a trader on his every wish. Should prices break out immediately, then that is just too bad. There are many ways to play the market and should a scalper have to forgo a particular setup, then he just moves on to the next tradable event. In this case, prices very orderly stayed within the boundaries of the low and high and even managed to produce 7 equal tests of the first high in the box, which is excellent. The stronger the significance of the signal line, the more traders will spot the break and have to react. Either to get in or to get out.

Within the setup, a number of higher bottoms can be counted (4, 5 and 6), lending extra credit to the possibility of a bullish breakout. As the coil is now being suppressed to the max, something has got to give. We can imagine it to be the signal line, but as clever scalpers we will never act before our turn.

Notice how gently the 20ema eventually guides the bars through the top of the box, literally pushing them out. The six small bars right before the break, five of them sharing equal highs, represent what we will refer to as classic *pre-breakout tension* (6). We could say it is a miniature box within the box itself. The subsequent reaction to the break speaks volumes. With the 1.3480 resistance area now cleared, prices were simply sucked into the vacuum below the round number zone of 1.35.

Note: Similar as in the previous chart (Figure 10.1) there is a little overhead resistance to be spotted to the left of the setup (1). Would that not be worrisome? To a tiny DD pattern it most probably would. There may just be too little tension building up within the dojis to counter the resistance overhead. But the BB pattern, in that respect, is quite different: it has tension written all over it. What's more, the most likely reason why the BB set itself up in the first place is because of that same overhead resistance. Which is also why the break of it stands to cause a sharp reaction. Once the defenders give up and step out of the way, the path is usually cleared for at least a number of pip.

Aspiring scalpers, when slowly taking a liking to this method, are recommended to study the characteristics of boxes like those of Figures 10.1 and 10.2 (and their reversed counterparts) with great attention to detail. Hardly a session will go by without these very tell-tale patterns showing up in the chart, one way or another. However, it is important to never lose sight of the overall pressure in the market, because that is what ultimately determines the future direction of prices. Obviously, assessing the overall pressure in a trending chart will not cause much problems. In more sideways progressions, this process requires a little more subtlety on the part of the chartist, as is the case, for example, in the next chart below.

Figure 10.3 When casually regarded, the sideways action before 05:00 could be interpreted as ordinary backing and filling; after all, price

merely dances above and below the sideways trailing 20ema without showing particular preference to go one way more than another. Still, the observant scalper may have already spotted a series of almost non-chalantly printed higher bottoms in this sideways progression (1, 2, 3 and 4). When that fourth higher bottom was printed, forming a cluster together with the handful of price bars next to it, things are starting to get interesting. Take a moment to compare the sharp upmove initiating from the second bottom (2) with the move that emerged out of the cluster (3 and 4). Although they look quite similar in their thrust, the first one shot through the average with hardly any buildup preceding it, whereas the latter first saw a cluster of bars build up tension before breaking out. As subtle as these differences may be, they are of great significance technically. Both moves seem to appear equally strong, but the one that emerged out of the cluster stands a much better chance of holding up. Not only does it stem from a slightly higher bottom, the fact that it broke free from a cluster puts a solid foundation beneath the current market. This means that if prices were to retrace back to where they broke free from, as they often do, they are most likely to be halted right at the level of the earlier break (resistance becoming support). After all, it is much harder for prices to dig themselves a way through a solid group of bars than when there is very little standing in their way. The mere implication of potential support can already be so strong that a market doesn't even feel the need to test its validity.

In a similar way, tension was also building up within the first BB set-up in the chart. No less than seven equal touches of the top barrier can be counted within that block before the market finally broke through to the upside. Notice how prices bounced off of the signal line, a few bars after the break, which clearly shows us the power of cluster support (6).

Have a look at the three very small dojis leading up to the break of the box (5). They are displaying in miniature the same pre-breakout tension as the complete box is displaying in the bigger picture of the chart (just wrap an imaginary box around the highs and lows of the price action from 04:16 to 05:16). At the risk of being overly elaborative, I am pointing this out for a very valid reason. If you learn to train your eye to recognize these subtleties in a live market environment, you will eventually be doing yourself a tremendous favor. The rise and fall of prices is not a result of somebody swinging a giant wheel of fortune. There are actual people in the market, trading actual ideas, feeling actual pain and actual pleasure. You may never know for sure what motivates them to do what they do at any given moment in time, yet of one thing you *can* be sure: their actions are reactions to other traders actions, which is why most of the time everything happens in such repetitive manner. Markets may be random, as it is often stated, but traders surely are not.

Despite the upward pressure, the cluster below and the magnetic pull of the round number above, with-trend participation after the break quickly died out. Eventually, this trade would have had to be scratched for a loss (where exactly to bail out on a failing trade will be discussed in Chapter 14 on Tipping Point Technique).

Although they clearly lost a round, we can expect the bulls in this chart to not just crawl up in a turtle position. Given all the higher bottoms earlier on, they will surely be on the lookout to buy themselves back into the market at more economical levels. The most logical area to pick up new contracts would be in the 1.3480 support zone. In fact, they didn't even wait for prices to hit the level spot on (7).

With the market traveling a few pip higher because of this buying activity, touching the 20ema from below, the bears were now offered a more favorable level to become a little more aggressive (8). And indeed, they managed to squeeze out one more low (9). They were given little time to enjoy that feat, though, as a large number of sidelines bulls quickly stepped in. It is the information necessary to keep a trader on high alert for another bullish attempt to take control of the market.

With no less than six equal highs testing one another, a scalper did not have to think very long about where to draw the signal line of the second box.

What is the major difference between the first box and the second? At first glance, box number one originated from a more favorable position (above the 20ema), whereas the second box popped up in sideways action (flat 20ema). Keep in mind, though, that the market couldn't care less about our 20-bar exponential moving average. That is only an instrument in our own personal toolbox. In fact, in a somewhat sideways environment, buying above it could at times be more dangerous than buying below it. Therefore, from a technical perspective, both patterns here are very similar in nature: sideways action, support holding up, a buildup of tension and a subsequent break. Take a mental note of the two little dojis right before the break of the second box (10). We will see this duo many times over throughout this guide. They represent classic *pre-breakout tension*: a final attempt of those who operate against the current pressure to keep the box from breaking. Both bulls and bears will be very quick to act, though, should the proverbial jack pop out. In the first block pattern there are even three of these dojis to be detected, together forming not only a higher bottom in the box but also the very welcome pressure underneath the signal line (5).

Figure 10.4 No less than six reasons immediately come to mind why this short trade has excellent potential to pocket a trader another 10 pip of easy profit. 1: The market gave up a rather lengthy support zone (first half of the chart). 2: Countertrend traders lacked enthusiasm to test the broken support properly (1). 3: Instead, a lower top got printed in what can only be described as a horizontal pullback (2). 4: Two tiny dojis represented pre-breakout tension (3, basically another lower top). 5: A solid signal line succumbed to the bearish pressure (4). 6: The magnetic pull

of the round number below may just finish off the job (1.31).

As pleasurable as it may be to occasionally stumble upon the near perfect trade, it also poses a rather interesting challenge on the topic of volume versus predictability. If we were to assign a rating to each individual trade—by counting the number of valid reasons to either skip or trade a setup—and came to conclude that the probability factor is apparently not a constant but varies visibly from setup to setup, should this not force an intelligent strategy to alter the volume per trade in compliance with the degree of predictability?

As you may recall, I strongly suggested to not put more than 2 percent of capital at risk on any one trade (when consistently profitable). I also suggested to cram as much volume in these 2 percent as allowed in order to exploit our edge to the fullest. If so, then that rules out adding anything extra, no matter how good-looking the trade, because the maximum amount of units are already at work. On the other hand, one could argue that if there is such a thing as a superior trade, then, naturally, there must also be its counterpart, the inferior trade (though still possessing a positive expectancy); when opting to trade the latter, could one not *take off* volume and tread lightly?

The true statistical mathematician, the one that eats bell curves and standard deviations for breakfast, would probably cringe at the typical layman's view on probability. And rightly so. Still, it remains to been seen whether his clinical calculations hold up in a real market environment, where nothing is what it seems, where dubious emotions play a major role in assessing the odds to begin with, and where his faithful law of probability may even be defied by the very same forces that are causing it.

Once again, my take on this matter is to not delve into the complexities of individual outcomes, but to at all times keep things simple, with the bigger picture in mind. Once consistently profitable in the market, even marginally, a trader could best explore every *valid* setup with appropriate passion and just load up. Whenever we picture ourselves to have an edge, each setup deserves to be treated with equal respect, no matter how shady or pretty its appearance. And that means assigning the maximum allowable amount of units per trade to fully capitalize on the principle of positive expectancy.

Note: Contrary to common perception, the least important of all your trades is the one you are currently in. All your previous trades, though insignificant by themselves, at least have a statistical relevance. Together they determine the power of your edge. Your current trade, on the other hand, has yet to earn its notch on the historical slate. It is just a trade in process. And it is totally irrelevant whether it will win or lose. In fact, in a consistently profitable strategy that has proven to stand the test of time, a losing trade is basically a false assumption. Why is that? Reflect for a moment on the following: if a 1000 individual outcomes would show an assembled profit of 2000 pip and your next trade came up a loser of 6, would you say you just lost 6 pip, or rather that you made another 2 on balance? Granted, embracing a losing trade as if it were a winner may be stretching it a bit. But the point does show the importance of a proper understanding of distribution in a probability play. All individual outcomes are just data. The only thing that truly matters is the collective result of all your scalping actions in the market.

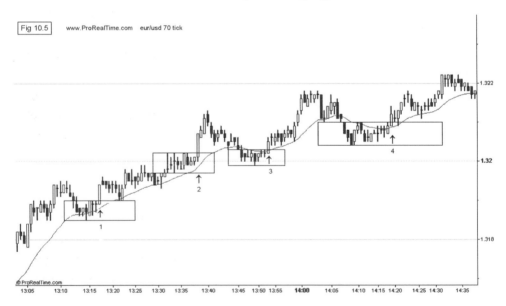

Figure 10.5 This chart offers a great example of the benefits of scalping with a predefined target objective: no stress, and with a minimum of exposure a trader could still participate in a big chunk of any solid move.

He does not need to wonder where to take profits. His only concern is how to get back in the market in case of a distinctive trend. Armed with a proper set of setups and aided by the fact that price seldom climbs or falls in a straight line, a proficient scalper should not encounter too much trouble in getting himself back in position. In this chart alone there were no less than four block break setups to be counted in the space of an hour. True, positions taken on box 2 and 3 may have over-lapped; still, it would have been rather easy to scalp 30 pip out of this chart, which is about the same number in pip the market managed to climb from the moment of the first BB setup (1).

By extending the boxes somewhat to the right, you can clearly spot the market's tendency to test almost any breakout before moving on. It is not uncommon to see a test to the exact pip, as is the case, for example, with the first and the fourth box in this chart. Note that this market doesn't care whether the boxes are formed from above a rising moving average or below a flattening one; to determine if the uptrend is still eligible for further advance, a quick look at the bottoms in it will usually be enough to make a proper assessment. In this chart, every noticeable bottom was put in at a higher spot than a previous one. As long as that is the case, we can expect the bulls to be aggressive and the bears to be in trouble.

On close inspection, we can see that the first box (1) contains a DD setup that would have already taken an alert scalper in the market before the box itself got cracked. It goes to show, though, that if for some reason a trade is missed, the market may still provide a trader with a valid opportunity to get in. Of course, it may come with the penalty of a less economical entry price.

The following box (2) contains a miniature bull/bear fight in the round number zone. Take note of the two little dojis right before the break. Preferably, these dojis have their extremes touching the signal line of the box, but things do not always have to be perfect in order to be tradable.

The third box (3) is an excellent opportunity to pick up a trade into the simultaneous support of a round number zone and some previous price action to the left; it more or less uses the cluster of bars within box 2 as support. Technical traders may recognize a tiny *reversed-head-and-shoulders pattern* within the box. Once again, two little dojis (the right shoulder) very typically build up pressure by pressing themselves against the signal line prior to the break.

The fourth box (4) makes a strong case for higher prices by not allowing the bears to test the round number zone to the pip (it uses the third box as support). Instead, the market prints higher bottoms within it and starts to work its way up to a top barrier breakout. Another very classic tell-tale sign.

Note: No matter how you look at it, break trading, when done properly, and in a favorable market, can be very profitable. The fact that so many traders are so paranoid about it, constantly dreading the notorious false break to haunt them, in many cases is only due to their limited understanding of what it means to have an edge. And yes, false breaks do occur on a regularly basis. But what exactly is there to fear when, on the whole, the odds are favoring a particular approach? Have you every seen a casino owner tremble in agony in the midst of his circle of roulette tables? He loves every spin of every wheel, win or lose. The same holds up in the markets once you put your edge to work. So there is no need for fear. Who should be fearful, though, are either those traders taking the other side of your contract, or those who do trade breakouts themselves but lack the ability to recognize an unfavorable condition. Have a look at the first and the third box again; the lows in both boxes represent typical false breaks to the downside. You may not think much of a candle dipping a mere pip below its companions, yet on a scalping chart these are false breaks nonetheless. And somebody traded those breaks or else the chart would not have printed these prices.

Figure 10.6 When confronted with a dull and rather lengthy non-trending market, like the first half of the chart above, it is not uncommon for a trader to start experiencing a somewhat uncomfortable mixture of impatience, boredom and even agitation. It can indeed be a mental challenge to have to sit out these times of inactivity, hoping for action and not getting any, especially to those traders who look upon their trading platform as a slot machine in a penny arcade. A word of caution may be in place here, because these sideways ranges do have the nasty habit of luring a trader in one of two very classic mistakes.

The first one is to start seeing and taking trades where there are none to be found. This warped sense of reality is typical for a trader who just *needs* action. And wrath be upon the market if he doesn't get it. Apart from the occasional winner that may come out of this, seeing a growing bunch of scratched trades eat their way into earlier profits will sooner or later present this trader with the unsettling notion of being reprimanded by the very market he is trying to punish. Needless to say that this sort of attitude towards trading is of the backfiring kind, and it remains to be seen whether this trader can pick himself back up in time for when the real action begins.

The second classic mistake is made by traders who on the surface seem to stay composed rather well in a sideways market. You won't catch them doing anything irrational like taking silly trades, nor will you see them get angry with the market or force their will upon it. They can watch the proverbial grass grow for what seems like an eternity without any sense of discomfort. Proficient enough to recognize the current indecision of the market as something that needs to be cleared by powers bigger than themselves, they simply sit back. Up until that one amazing moment that boredom abruptly kicks in. For reasons unbeknownst to themselves they suddenly have to get up to make these phone calls, do their exercises, watch the news on the TV or even take a stroll outside. Anything to get away from that screen and that market!

Although not nearly as detrimental to a trader's overall results as the other case, giving in to a sudden burst of boredom after a prolonged spell of inactivity is like walking away from an investment that is just about to sprout. It is a pity that traders are so caught up in the notion that trading trending markets is the only way to go. Contrary to popular believe, sideways markets deliver excellent opportunities, for the simple reason that they have to break out eventually, just like a trending market will eventually come to a halt or even reverse. Whereas it is impossible to define the exact moment when a trending market will move into the sideways phase, the sideways market, on the other hand, can give off very strong signals that it is about to move into a trending phase.

A good example of such a predictable breakout can be found in the chart above. The first hour of price action obviously shows the market in consolidation mode. With the moving average traveling sideways and price bars alternating above and below it, there is not much to make of it. This is your typical round number zone tug-o-war in the absence of a clear incentive (1.3150). But of one thing we can be sure: unless it is a national holiday, late Friday evening, or lunchtime in an already dead Asian session, price will not stay put for hours on end. Sooner or later some party will give the market a push and that will be incentive enough for others to react.

The trick is to recognize the buildup that most often precedes it. This is why it is so important to familiarize yourself with *pre-breakout tension*. What will help is to draw, or imagine, a box around any clustering

price action that might lead to a break. It may take some practice to recognize the right set of bars to wrap a box around, but essentially there
are not too many variations to grasp. The first box here, for instance,
is almost an exact copy of the fourth box in the previous chart (Figure
10.5, box 4).

By extending the signal line to the right, we can see that the pullback
following the break successfully tested the breakout level as well as the
broken round number of 1.3150 (1). That will certainly have inspired
a number of bears to just throw in the towel. And a number of bulls to
quickly enter the ring. However, despite this potential for double pressure, markets do not always immediately pop. In this chart the bears
still put up a reasonable fight, as we can tell by the cluster of hesitating
bars (3) that eventually led up to the forming of the second box.

If you look closely, you can see that the top barrier of this second BB
setup is not exactly running across the absolute high (2) but one pip
below it, across the equal extremes of four consecutive bars. As much as
it may be preferable to see a signal line unbroken by an earlier bar, we
definitely do not need to see the perfect box in order to trade. Whenever
there is room for a little doubt regarding the actual breakout level, it is
best to let yourself be guided by technical logic. Here it seems logical
to put more weight to the four equal highs than to that one single high
sticking out on the left. It would be overly prudent to wait for this high
to be taken out, too. But let us ignore our setup for a moment and see
what the market has to say about this: it put in a series of distinctive
higher bottoms within the course of two hours; it broke a round number
zone and saw it successfully tested; it built up towards a possible bullish breakout and now it breaks a cluster of four bars with equal highs.
I think it is telling us to trade.

Figure 10.7 Notwithstanding the very bullish trend earlier on, it is hard to miss the obvious signs of resistance on top of the round number line of 1.36. A triple top, a M-pattern, an extended head-and-shoulders pattern—no matter what you call it, the action between 05:12 and 05:30 represents a serious attempt of the bears to put a lid on the bullish fun. Does this mean the bull party is really over and we should go about shorting this market at the first sign of a countertrend setup?

As you may have gathered by now, I am not particularly fond of countertrend trading; but there are situations in which a setup against the trend can be just as tradable as any other valid pattern. However, since it is a somewhat riskier undertaking, it will pay off to carefully assess the overall conditions because the mere appearance of a setup alone is arguably not enough.

One of the simpler ways to figure out the validity of a questionable setup is to balance out the pros and cons of forces in the market and then see if the scale is tipped in favor of either aggression or prudence. When applying this tactic to the chart in question, while considering a countertrend trade, we first need to take into account the exact breaking point of the box. Ideally, we want to see the break occur immediately after some significant support gets taken out. Although we may only strive to take a quick 10 pip out of the market, the longer we postpone entering against a strong trend, the harder it will be to reach our desired profit target. For a strong up-market, at some point, *will* be bought. When trading countertrend, it is vital to not mistake the trade for a with-trend trade in the other direction. A countertrend trader should go in and out and be as nimble as a thief in the night. After all, if the real trend is any good, the countertrend, quite logically, can be expected to have a rather short life-span. Therefore, the validity of the countertrend trade, and particularly its entry point, is best based on the price action sentiment directly to the left of it, not on overall conditions that seem to have turned against the trend. If that was the case, the trade could better be considered a with-trend trade, at least from a scalper's perspective. Scalping a quick 10 pip *against* the trend, that is the objective of a countertrend trade.

What can we bring to the table to defend the idea of a countertrend scalp? How about the lower top next to the earlier triple top formation (3). With a bit of imagination (and a touch of self-deceit) the initial triple top could still be regarded by a bull as just a temporary pause in the bullish trend. Although a true technician would probably cringe at the mere thought of it, there is something to be said in defense of that idea—the bulls do have the trend on their side. And trends are known to continue rather than reverse. And indeed, should a BB setup have been formed underneath the *top* barrier of the triple top range—as a mirror image of the actual BB resting on the *bottom* barrier—a scalper may very well try and trade a break to the upside. Technically, though, after a triple top, the lower top is the more likely variant. Any bull not paying attention to the waning resources of his fellow companions (which is what the lower top represents) might be up for a rude awakening should he decide to stay on the bullish team. Fortunately, there is no such thing as honor, duty or moral obligation in this trading business. Most bulls will simply abandon ship on seeing that lower top appear and many of them will even start to join the other side.

What else can we make out of this chart? How about the fact that the bottom barrier of our box not only coincides with the strong support to the left of it, but also with the round number support in general (1.36).

On seeing it crack under downward pressure, we can imagine a large number of bulls to pull the plug on their positions.

From the perspective of the trapped, the reaction to a pattern break is usually a three-step process. The fastest traders react to the break almost instantaneously by dumping whatever they own. Another group of individuals often grab their chance in second instance should the market be so forgiving as to kindly revisit the breakout level. Then there is the confused and slightly surprised trader who, in the absence of a bailout plan, will try to hang on to his losing positions for as long as possible, hoping for the market to turn around. And yes, miracles do happen on occasion, but usually not before a tormented trader has dumped the last of his remaining contracts in an act of disgust.

Quite similar to this three-step process of bailing out, those who want to get in on the break also move in stepwise formation; either (a) instantaneously, (b) a bit more conservatively, or (c) quite late to the party. Bear in mind, the fastest ones are not always the happy bunch, for they can be trapped equally fast in a premature break. Therefore, to maximize the potential for a successful trade, we have to pick our spots of entry with sniper precision. And in this process of trade selection, proper buildup is always our best ally.

A good example of why this is so important could not be better illustrated than by the earlier false break through 1.36 (2): the market fell from the high of the topping pattern straight to the bottom of it, and then almost immediately dipped below it, completely lacking buildup. Prices were quickly bought up. A classic bear trap.

What else do we have to support the idea of a countertrend trade? How about the fact that, in case of a trade, the first real resistance to be encountered on the way to the target lies about 10 pip below the entry point: from a technical standpoint, we can imagine the clustering group of bars of (1) to offer some support to a falling market. It is a bit tight, but it may give the trade just a enough room to reach target before the anticipated buying pressure could possibly ruin our fun.

It may seem like quite a task to weigh these pros and cons of a countertrend trade when under pressure of having to decide what to do. In practice, though, this may turn out to be a lot easier than one might think. Just imagine the myriad of information that comes to you when you are about to cross a street. There is traffic and sound coming to you from every possible direction—a slow car, a faster car, a biker, an old pedestrian, a honking horn, a bunch of kids, a runaway ball, a truck unloading—yet somehow all this data is processed within your brain in a matter of seconds, allowing you to safely cross that street without so much as slowing down your pace. It is the same thing with the market once you have trained your eye to automatically sift through whatever information it throws at you. When reaching that desired state of proficiency, you will often find that the setup itself is only the finishing touch to what you are already anticipating for minutes on end—more like a crown on your analysis, as opposed to a wave of new information that needs to be processed before the dreaded deadline of a break.

Let us look at the BB setup in question and see how the signal line was derived. The earlier false break (2) was basically ignored and so the line was drawn across the five equal lows two pip higher—the most logical level, which also happened to coincide with the earlier lows of the M-pattern, just a pip below the round number.

Having gone over all the technicalities at hand, it is safe to say that this countertrend option had all the makings of a valid trade. But it did lack a welcome ingredient, proper pre-breakout tension. As much as any box, as a whole, represents pre-breakout tension regarding the bigger picture, a little miniature pre-breakout tension within the box right before the break really puts the pressure up. Therefore, it would have been preferable if prices in the bar of (4) had not dipped below the signal line at that moment in time but maybe one or two bars later. Can you visualize how nicely the 20ema would have squeezed two more dojis out of the box?

Unfortunately, as already stated, the market is not always so kind as to print our setups in the most desirable way. The good thing is that a conservative scalper can always decide to pass up on a trade if he does not perceive the odds to be favorable. A more aggressive scalper could have fired his short as depicted, to capitalize on a quick countertrend opportunity. He must have kept his cool, though, when prices decided to crawl back in the box immediately after the break. Should you get caught in similar fashion (and you will), the first thing to monitor is the 20ema. As long as the average manages to cap the little false break and then slowly starts to push the bars out of the box again (as a figure of speech), the trade stands a solid chance of working out still. Don't be tempted in these situations to bail out within the box for a minor loss of, say, a pip or three, fooling yourself to get off cheaply. As is the same with any other setup, a little fight around the entry point is all part of the breaking game.

Final note on the first BB trade: After the market broke out of the box a second time, persistent bulls still stubbornly tried to force prices back up, but this time they could not get any further than a test of the break-out level (5). All very standard price action, and I probably wouldn't have mentioned it, if not for one last bullish attempt: that lovely false upside break back through 1.36 a few candles later (6). What a classic bull trap. In order for a trade like that to succeed, it would have to dig its way up through a giant wall of resistance (the triple M-pattern and the lower top next to it). Apart from the fact that anything can happen, trading such breaks is a losing proposition in terms of probability. Sure, the overall trend was up, but initiating a long at that moment in time is simply trading along the path of *most* resistance.

As a side note: It is hard to tell whether this countertrend trade actually reached target or not. If not, it sure came close. Assuming the trade did not get filled on target, an alert scalper would have scratched it for a tiny profit at the very level of the entry on the second box (10). But it is best to not concern ourselves with exits at this point in time.

If you look closely, the second box in the chart is actually part of a little *triple bottom reversal pattern* (7-8-9), in essence, a smaller mirror image of the earlier triple top. Seeing a W-pattern develop, not only in support but also in what could very well be the end of a pullback (a more or less 50 percent retracement in a distinctive trend), an alert scalper should start to set his radar to the long side again and monitor the action attentively.

If we examine the total pullback for a moment, from the top of the M-pattern to the bottom of the W-pattern, we can see that it very technically produced nothing but lower bottoms and lower tops, all the way to the end of it. These are the typical seesaw characteristics of a downtrend. But since this downtrend is actually a countertrend in an uptrend—even on our chart—it is safe to assume that a vast number of smart traders are patiently awaiting their chance to buy themselves back into the market again. They only need a valid incentive.

To some, recognizing the bottoming pattern in support (no more lower lows) may be all the incentive needed to warrant a bullish position, hence the stalling of prices in that area (the second box). But the majority of traders will most probably not act upon their hunches until they see a very classic break of a previous top, too. After all, that would fully negate the bearish pattern of lower lows and lower highs and thus offer a huge technical incentive to bears and bulls alike. To the bears to get out, and to the bulls to get in (10).

Note: If you shorted the first box and had to bail out on the break of the second, do yourself a favor and click on the buy button twice. That will close out the short and initiate the long.

Figure 10.8 Since there is no way of knowing how a market will respond to any individual break, whether substantial or minor, there is no point in expecting things to happen. That will only lead to disappointment

and confusion, or even worse: bias. All a trader can do is simply follow the price action before him and act according to his own personal
approach. Whatever tricks the market may have in store, to the disciplined trader it is all the same. There are no mysteries to be solved.
No surprises to fence off. No scary monsters to beat. Just a bunch of
candles marching through the chart.

Could a scalper have predicted the trend in Figure 10.8 to almost fall
off the charts like it did? Not in any way. Was it very hard then, to trade
the market from the short side and scalp 20, if not 30 pip out of this
little mini crash? Not in the least. Should a trader be annoyed that he
only pocketed about half of the size of the trend? Of course he should
not; he can only act on what is offered.

These fine BB setups above are almost self-explanatory. Being a mere
three to four pip in length, the candles within the boxes have no option
but to present themselves as non-descriptive dojis. Still, it was very
easy to wrap an imaginary box around them or to draw a horizontal
signal line below the many equal lows.

There are two events here that deserve a little attention. The first one
is of a practical nature and is good to point out on account of it occurring regularly in many similar situations. As I mentioned earlier on, my
intention is to take the element of surprise completely out of the game,
so allow me to pose the following hypothesis. Imagine yourself to have
shorted the break of the first block (1). Depending on your fill, your current profit is about 6 pip when the market starts to show some sideways
motion (forming the second box). For argument's sake, let us say the
current profit is about 8 pip, so very close to target. After seeing the little
horizontal pullback appear within your running trade, chances are you
may be dealing with another BB setup. Assuming that all of your assets
are caught up in your one running position (as we discussed before)
there will be no double trading this market should the second box break
to the downside. Your margin will only become available again when
your current position hits target. But that does not mean you are out
of options when it comes to participating in that second BB. You may
have to be nimble, though, for the trick to work. Here is what you could
do: the moment that second box cracks and the market slips a few pip

to the downside, you make sure you are filled for a 10 pip profit on your first trade (2). Instead of doing something silly like celebrating or uttering sighs of relief, it is best to stay super alert because any moment the market may tick a few pip back up, even within the same candle that broke the box and filled your first trade for a 10 pip profit. That would be an excellent opportunity to get in on that second BB after all, sometimes without so much as paying a penalty for coming in late. As we have already seen so many times, breaks do get tested a lot and these tests make for excellent entry points, provided the price action has not altered the outlook of the trade. That is an important distinction. To give an example: you missed a short trade and 7 pip below your missed entry the market now starts to print a little double bottom. Should the market trade back up to the bottom barrier of your box, things are not quite the same anymore. Now this short trade has to eat its way through a potential reversal pattern (the double bottom) to get to target, which usually reduces the odds of a winning trade considerably. In general, one could say that within the first couple of bars after a missed break (sometimes even within the entry bar itself), the odds of a belated entry are just as good as those of a trade at the original break. In most other cases, the situation is best assessed anew, just like a trader who did act on the initial break would have to assess whether it is wise to stay in the trade or best to bail out. Anyway, always be alert when a profit fill on a current position is very close to, or accidentally coincides with, an entry signal to another trade. With a bit of luck you can enter on the second trade, too.

The second point of interest in the chart is of a technical nature and concerns the third box in the trend. If you ever wonder whether you should go on trading to the downside when a market has already sold off so much and so fast, my advice would be to not burden yourself with such futile reservations and just keep trading what you see. That same perception—that a particular trend is way overdone—is actually the main reason why these trends are so persistent. I am sure the early-bird bull, who traded the false break of the third box to the *upside* (3), can not appreciate that irony when forced to close out his contracts for a loss, contributing to the very trend he tried to fight.

Chapter 11

Range Break (RB)

It has been my intention from the very onset of this book to not just hand the reader a bunch of workable setups to only play certain phases of the market, but to present to him a complete series of scalping techniques that, when properly applied, could be set to work in virtually any kind of market, be it a trending, a countertrending or a non-trending one. The reader should bear in mind, though, that the key to sophisticated scalping is not found in the mere ability to recognize these setups, but to truly understand their role in relation to the overall picture. Disrespecting this subtle distinction, or being fully ignorant of it, could very well mean the difference between marginal and extraordinary results. For example, acting on an otherwise excellent pullback setup in an environment that does not allow for immediate continuation can seriously hurt a scalper's performance, and not uncommonly without him really understanding why.

Particularly in a sideways market, a scalper's all-round proficiency, or lack thereof, is easily brought to light. The novice, on average, finds it much harder to reap profits from a ranging market than from a trending one. Whether it is discomfort, fear, hesitance, or simply a lack of understanding of price action principles, it is not uncommon for the struggling trader to even decide to skip the ranges altogether.

Although very understandable—after all, trending markets do possess a visual clarity that is not easily matched—this inhibition towards trading the non-trending phases of the market is totally unnecessary. In fact, the progressive nature of the ranging market offers a huge benefit over trend trading, because it allows a scalper ample time to assess the current price action and to pick a moment of entry with sniper precision.

No matter what preferences the aspiring trader may secretly entertain—whether he favors complexity over simplicity, speedy markets over dull ones, trends over ranges, countertrend over with-trend—his overall results are best served by mastering the full array of trading techniques available to him. After all, remaining on the sidelines for countless hours on end, waiting for a pet setup to appear, could not be the intention of scalping (although at times there is no way around it).

After having studied the Double Doji, the First Break, the Second Break and the Block Break setups, it is now time to take a look at the very interesting Range Break setup (RB). Believe it or not, most of our trades, one way or another, will be related to a sideways pattern of sorts; the block break pattern, for instance, is nothing other than a miniature trading range. But even the very trendy double dojis appearing in the end of a pullback could also be regarded as a trading range, though be it on a micro-level. It all depends on whether one is looking at the market through a telescope or a microscope.

For our purposes, a range could be defined as a somewhat extended sideways market phase in which prices seem to be contained between a horizontal top level and a horizontal bottom level. Ideally, these barriers are very straightforward, with at least two equal tops and two equal bottoms touching them, but in practice we will often find the ranges not to be so textbook defined. Still, a range by itself should be easy to spot, its main characteristic being a lacking of trend. A very wide range could easily have trends in them, but unless the highs and lows are clearly visible on our scalping chart, we scalpers may be totally unaware of these wider patterns. On a 70-tick chart, range formations usually last anywhere from a around 15 minutes to a couple of hours, with the best part of an hour being a very good average.

Its most splendid characteristic, and the one a scalper should try to exploit to the fullest, is the simple fact that the range will ultimately crack. The longer it lasts and the more defined the barriers can be drawn, the more players will spot the same break, which will enhance the likelihood of necessary *follow-through* (a term for visible market participation in the direction of a new event). But not all breaks are created equal. As is the same with the BB setup, pre-breakout tension is one of the better leads to a dependable breakout. In Chapter 10 on Block Breaks we have observed the interesting phenomenon of how a small set of little dojis underneath a signal line often acts as a precursor to the upcoming break. This concept holds up for the range breakout as well, the main difference being that there are usually more bars involved to build up sufficient pressure to warrant a break. Yet the price action principle behind the event is completely identical. If you grasp the concept of the BB setup and the typical way it is broken, then you will understand the range and the nature of its breaks as well.

But does that make the range breakout as recognizable and tradable as the average breakout of the smaller block? In most instances, very much so. But there are a few things to consider. First of all, as is the same with the signal line of the BB setup, we may have to apply similar flexibility when it comes to drawing the smartest barriers. It is not uncommon for the range box to show the majority of equal highs at a level one or two pip below the absolute highs; or show the majority of equal lows at a level one or two pip above the absolute lows. In other words, it demands flexibility and technical logic on the part of the scalper to pick the most strategic highs and lows to draw the barriers by. In general, the absolute extremes should be our first choice, but every now and then we may be able to create a better barrier, and thus a better entry level, by squeezing the width of a box a bit. This tactic is most useful in the more volatile markets where the absolute extremes tend to be a bit spiky and may not even be duplicated by another bar. When dealing with very slow or compressed ranges, it may pay off to just concentrate on the absolute extremes instead of opting for a more economical entry below or above them.

The usual starting point of a range barrier is often a visible top or bottom from which the market clearly bounced. As the forming of the range progresses, new highs and lows get printed, often very close to or equaling previous ones. It is very common to have to adjust the barrier levels along the way as the market slowly defines the most prominent highs and lows (by respecting them) and dismisses the less significant ones. On average, the majority of ranges will be rather straightforward and their boxes can be drawn with little room for debate. And even if a barrier is slightly off, it may still offer a tradable entry level, especially so since the underlying forces will be pushing in the direction of the trade (when scalping along the path of least resistance, that is). Overall and with a little experience, a flexible chartist will not encounter much difficulty in identifying the proper extremes to draw his barriers by. Usually, the barrier from which a potential break is to be traded will show the most streamlined resistance, whereas its counterpart on the other side of the box can be very choppy or not even have one high or low match another.

When it comes to trading range breaks, however, a scalper's biggest challenge is not how to draw the ideal box, but to be able to identify, in time, two very tricky phenomena that are definitely known to wreak havoc amongst those traders not yet fully up to date with range break tactics. I am referring to two typical traps that appear on a regularly basis and the scalper is best advised to study them with some extra attention.

The first one is the notorious *false break trap* and the second, less malign but deceitful nonetheless, I have come to address as the *tease break trap.*

Let us look at the false break version first. The reader may remember the false break discussed in the previous chapter (Figure 10.7, 2), where the market came down from the high of a pattern straight to the low of it and then went on to break that low almost instantaneously. That indeed is a terrible way to set a break and it often leads to a very classic trap. With next to none pre-breakout buildup, prices that break through a pattern barrier are highly prone to have exhausted themselves; this offers countertrend traders excellent odds to do what they love to do, which is to prove the break false. They may only be successful to a certain extent, but their activity is usually forceful enough to shake at least a large number of unsophisticated break traders out of the market.

Getting trapped in a false break is arguably the main concern of any trader exercising a pattern breakout strategy. After all, there are always two opposing forces at work: traders that anticipate the barrier to fail and those that trade in the opposite direction, anticipating the barrier to hold, even despite a temporary breach. The good part is that both parties can buy and sell contracts from each other without having to chase price (they just exchange their opposing ideas); the bad part is that one of these parties will soon be on the wrong side of the market.

But what is wrong and right in the melting pot of strategies, time frames, opinions and perceptions? Of course, we can only look at this from the perspective of our personal chart. But even though we may technically put on a trade in the right direction of the market (in terms of overall pressure), when our timing is seriously off, it is nothing other than trading along the path of *most* resistance, and that is certainly a folly to avoid. It stands to reason that in the face of any faltering trade, a scalper with a tight stop is in much more danger than someone trading the same break from a bigger frame or with a much wider stop. This is the reason why timing the entry on a trade correctly, to any scalper, is so crucial. In the market, it can be a costly proposition to be at the right place, but at the wrong time.

As we have already reflected on, our best ally in a breakout trade is the occurrence of pre-breakout tension leading up to the break. Not only may it cause prices to literally jump out of the box, very often it will also hinder the market from crawling back in afterwards. After all, it is much harder for prices to eat their way back through a cluster of bars that led up to a break than when there is nothing standing in their way. The forming of this pre-breakout tension is actually such a visual process in the chart that getting caught in a break that shows no buildup, or just too little of it, should essentially be a non-issue. We just don't trade that.

I hope the point is noted, though, that there can be no avoiding the false break entirely. Even the best looking trade in the field could still turn out a loser. But there really is no reason to let ourselves get caught in the obvious traps.

Not nearly as dangerous as engaging in what could be a typical false break trap, but still very much to avoid if possible, is getting ourselves tricked in the tease break variant. This break has almost all the makings of a valid trade, yet is technically still bordering on the premature side of things. At times, it can be a thin line, though, between a valid break and a tease break trap. Usually some tension has already been building up before the break will take effect: a number of bars hanging below a top barrier (for a possible long) or resting on the bottom barrier (for a possible short). However, what should be missing in the picture for our break to deserve the tease status is what we can refer to as a proper *squeeze*: prices being literally sandwiched between the 20ema and the barrier line. When they are contained like this for at least a handful of bars, then things are building up nicely towards a potential break; but it should be added, though, that pre-breakout tension does not always show up in its most ideal form and sometimes we may just have to accept the middle way between a tease and a proper break.

On occasion, it can be a delicate choice between risking to miss a range break entirely and acting prematurely. However, the less malign characteristic of the tease break trap, as opposed to the meanness of the false break variety, is displayed in the fact that the market tends to be a little bit more forgiving on the part of this premature entry. The break is usually not so violently countered as its uglier counterpart. Practice shows us that a faltering trade of this type still has a reasonable chance of working out, even though prices may come dangerously close to a scalper's protective stop. Regardless, we should definitely aim to avoid the tease break trap as well.

As we have already noticed when studying the BB setup, the 20-bar exponential moving average can be an excellent aid in not only pushing prices through a barrier defense, but also in keeping them from slipping back into the box after a break. In the RB setup, it often plays a similar role. Of course, it is not the 20ema itself that has such magical powers, but the visual illusion can be so impressive that it is easy to forget that the average is merely a reflection of what the bars are already showing us.

All of the above is going to make proper sense, I am sure, once the reader gets himself acquainted with the Range Break setups in the charts. It will pay off to study the coming examples with great attention to detail, because we can expect these ranges to pop up multiple times in any 24-hour session. Also take note of the vertical price axis in all of the coming charts, because more often than not the 00 and 50 round number levels will play major roles in the forming and breaking of a range.

Figure 11.1 Let's start out with an almost picture perfect, yet very common range formation. The action within the box is about an hour's worth of price data. I am sure you can see why the barriers are drawn as depicted. When you are watching this develop in real-time there is no way of knowing, of course, that the market will set itself up in such orderly fashion. In many instances, the initial extremes that mark the beginning of a range do not hold up and so a scalper has got to be flexible in drawing his barriers and be ready to adjust them along the way.

In this chart, the initial levels were very well respected. The bottom barrier is the first to appear. A scalper could have immediately drawn it below the first lows in the chart after prices bounced up, but only once they came to challenge this level again and bounced up once more did the barrier truly earn significance (1 and 3). The top barrier may already have been plotted the moment a first top was put in (2), but most certainly after a second top matched the earlier one spot on (4). With two highs suggesting resistance and two lows offering support there is not much to make of this chart in terms of future direction. All we can do is watch the action with an open mind and let the market run its course. Prices will not bounce back and forth between the bottom and top of a range forever. If they do not force themselves out in an overly eager one-directional attack, then at some point they will either start to stall below the top barrier, or somewhere above the bottom barrier.

When the market came down from the second top but could not proceed beyond the level of the 20ema again, things started to look up for the bulls (5). If nothing else, at least they got clarity on the job ahead, which is to keep the market in the top right corner of the box and aim for a clever bullish breakout. Now that they've got themselves a slight advantage over the bears, it would be a strategic default to let prices fall below the average once more. That would put more significance to the second top of (4). In fact, the chart would print a bearish double top below a round number zone (1.3250), which would not look particularly pretty from a bullish perspective. It may very well provoke new bears to start selling more aggressively.

So the bulls have a task: keep prices in the top of the range, preferably at all times above the average, and then slowly work themselves a way out of that box. The bears, of course, have a task of their own: to prevent that from happening, and sooner rather than later.

As you can see, when the barrier on the side of the break is of exemplary quality, it is very easy to determine the point of a RB entry (7).

Was there anything the bears could have done to prevent that break from happening? Of course there was. They only needed to sell more aggressively than the bulls were buying. Apparently something in the chart kept them from doing so.

Was it our squeeze (6)? Who knows. A technical pattern trader may have recognized the bullish implication of a *cup-and-handle* pattern that formed itself in the last third of the range (3-7). Taking a step back, he may have spotted the elongated and rather tell-tale W-pattern stretching itself throughout the box from left to right. Others may have noticed a lack of follow-through after the market drifted below the 50 round number zone in the beginning of the chart, which implied very little selling interest.

No matter how much the individual setup, as a stand-alone event, may already serve the trader well, it is an absolute necessity to look at the complete picture in the chart. Only when the setup complies with the bigger forces at work should a trade be considered.

Figure 11.2 This chart is almost the mirror image of the previous example (Figure 11.1). Once again, the breaking of a round number zone trapped traders on the wrong side of the market. In the previous chart, it was a downward break through the zone that not long after turned bullish, here it was an upward break that soon turned bearish.

Is there a reason these round number breaks don't hold up? Probably no more than there is to any other break or move that fails or falls short: a lack of follow-through. It is not uncommon to see enthusiasm dwindle in rather subdued markets, or in situations where the round numbers are more of a symbolic nature than that they actually represent true technical levels of resistance and support. In these cases, it is fair to assume that not too many stop-losses reside above or below the levels. As a result, the price action remains calm; as much as those in position do not see the need to get out, those on the sidelines are not exactly scrambling to get in, either.

More practical than trying to figure out the reason (foolish in any respect) is asking ourselves if these failed round number breaks could somehow be anticipated and possibly exploited. Interestingly, in the majority of cases there is indeed a pattern to be spotted. First the round number is broken, quite often with hardly any fight. Not much later the break is tested, usually successful. On seeing this, a number of new players step in, thinking they're in for a treat. And then, for some reason or another, the play dies out like a flame. Traders at any moment in time may buy as cheaply or sell as dearly as the market allows them, but if no new players pick up on their idea of direction (follow-through), they are trapped on the wrong side of the field. All of this is not uncommonly captured within the confines of an unmistakable range very close to the round number of interest. It is a scalper's task to figure out when the predicament of the trapped becomes unbearable from a technical perspective. Naturally, the idea is to capitalize on their instinct of flight.

Everything is very easy in hindsight, yet if you managed to grasp the concept of the forces in play that caused the upside break in Figure 11.1, I am sure you can also see why this particular range, halfway through, started to develop a fancy for a downward break.

Let us examine up close what exactly went on from the moment the third top was set (4). It started to go wrong for the bulls when the reaction to this top (a tiny countermove) was not being picked up by new bulls in the 20ema a few bars later. That would have been a perfect opportunity to swing prices back up. From there on, they could have created themselves a nice squeeze by not giving in to whatever bearish pressure and then force themselves a way through the top barrier of the range. In fact, the three earlier tops (1, 3 and 4) would have made for an excellent barrier to trade that upside break from.

However, instead of working on that upside break, the market set out on its way to the bottom of the range again (5) and now even showed a classic triple top in its wake. These are not bullish signs.

But there was hope still. After all, the round number zone was cracked to the upside and successfully tested earlier on, and that should at least amount to something. If somehow new bulls found it in their heart to aggressively step in above the 1.33 level, inspiring even more bulls to jump in after them and bring prices once again to the top of the range, the chart would show an unmistakable double bottom in round number support (2 and 5). And that would look quite bullish.

Sometimes it only needs one bar to turn pleasurable hope into the idle variety. How about that little doji (7) that stuck its head a pip above the high to the left of it (6). A higher high in a bullish market after a possible double bottom in round number support, that should have attracted new bulls to the scene. What kept them away? We can imagine it to be the triple top pattern to the left; but it is not our business to decipher or explain the actions or non-actions of our fellow traders. Everything is just information.

As observant scalpers our task is not just to monitor a chart, but to look for clues in it. The more crucial the signs we can assemble, the more we can solve the puzzle of who is possibly toppling who in the market. Any sign or hint that leaves a distinctive mark in the chart will work to the benefit of our assessment. These signs, at times, can be quite obvious, like triple tops and other well-known reversal patterns, but they can also be rather tiny, like a one pip false break. The best indication to determine the value of a particular chart event is to consider its place in the chart in relation to whatever price action preceded it. To give an example, the tiny false upside break of (7) would have been considerably less indicative had the market not printed that triple top shortly before.

With prices now trapped below the 20ema, the market was on the brink of being sandwiched into a bearish breakout through the bottom barrier of the range.

That brings us to the interesting part that you may have already spotted: the first breakout below the barrier. Why did I mark this one as a tease (T).

Granted, this one reflects the proverbial close call and I couldn't really argue with anyone looking upon it as a valid break. For my own personal comfort, I would like to see prices get squeezed a little bit more before breaking down. Preferably, I would like to see the market print a couple of dojis right on the bottom level of the range (as in a regular

BB setup). It must be stated, though, that a conservative stance is not always the most successful approach.

It would be nice if we could really put a rule of thumb on these false breaks, particularly on the tease variant, but alas, it often depends on the situation at hand. Here the market was extremely slow and the price action very subdued (almost every bar a doji). That makes me want to wait for superior conditions just a little bit longer than, for instance, in case of a speedy market, where I might run the risk of fully missing the break on account of being too conservative.

Note: As for the difference between the false break trap and the tease break variant, imagine for a moment the 05:00 low (5) to have dipped a pip below the range barrier. That would have turned it into a false break of the earlier bottom of (2) and not a tease. Why? Because prices came straight down from the high of the pattern (4) to the low of it and then immediately broke through without any buildup. That typifies a classic false break (in terms of potential, of course, for any break, even a silly one, may find follow-through and prove itself true). When it comes to the tease break, on the other hand, the cracking of the range usually starts with a move that originates not at the top or bottom of the pattern, but more from the middle of it, or at least from the 20ema zone. In case of a downward break, for example, before breaking out, prices usually first touch the bottom barrier and then bounce up to make an intermediate high in the 20ema. From that point on there may be some squeezing between the average and the bottom barrier, but usually too little of it to consider it sufficient buildup to a tradable break. It would be preferable to see prices bounce up and down at least a few times between the bottom barrier and the average, until they are finally being squeezed out. And that makes sense; the more contracts change hands in the squeeze, the more traders will find themselves on the wrong side of the market once support gives in. And most of them will have no choice but to sell back to the market what they had bought at bottom prices just moments before. Add to this a number of sideline bears eagerly stepping in and we have ourselves the perfect ingredients of double pressure and thus follow-through.

At times, the anticipation of this little chain of events is very straightforward. At other times, the assessment of the squeeze can be a lot more subtle and it may leave a scalper wondering whether or not to trade. Particularly when the space between the 20ema and the barrier line is no more than a few pip in width, the tease break may be almost indistinguishable from a valid break.

If you ever find yourself caught in a tease break, or in any other valid break that acts as a tease, similar calm is required as in the case of the BB trade where prices break out of the box and then crawl back in. As we have seen already in several examples, the 20ema, just like in the chart above, can still guide prices back out in favor of the trade. In many cases that is also the final incentive for the market to really pop.

Take a moment to compare the string of black bars after the break in this chart with the string of white bars after the break in Figure 11.1. What do these moves represent? They clearly show us the unwinding of positions of those traders trapped on the wrong side of the market. In the chart above, for instance, *all* scalpers that picked up long contracts inside of the range are carrying losing positions the moment prices break down below 1.33. That string of black bars represents their predicament and their panic, so in essence a rapid unwinding of long positions that are being sold back to the market. Naturally, clever bears on the sidelines, smelling blood, will be happy to add fuel to the fire by quickly selling contracts to whoever still entertains bullish fantasies. Of course, even a falling market will always find traders ready to buy, but these bulls will not be so eager as to not demand lower prices to trade at. As a result, prices will fall even more until eventually the market calms down and more bulls than bears are willing to trade. This, in short, is the principle of supply and demand. It works the other way around in equal fashion. And it is our job to anticipate it before it even takes place. To the non-initiated this may seem like quite a daunting task. Yet those who observe, study and learn will most likely come to see the repetitive nature of it all. And soon they will be able to exploit those who do not.

Figure 11.3 Anyone who has ever studied the eur/usd pair on intra-day basis will surely have noticed this market's remarkable tendency to move in stepwise increments of 20 pip. For example, if, say, 1.3120 is cracked to the upside, as in the chart above, and then tested back and proven sound, then, more often than not, the market's next stop will be 1.3140. Variations on this pattern repeat themselves with such relentless persistence that it is not hard to imagine how numerous intraday strategies are solely built to exploit this phenomenon. And yes, the market's fixation with these round number levels at times is truly astonishing. Of course, as scalpers we are only interested in one thing: can we exploit it?

Psychologists have us believe that the omnipresent round number effect, visible also in many other aspects of life, has no coherent relation to value whatsoever but is simply a way for the human brain to filter out noise to protect itself from information overload. From a practical per-spective, there may even be a strong self-fulfilling aspect attached to it: if we all believe that round numbers bear significance, then, naturally, our actions concerning these numbers bring significance about. Any-how, if nothing else, round numbers do have the pleasant side-effect of framing things in organized manner, just like wrapping boxes around ranges gives us clarity on resistance and support. When it comes to the 20-levels (00, 20, 40, 60 and 80), you will have noticed that I have set up my software to plot these levels thinly in the chart; but I use them solely for guidance and try not to look upon them as absolute levels of resistance and support. They may do so at the moment, but I rather leave that to the price action itself. Frankly, in the never-ending quest for simplicity I have tried to scalp with a clean chart, meaning without the 20-lines in it, but somehow my conditioned brain felt less comfortable without these levels framing the action. This may very well be a personal quirk and any scalper can try for himself what suits him best. One last thing: on the road from 40 to 60, and the other way around, things can get very tricky. Currency trading, like it or not, is a big players game, and the 50-level is arguably their favorite toy. Unlike the 00 round number, this level is not a 20-level itself. Hence the occasional conflicting mishmash between 40 and 60. However, do not *expect* anything to happen around this level. Just be on the alert. Always monitor any action carefully, but keep a special eye on the two major round number zones of 00 and 50. More often than not, these levels are what the bigger chart is all about and why we see so many ranges appear as a result.

Let us look at Figure 11.3 and see if that RB trade was easy to spot. Halfway through the chart, the options are very much open. There are no trades near and a scalper should just relax and apply patience. To obtain an idea on support and resistance, he may have already drawn a horizontal line across the first top of (1) and then another below the low that followed it (2). Tip: you do not necessarily need to draw boxes, a horizontal line across the tops and one beneath the lows will do just fine.

At any moment in time there are always three ways to look at a chart. Through bullish eyes, bearish eyes, or neutral eyes. Needless to say, observing the price action with a neutral disposition is the way to go. Many traders, however, can't help themselves looking at the market from the perspective of their current positions (or intentions), so either from a bullish or a bearish stance. It is a bit the same as with the novice chess player who only moves his pieces around in order to attack; this player usually pays very little attention to position play or even to the many gaping holes in his own defense.

When biased towards the upside, a bull may view the triple bottom pattern (4, 6 and 8) as a very healthy token that the market is building up towards a bullish breakout. And with reason; the market definitely shows signs of support in the 1.3120 area. Should it continue its pattern of slightly higher bottoms, then breaking out to the upside, eventually, would technically be the most logical result.

When looking at things from the bearish side, traders may find comfort in the triple top pattern (3, 5 and 7) that appeared on a lower level than the earlier, more dominant top of (1).

As neutral scalpers, we can only sit back and enjoy whatever the market has in store for each party. If you place your thumb on the chart for a moment, to block the prices after 17:00, you can see that it wouldn't have taken that much of an effort from the Powers That Be to give this chart a more bearish look; cracking the 1.3120 level by a few pip would have probably done the trick. One thing is of importance, though, and that is to not walk away from this chart in a silly act of boredom. If the bulls show a bit more persistence, particularly when entering a potential squeeze phase, we may have a trade on our hands in a matter of minutes.

The first break through the upper barrier could be classified as a typical tease on account of it not originating from a proper squeeze situation yet (T). In order for the market to deliver a more reliable break, it is preferable to see prices first retest the 20ema again and then attack the barrier in buildup fashion. As a matter of fact, the subsequent price action after the tease, that is the perfect squeeze that led to an excellent textbook RB trade (9).

If these tease breaks, after breaking back, are so often caught by the 20ema and then still manage to break out eventually, couldn't we just always look upon them as valid breaks and trade them no matter what? That is a very fair question. So far the examples here show outcomes that point in favor of that option. It is my observation, though, that in most cases you can get away with being a little more patient. In other words, missing a range break trade due to a conservative stance is less common than one might think. Secondly, there is also the matter of protection to take into consideration. As we will see in the section on Trade Management, squeezes provide excellent levels for stop placement. Conversely, a tease break situation, in essence a somewhat hastier break, seldom delivers the same technical clarity in terms of where to place the stop. When trading breaks, patience truly is a virtue. Therefore, my advice would be to shun the non-buildup breaks entirely (false break traps) and those resulting from little buildup as much as you can (tease break traps).

Note: If prices after a tease break are pushed back inside the range but not much later break out again as in a valid RB, then it is not necessary to postpone entering until the tease level is taken out, too. It is usually best to just take the trade as if the tease had not occurred, which means firing a market order on a break of the original range barrier. An exception would be if there are multiple tease breaks in a row that together form a new barrier by themselves. Then it may be recommended to assess the situation from the perspective of that new barrier (see Figure 11.6 for a good example).

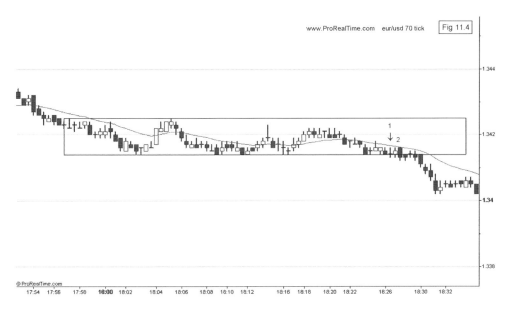

Figure 11.4 On a bigger time frame this kind of price action could be seen as a just a brief stalling of prices before the market continued its

downward momentum. It is not hard to imagine two little doji bars, for instance, representing the action from 18:00 to 18:30 on a 15-minute chart. Sometimes a trader cannot help himself noticing things that have no informational value regarding his method. A good example would be for a scalper to accidentally spot a huge reversal pattern on a daily chart. That sort of information may easily inspire him to enter his next session with strong directional bias, if only on a subconscious level. A scalper is best advised to not look upon himself as being immune to this trait. My personal take on how to protect myself from the dangers of intuitive bias is to acknowledge that I am only human and thus prone to the folly. As a countermeasure I do not read or watch other people's market opinions and deliberately curb any unnecessary information by having my 70-tick chart show me no more than about two hours of data in one go, which is about twice the size of the overall chart in this guide. On average, a couple of hundred of printed bars will suit our scalping purposes just fine. In terms of individual bars, you could compare it to at least nine months of price action on any daily chart.

It remains to been seen, though, whether any nine months worth of daily data would be able to print such a picture perfect range formation as depicted in the chart above. No less than 12 equal touches made up the bottom barrier of the range before prices finally gave in to the downward pressure.

Hopefully you can see why there is no need to postpone entering here in fear of a tease. The bears dealt the bulls a perfect little squeeze that is best acted upon straight away (1). There is never a way to foresee a market's reluctance to accept its most likely fate (2). Whatever happens, happens and, whether in or outside of the market, we also have to accept. The next few bars remained capped very well, though, by the 20ema, as is often the case, and since no new bulls came to the rescue, eventually prices chose the path of least resistance.

The round number zone about a dozen pip below the bottom of the range will surely have contributed to the success of the downward break, simply by hauling prices in through the vacuum above it. Why the vacuum? You will not find too many traders ready to buy in front of a round number level with so much resistance (the broken range) hovering above them. They rather wait for the round number to be tested first, or even perforated. Hence the so-called vacuum, which, of course, is nothing more than a temporary shortage of buying interest.

Note: Maybe this is a good time to address a little luxury problem that may arise when confronted with an almost perfect vacuum trade in front of a round number. For the sake of a hypothetical argument, let us imagine we get filled on a short at 13 pip above a 00 number. With the touch of that round number as one of the most likely occurrences in case of a proper break, would it not be a smart idea to stretch our 10 pip profit target by another 2 pip to capitalize on the odds of that 13 pip move?

Let us do the math and see if we can come up with a satisfactory answer. If the trick works, then that pockets 2 extra pip. If the trade offers 10 pip of profit but then starts to turn sour and somehow needs to be scratched, say, for a 2 pip loss (a pretty good scratch), then that pockets a 12 pip loser (10 pip of missed profit, plus a 2 pip loss). So, in order for this strategy to break even, a trader needs to successfully repeat this little act of greed no less than six times for every time it fails. And that is just to break even from a clinical viewpoint. It is not hard to imagine the original loss being accompanied with a loss of emotional balance as well. And that needs to be regained, too. After all, not sticking to the plan and seeing it backfire is a true classic and known to torment a trader way beyond the actual damage done.

Of course, you could alter the numbers here and try again. But remember that the odds for a winning trade diminish in tandem with every pip you think to add to your original target.

My advice would be to sooner stick to what is already working well than to try and force some extra profits out of the market by deviating from an already sound strategy. Over time, improvements can be made to even the best approach, but these changes will usually come about gradually through a growing awareness, and should better not stem from an impulsive need to score more pip. Once consistently profitable in the scalping field, volume, of course, is free to be adjusted to keep up with a growing account. If a profitable scalper works up to bigger volume by progressively trading more units per trade there is simply no need to score more pip.

Figure 11.5 The chart above, on the whole, does not exactly paint a very vivid picture of market activity. The bars were printed in an almost lethargic fashion and the range that came out of it took over two and a half hours to crack (more than twice the average). But this is what we get every now and then, particularly during the Asian sessions, and it couldn't hurt to go over some of the technicalities in play to see if maybe a lesson or two could still be learned from it.

Without too much of a fight, the market had fallen through the round number zone of 1.34 in the beginning of the chart. As has already been stated, this does not necessarily mean the round number is truly given up; but from a technical viewpoint we should regard it as such until proven otherwise. Here the bulls, initially, seemed rather reluctant to prove the break false. A first and rather weak attempt to bring prices up for maybe a retest of 1.34 was easily countered in the area of the 20ema (1). Not long after, the market slowly drifted lower to a level below the previous low (2). Another round won by the bears.

Despite the technical incentive of a lower low in a slowly falling market, bearish follow-through turned out to be almost non-existent. This is interesting info and it will not go unnoticed by the ever-present countertrend opportunists lying in wait: to them, it may be just the incentive needed to try and swing prices back up.

In the marketplace, the best way for one party to regain possession of lost territory is to move in on the opponent in a stepwise fashion. With prices well below the 20ema, for instance, it is seldom a smart idea of the bulls to buy themselves so aggressively into the market that prices spike through a bearish defense, only to exhaust themselves. That is asking for a good whack, and not seldom after a false break of some kind.

The first step in taking back some control over the direction of the market starts with re-conquering the 20ema. One of the better ways for the bulls to convince sideline watchers to join in on a countertrend mission (and provoke with-trend players to exit) is to first print some sort of technical sign below the 20ema as a token of support. This could be a very tiny double bottom, a higher low, a strong doji in technical support, or basically anything that stalls, at least temporarily, the bearish momentum. Here it was a tiny higher low (3).

The next step is to try and perforate the 20ema, a crucial moment in the counterattack because this area is so often used by with-trend traders to deploy a new wave of activity in the direction of the trend. Regaining control over the average will definitely earn some technical respect and convince at least a part of the market to exit their with-trend positions, and another part to enter on some countertrend ones. In that respect, the first attempt after the higher bottom to take out the 20ema was pretty convincing (4). One only needs to look at the very bullish bar—more than twice the size of its neighboring candles—to acknowledge that bullish feat. Is this the sign needed to convince the market that the bearish party is over? Not in the least. But it did flatten the momentum and take away the bearish advantage of having prices below the 20ema.

Trying to immediately push through and attack the earlier high was a bit on the greedy side (5). A smarter idea would have been to calmly establish the re-conquered 20ema as a base of support by printing some candles on top of it and then take it from there. It is all about slowly convincing other parties to join in, for hastiness usually backfires pretty fast. The failed attempt did present the market with an equal high, though, confirming the level of resistance suggested by the earlier top of (1). In case of a potential range breakout to the upside, a scalper now has something to go by: a proper barrier connecting two stand-alone tops.

Had this market been of a faster pace, a scalper may have placed his top barrier one pip below the range extremes. Even before 04:00 this level seemed to be way more respected than the actual highs a pip above it. Still, with a market running so slow as this one, a scalper is recommended not to try to front-run the breaking of the actual extremes, certainly not by a mere pip. Even so, just in case a trader had opted to draw his barrier a pip lower than depicted, the new high peeking through it (5) would not have been a valid breakout but more a midway between a potential false break trap and its tease break cousin (false, because the move that led up to it originated from the bottom of the range; tease, because prices did attempt to form a bit of sideways tension before breaking out topside).

Next up in the range is a dull half hour fight over the 20ema (6-7) that eventually got resolved in favor of the bulls. They not only managed to keep the 20ema sloping up, they also had two higher bottoms to show for it (6 and 7).

All in all, the activity within the range, though tedious to some, is slowly starting to tip its hand. Technical chartists may have already recognized the very familiar, and quite dependable, *reversed-head-and-shoulders* formation stretching itself throughout the box. No doubt the reversal implication of the pattern must have inspired some bullish enthusiasts to aggressively force a break through the top barrier without the proper buildup necessary to accompany such an attempt (no squeeze whatsoever). The result: a typical false break that we can classify as a tease since it originated from the area of the 20ema (T).

Had there been sufficient tension building up below the top of the range, then the expectable resistance of the 1.34 round number level a few pip above it (8) should not have kept a trader from trading his RB. However, starting from 10 pip below (7), breaking a range in the process and expecting the bullish strike not to run out of steam at 1.34 is just asking for more than a calm market will normally give. It took a few bars, but eventually prices re-entered the range, proving the break false.

Apparently, this did not demoralize the bulls for long. Prices, though back in the range, kept themselves glued to the top barrier, also forming another higher bottom in technical support (9). The fact that the 20ema did not squeeze the bars out so nicely as in some of the previous examples bears little significance (10). It is mainly due to the hesitance of prices to crawl back into the box after that earlier tease. With six consecutive candle closes above the barrier line, the average had no choice but to follow and lift itself up. But bear in mind, the aid of the average, though remarkably visual and accurate at times, is not a requirement to trade. We will always base our decisions on the price action itself.

There is no escaping these long ranges, even as a scalper. It is important, though, to not let impatience disturb your analytical skills or make you feel grumpy with the market. You do not always need to trade. Other traders do not move the market just to oblige your scalping needs. They need a good reason to step in. If you don't see one, why would they.

Figure 11.6 Before delving into the specifics of this particular RB entry (10), let us take a step back and look at some of the technical key points in the first half of this chart. Obviously, things started out rather well

for the bulls. Not only did they manage to break the round number of 1.33 in quite a daring move, the bears couldn't even produce a noteworthy pullback in return. Instead of retracing, prices merely drifted sideways, forming what is widely known as a classic bull flag pattern (1). This pattern broke in textbook fashion, but the moment the new thrust of buying activity fell short of breath (2), countertrend traders immediately sprang into action and started slamming the market to make some decent profits themselves. Although prices tried to bounce up from this in the first 20-level they came upon, the bearish pressure remained persistent and did not falter until the market was brought all the way back to test the only valid level of support in sight: the top of the bull flag (3). Not only was that an excellent spot to pocket some countertrend profits, it offered a sideline bull a perfect opportunity to pick up a with-trend position. We could even imagine a very nimble scalper scoring a number of pip on the way to support and then profiting again as a with-trend trader in the subsequent technical bounce. Scalping can be fun to those apt and able.

But it is not our business to speculate on how other traders make their living. Our task is to observe the price action from our own perspective and then see if anything develops that may lead to a textbook trade. So far, things were evolving in very technical manner. In a bullish looking chart like this, our radar should naturally be scanning the horizon for trades to the long side. This is not to be confused with entertaining directional bias. It is simply based on an assessment of *current* pressure. To understand the importance of that distinction, we only need to cast one look at the second half of this chart; it shows us a stunning example of how even a very trending market can falter and crumble in just a matter of minutes.

Was there any way a scalper could have seen that shift in prospect coming? To answer that, let us pick up the action from the moment the market put in that second top (4). The fact that it fell a few pip short of the earlier top was not a problem at that point. But it would have been nice, for the bulls, to see new players step in when prices retraced to the 20ema. That level would have been an excellent stepping stone for yet another bullish attack and maybe one strong enough to take out the earlier highs. Instead, prices slid all the way back to support for a second time and even managed to dip a pip below it (F). A round won by the bears. However, those bears late to the party immediately saw themselves caught in a classic false break trap (F). But they only had themselves to blame; with no buildup whatsoever to back up that break through support, shorting a bullish market at that level makes for terrible odds. Clever bulls did not have to think twice about what to do and thus the market quickly moved up once more. A round won by the bulls (5).

But things were about to get ugly pretty fast for the latter party. To answer the question of whether is was possible to identify the shift in momentum from bullish to bearish (at least in time to trade that break), we only need to follow the price action as it developed in the next ten minutes of trading. Granted, despite the resistance they encountered, the bulls kept on buying in support, which showed their resilience and their belief in the earlier trend; but the bears kept shorting at lower and lower levels, which obviously showed they cherished some beliefs of their own. In fact, that series of lower tops popping up in the 20ema slowly formed a textbook squeeze (though a bit rough) and sooner or later something had to give. Either the bulls would give up on defending their beloved support, or the bears would come to see the folly of shorting into it.

Allow me to dig into this particular squeeze for a moment, because there are some interesting little clues to discover that may be worthwhile remembering for future purposes. As you can see, the original box could be drawn the moment a third low in support matched the first (6 matches 3). At that point, the false break level of (F) had no low to connect with, so it makes sense to ignore it for the moment and draw the barrier a pip above it.

Not much later, after yet another lower top in the 20ema, a fourth low hit support (T), and this little tease matched the level of the earlier false break (F). That's interesting, because now there are two equal lows below the original barrier, and this last one, too, is obviously respected and being bought. Frankly, this situation clearly shows us the tricky proposition of considering a countertrend trade against a strong trend:

if the trend is indeed any good, traders will keep buying into support and they may even buy below it; therefore, it is much harder to tell a true break from a tease break trap.

After seeing that tease successfully test the earlier false break, it may be wise to reconsider the level of support. It is fair to say that the actual extremes (F and T) have earned themselves enough credit to justify lowering the barrier to the level of the dotted line.

Although on the alert for a bearish break, let us not underestimate the bullish resilience just yet. As long as their support is holding up, there is a fair chance that they may still worm themselves a way out of that squeeze. As a matter of fact, they produced an interesting little feat just moments after bouncing up from the dotted line: a higher low (7) and a subsequent higher high (8).

And this brings us to another technical marvel that is certainly worth reflecting on. When prices are caught in a momentary impasse between bullish and bearish forces, the market often needs an incentive, either way, to convince those in position as well as those on the sidelines that a particular play is over. This could be an obvious break, a reversal pattern, a sudden spike, a false break, a lack of follow-through, basically anything, but usually something either very obvious or odd.

In situations that deal with a possible with-trend break, the obvious incentive will usually do just fine. A good example would be a pullback petering out and then a break in with-trend direction. But when contemplating a *countertrend* trade against a relatively strong trend, it is a nice bonus to first see an odd event defy the obvious. For the sake of explanation, bear with me for a moment and consider the following examples. Imagine a trend to be *down* and price to have found support at, say, 10. Then the market goes up to 13 (against the trend), back to 10, up to 13, back to 10, up to 11, back to 10 and down to 9. Shorting at 9 probably makes for an excellent with-trend trade (the obvious). No problem there. Now imagine the trend to be *up* and price to have found support at 10 again. Then the market travels up to 13 (with-trend), back to 10, up to 13, back to 10, up to 11, back to 10 and down to 9. This may seem like a similar obvious short to some, but based on the fact that the trend is *up*, this break below 10 runs a much higher chance to be proven false than its with-trend counterpart in the earlier example. Because it concerns a countertrend move. Now let's get to the odd situation; imagine to trend to be *up* again and price once more finds support at 10, goes up to 13, back to 10, up to 13, back to 10, up to 14(!), back to 10, up to 11, back to 10 and down to 9. All else equal, seeing that break at 14 being pushed back, turning it into a false with-trend break (the odd), I would now be more comfortable taking that countertrend short at 9. Another way to put it, purely from a technical standpoint, is to say that when the obvious event fails, a subsequent not so obvious event looks more credible as a result. In a bullish environment, this translates to the following: if an upside breakout gets forced back, a downside breakout may catch more follow-through.

This does not mean that we need to see an obligatory odd move first before even considering a countertrend break. Of course not. Any solid reversal pattern would probably do the trick. The point is to not look upon the countertrend trade as a with-trend trade in the other direction. With-trend trades do not require nearly as much technical backup (or clues, if you wish) as do the countertrend trades. After all, countertrend trades, by definition, will always suffer a major disadvantage, and that is the undeniable fact that prices have to travel against the trend.

All in all, trading in general, and scalping in particular, is just a matter of picking up clues from the chart, and the more we can assemble, the better our assessment of the current situation. For example, seeing the bulls finally crawl away from underneath the groping claws of the squeeze (8), only to immediately get sucked back in again (the odd), is a nice little clue that will warm the heart of any scalper contemplating a downward break. Events like that, though tiny in size, can have a devastating effect on the bullish morale. It may just be the incentive needed to finally give up on that support.

In this particular situation, it was rather easy to define the exact moment to fire off that RB short (below the dotted line, 10). But what about if the last low before the barrier break (9) had not bounced up from the dotted line but immediately dipped below it; would that have been a valid short as well?

Fair is fair, since our objective should be to study all eventualities as they may appear in the actual market, we have no option but to also consider the possibility of that less desirable break. If we imagine prices to have dipped below the dotted line at (9), then we couldn't really argue with anyone looking upon it as a tease. On the other hand, a more aggressive scalper would probably see no problem in shorting that break straight away, particularly in the light of that last little clue, the false upside break. So who is right in this respect? Unfortunately, there is no one definitive scalping approach that could ever rule out the validity of another. Because even traders with very similar methods always have a choice between aggression and prudence. And it is very hard to tell which approach will come out ahead in the longer term. Specifically when dealing with ranges, things are not always so evident as for instance in a DD setup where both type of players will probably hit the button at the exact same moment.

Trading textbook range breaks, like the earlier one in Figure 11.1, for example, will most probably not even confuse the absolute novice. But when it comes to handling the somewhat tougher ranges, it may prove wise to remain very conservative until you truly feel comfortable trading them. Rather trade the extremes than front-run the break. And sooner wait for some extra buildup than act on a break that shows too little of it. Keep in mind that even though things may look pretty obvious in terms of directional pressure (they often do), range barriers can be very resilient, particularly when the actual boundaries are open for debate. Trade your range breaks only when you picture yourself to have an edge in the venture: a clear barrier, a nice squeeze and underlying pressure in the direction of the trade. And remember, you do not *need* to engage. A scalper's true virtue is not his technical grasp of knowing when to enter, but more his understanding of when to stay on the sidelines.

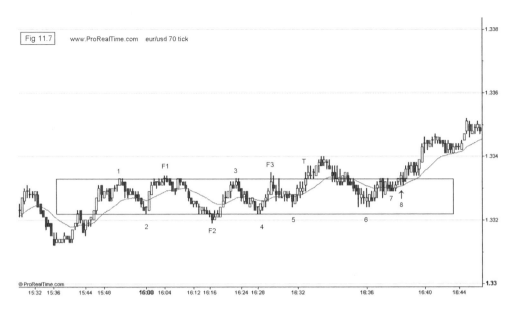

Figure 11.7 This range may look a little rough around the edges but all in all it contained pretty straightforward price action. Despite the many false breaks, there was no need to get caught in any of them. In fact, a scalper would probably not even have started plotting his barriers before the top of (3) equaled the top of (1), and the low of (4) equaled the low of (2); and that would have already eliminated two false breaks (F1 and F2).

This chart, obviously, shows the market being a bit nervous. If you look closely at the time scale below it, you can see that the second half of the range printed the bars about three times as fast as the first half of it. By that information alone, it is quite safe to assume that halfway through it, the market was bracing itself for a typical news release. News releases bear an intrinsic potential to really rip a chart apart. They are mostly dreaded by those in position, of course, for there is no way of telling how hefty the market will respond. The first sign of news hitting the market is the way the chart speeds up. It means that contracts change hands so feverishly that it looks like the bars are literally being spit out on the screen. Seeing them get printed ten times as fast as their normal production rate is definitely not uncommon. It is also the time when you can really tell the difference between a tick chart and a time frame chart; tick charts can still show the ebb and flow of even the wildest markets, whereas a 1-minute chart, for example, may just show a huge 1-minute bar. A second characteristic of news hitting the market is that resistance and support levels can evaporate in a matter of seconds, regardless of their earlier significance. And then there is the potential for huge spikes, even 50 pip or more; these arrows of death are not only known to shake traders out of their positions at the speed of light, they tend to cause enormous slippage to boot. Not seldom, these spikes are extremely short-lived, but that is of little consolation to those shaken out. All in all, news breaks offer a dangerous environment to scalp in. To avoid getting caught by surprise, traders can check the economic calendars (freely available on the web) for the exact moment of *major* announcements (like interest rate decisions and non-farm pay-roll numbers). If caught anyway, and not immediately shaken out, just remain calm. Always aim for a technical way out of a trade. With a bit of luck the market hits the side of the target first. If it shoots off the other way, then there is always the automated stop to prevent excessive damage. It may get hit with slippage, but that is just part of the game (and a good incentive to be more cautious next time).

But the market's erratic reaction to a news release may not be the only danger to worry about; retail traders trading through a no-commission retail broker are advised to check their company's policy on spread mark-up, because some spreads are known to go as high as 10 pip during news breaks. Of course, traders should avoid these brokers in the first place. But then again, trading through a retail broker is a game of give and take. If the broker is okay in any other respect, offers a solid platform to trade from and keeps the spread at 1 pip throughout 99 percent of your sessions, then a simple solution would be to avoid the occasional mark-up by simply not trading during a hefty news release. The brokers to absolutely avoid are those who mark up their spreads more sneakily for no particular reason and for hours on end. Even if they just add a few pipettes either side, it can have a devastating effect on even the best of scalping strategies.

In terms of turmoil, the reaction to the news in this chart was rather subdued. But not without tricks, though. First appeared another false upside break (F3), which got slammed back pretty fast. Next in line was the tease break (T) that suffered a similar fate.

We have to give the bulls some credit for not throwing in the towel then and there. Instead, they played their last trump card, which was to keep the pressure up by not allowing prices to slide below the last low in the range. And that worked out wonderfully well. The low of (6) matched the low of (5), forming a double bottom, and not much later prices were pushing against the top barrier once more (7). Notice the pretty little squeeze and how nicely the 20ema guided prices out of the box. Out of all the breaks through that top barrier, this was the only one that deserved true RB status (8).

Figure 11.8 This range is almost self-explanatory. You may have noticed already that when the round numbers get broken or are being approached, the market does not necessarily tests these levels to the pip. Quite often you will see a range appear with a rather straight-forward barrier a few pip above or below a round number level. The technical implications are nonetheless the same, meaning we should try to trade the breaks of them regardless of the fact that the absolute round number may cause some resistance a few pip away. In the chart in question, for example, the 1.3650 round number resides about 4 or

5 pip below the range, but that should not keep a 10 pip scalper from trading this very valid break. If you think about it, that makes sense. The true technical support in this chart is unmistakably displayed by the actual bottom barrier of the range and not by the round number below it. Or look at it this way: if you imagine yourself to have picked up a long position somewhere inside of that range, would you still hang on to it after the market broke the bottom barrier; would you really hope and pray, as your losses mount with every pip down, that sideline bulls will come to your rescue in that round number below? Or would you dump your long contract then and there and be done with it.

If you can see the logic behind a scalper's reasoning to sell out his position on a break of the box, then you might as well rise to the occasion and short the market yourself, regardless of what lies below (1).

Figure 11.9 This is a very textbook range. Let us look briefly at all of the technical clues in it and see if the pattern was also easy to trade.

The beginning of the chart immediately shows us two classic technical chart patterns, known as a *bull flag* (1) and a *double top* (2-3). The first is regarded as a continuation pattern, a temporary stalling of prices before the market picks up the trend again. The double top, on the other hand, is known to indicate a possible reversal. A pattern like that doesn't necessarily have to reverse the trend completely, but its mere presence can be powerful enough to at least put a temporary damper on it. That brings us to a third and also very technical feat: a *pullback to support* (3-4). Support was offered by the top of the bull flag pattern.

Despite the fact that prices had now arrived at support, the bulls had trouble trying to bounce up from it. Either the level could not attract sufficient follow-through, or the bears were just more aggressive shorting into it. From (4) to (6) they kept the bulls trapped in a squeeze between the 20ema and support. What's more, they even managed to slam back a bullish outbreak (5), causing the much dreaded false with-trend break. But the bulls were not beaten yet. As long as their support held up, they still stood a pretty good chance of breaking free and hurting the bears in return.

Look at that move from (6) to (7). That typically shows us the unwinding of the squeeze. But this time, instead of forcing the bulls out of the market, the bears had basically trapped themselves.

But then the bulls made a classic technical mistake. It wasn't so much the fact that this new top of (7) fell short of the earlier two. In a sense, that was even healthy, because we all know what tends to happen when the market takes out a former extreme in an unsustainable one-directional move. But when the mini spike out of the squeeze fell short of breath, the bulls really should have tried to not let prices slide all the way back to the bottom of the range again. It truly betrayed their lack of enthusiasm to not make use of the technical support offered by the 20ema in conjunction with a 20-level and the cluster of bars to the left. As a result, the bears quickly took over and they even managed to break the earlier lows by a pip (F). If all of this rings somewhat familiar, have a look at Figure 11.6 again and the false break in it (F).

Of course, despite the lack of bullish enthusiasm, a disciplined scalper would certainly have recognized the danger of shorting straight into that support without seeing any sort of buildup first. But not all scalpers are created equal and those trapped in the false downward break immediately had to pay the price for their incompetence, all the way up to another lower top (8).

At that point in time, the market could really go either way. In the chart we could already plot a nice bottom barrier below the lows of (4) and (6). At the other side of the range, a possible barrier could be drawn across the highs of (3) and (7), or maybe a pip higher, as depicted. Naturally, as neutral scalpers we entertain no preference as to the side of the future break. Granted, there is no denying the series of lower tops (2, 3, 7, 8 and not much later 9) as the range slowly progressed. But then again, support was holding up pretty good. It's a scalper's fine prerogative to just watch and see how things develop.

Although ultimately the range break was one of textbook variety and should have caused a scalper no trouble trading it (11), there are two eventualities that may be worthwhile to address: what if the bar of (6) had broken the barrier to the downside and what if the bar of (10) had not bounced up (for a better squeeze) but broken the barrier straight away?

Let us start out with the possible break at (6). Obviously, the bars caught between the 20ema and the range barrier formed an excellent squeeze (reinforced even by the false upside break of 5). That leaves us solely to address the question of whether the technical clues, at that point in time, were supportive enough to risk a trade against the trend. To answer this, let us compare the action between (2) and (6) in this chart with the action between (2) and (9) in Figure 11.6. Evidently, the price action similarities are quite striking. However, the bearish pressure in the earlier chart is much more outspoken, even despite the fact that the uptrend was pretty strong. The double top, for example, was huge and therefore may have kept a large number of potential bulls stuck to the safety of the sidelines. And the squeeze, too, seemed more powerful and determined; the fact that a false break below initial support and then two subsequent tease breaks could still not hold the market up were unmistakable clues of bearish perseverance. Conversely, the bearish pressure in the chart above, though present, somehow lacked the fervor necessary to deem a downward break at (6), had it occurred, convincing enough to risk a countertrend trade. Even despite the false upside break of (5), which would have offered extra credibility to a downward break (remember the principle of the odd versus the obvious as discussed below Figure 11.6), going short at that stage seems very tricky.

Had I carried a long position, though, the break would certainly have inspired me to exit.

Now, I do realize that this answer is not devoid of selective reasoning and it may not appear solid enough for an aspiring scalper to heed its content. But allow me to add that in the business of scalping the line between skipping and trading a break can be extremely thin, even if I was to provide a more satisfactory answer on the particular matter at hand. Regardless of a scalper's degree of proficiency, he will always have a personal way of looking at things, and what looks good to one, may look dubious to another. Fortunately, there is a simple solution to solve the issue of a questionable trade when confronted with one; and that is to only trade those breaks that leave absolutely no room for dispute. Such a trade may still look dubious to another trader, but that is irrelevant from one's own individual perspective.

The second eventuality, that of a possible barrier breach at (10), is a little easier to reject. Had the bar pierced through the barrier at that point in time, I would have looked upon it as a tease. Rejecting a tease, only to see the market shoot off without looking back can be a bit disheartening at times. But bear in mind that things in the market are only favorable for trading if the chart also provides a favorable setup to join in. And the typical tease does not qualify in that respect. So rejecting it is the proper thing to do.

Figure 11.10 Let us close up this chapter with a pretty common range and one that should not cause too many problems finding the right spot of entry for the RB trade. Compared to most of the ranges we have discussed so far, this particular formation, about half an hour in length, is more like a midway between a range and a bigger block. It does not take much technical insight to classify this range as a potential *continuation pattern*. When prices go sideways after trending, not able to run any further but not significantly pulling back either, it usually forebodes another trending run in the direction of the earlier trend. In fact, a chart like the one above is highly prone to reveal what we can refer to as a *trend-equals-trend* formation, meaning that the move after the range is likely to mirror the one that came before it. This is more common than one might think and it is also highly anticipated. In that respect, we can be certain a large number of traders, in position as well as on the sidelines, will be following this market's next steps with close attention, even more so because the current sideways battle revolves around the 1.3150 round number level (with possibly many stop-losses floating above the area).

The reason prices so often stall in the round number zones is not solely attributable to a flood of incoming activity from players who like to swim against the tide. The fact that those in profitable with-trend positions can only cash in by flattening out is just as much responsible for the market to halt, or even reverse. For instance, in the chart above it is not hard to imagine a number of happy bulls exchanging their paper profits for the real variety, if not at the very moment of prices hitting the level, then certainly somewhere in the area when they start to stall. As always, the question of who causes what in the market represents a classic hen-egg situation: are the bulls stepping out because the bears are stepping in, or are the bears stepping in because the bulls are stepping out. That is a nice riddle to solve and one not devoid of irony. After all, from a transaction perspective, a bull stepping out is essentially a bear, and a bear stepping out is no more than a bull, even when both players carry no positions after the fact. The market will simply not be able to tell the difference between a trader flattening out and one taking a new position. It is just another transaction in the marketplace.

Apart from a technical tendency, was there any telling beforehand that the box in the chart was going to break to the upside, at least more likely than to break down? To answer that, let us assemble the clues that point in favor of the bulls and then those in favor of the bears. These are the bullish signs. 1: The trend was up. 2: The bottom of the box rested in technical support (the rather flat bull flag that got formed in the twelve minutes before 12:00). 3: Prices tightly circled around the round number level but could not really sink through it. 4: The box showed excellent support (a number of equal lows) and even a false break to confirm its validity (F). 5: The complete range showed a compressed yet unmistakable W-pattern. 6: Some pre-breakout tension preceded the break (not very extensive, though, yet a nice looking little doji after the tease). 7: The moving average guided prices upwards in the top right corner of the box, basically pushing them out.

As for bearish signs: the possible resistance of a round number level. Can't think of anything else, really.

With so many bullish signs pointing in favor of an upside break, it is still important to not get cocky and to patiently await the right moment to acquire your contracts. Therefore, disciplined scalpers (bar the very aggressive ones) would probably have passed up on the slightly premature tease (T), no matter how much this market looked like it was about to pop.

Note: The *most* important reason not to trade the tease in this situation is not out of fear for a counterattack that may force the trade to be scratched for a loss. It is simply to not teach yourself the bad habit of acting before your turn. If you allow yourself to do that, to stray from your strategy on a whim because the technical signs indicating a possible event are just *so* overwhelming, then, before you know it, you will be doing this all over the place and end up hating yourself every time it backfires. Peace of mind throughout your trading by sticking to your plan is of crucial importance. If you knowingly deviate from your plan by trading prematurely, then your impatience is simply stronger than your calm. Conversely, if you knowingly deviate from your plan by not trading a valid break, then your calm is probably bested by your fear. In either case, what you are essentially doing is trying to outsmart the odds by predicting when a valid setup will fail and when an invalid one will work out. Wouldn't life be much simpler if we just regard all valid setups as valid and all invalid ones as not. Why not relieve ourselves from the fruitless task of prediction and let probability do the thinking.

Chapter 12

Inside Range Break (IRB)

The Inside Range Break setup (IRB) shares many characteristics of the original RB setup discussed in the previous chapter, as well as those of the BB setup examined in the chapter before that. The idea is to explore the possibilities of the sideways market somewhat further. So far we focused on how the ranges are formed and how to go about trading them when their barriers are likely to give in. But what about all these situations in which we can picture these barriers to hold; wouldn't it be nice if we could find a way to trade that as well? And how about looking for a trade in the middle of a range, or getting ourselves positioned for a potential breakout while not even close to the barriers? As we will see, the IRB setup could serve our needs in many respects and it will benefit all scalpers to study its specifics in detail, for it is hard to imagine a day to go by without this pattern showing up in the chart.

One of the functions of the IRB setup is to capitalize on the tendency of prices to bounce back and forth between the top and bottom barrier of a well-established range. From a technical viewpoint that makes sense, since these barrier levels, by their very nature, display clear areas of resistance and support that are widely respected by traders all over the market and hard to miss on a technical chart. How many times, for instance, haven't we seen the top sides get aggressively shorted and the bottom sides aggressively bought. It is not for nothing that it takes such careful planning to break a range successfully. It could safely be stated that the typical range, before ultimately overstaying the hospitality of the market, is more keen on preserving its existence than provoking its demise.

Admittedly, there is no escaping the irony of paradox in the above-mentioned statement, for naturally anything with an expiration date is also ultimately moving towards its own termination. It is the same principle as with the notorious trend: the more prominent it is displayed in the chart, the more it is perceived to continue, while at the same time the inevitable turn is more and more at hand. No matter how a scalper looks at these things, his decision-making process should never be affected by, or based upon, the vagaries of personal perception. There exists no such thing as a range lasting too long or an overextended trend, simply because it is not a trader's call to decide on these matters. That part is already very well taken care of by the market. The scalper should stick to his own task, which is to find and trade setups in a favorable market. Therefore, it is strongly recommended to regard all *valid* setups as equal and not think in terms of safe and lesser safe trades.

The observant chartist may have noticed that the most explicit barrier bounces tend to be quite elusive and rather hard to capture if one does not apply a very aggressive strategy of shorting resistance and buying support. This is quite true indeed. However, as we will shortly discuss in more detail, there are ways for even the conservative scalper to capitalize on the potential boomerang effect between the top and bottom of a range. The trick, as usual, is to be patient and wait for the market to set itself up favorably.

Quite similar to the price action in a regular BB setup, the bars in the IRB are often printed in a compressed but orderly fashion, with either a bunch of equal highs or equal lows capping the tension on the side of the future break. And just like in a BB trade, a trader could wrap a box around this price action to isolate it from the neighboring activity, creating also a clear signal line to trade a break from. When this block of price action—a mini range by itself—appears, for instance, in the area of the top barrier of a bigger range, the tension in it will often push prices out in the direction of the bottom barrier again. And vice versa when a mirror image of this block shows up in the lower region of a range. Hence the boomerang principle. Although the actual setups all have their own individual characteristics, oftentimes we can regard them as failed squeezes that break out the other way. At the break of the IRB setup, a scalper can enter at the market and trade the pattern just like any other setup.

Naturally, we like to see as little chart resistance as possible on the path to our profit target. Therefore, when opting to engage in a boomerang play, the vertical span of the range needs to have sizable width to allow for prices to freely swing within it. If we were to subtract the average width of a setup from the total span of the range and still have adequate room left for a 10 pip ride, then we are easily talking ranges of close to twenty pip and up.

Another way to use the IRB setup, and particular handy in the heart of a much wider range, is to play the pattern as a regular BB trade and not be too concerned with the barriers on either side. As we have already observed many times, prices inside a range do not just swing from top to bottom and back. The wider the range, the more this holds up. Quite often we can see a familiar cluster of bars take shape somewhere halfway or thereabouts. When this pattern is carefully built up and supported by underlying forces, a scalper could wrap a box around it and trade it just like any other BB setup. It is not uncommon for prices, once broken free, to accelerate towards the nearest barrier.

In the wider ranges, the profit target may be reached without having to crack the range's protection shield, but that is not to say that the narrower ranges, on occasion, cannot be played in similar fashion. In fact, a third and much used function of this splendid little setup is to anticipate an actual range barrier break, not from the position of one of the barrier levels, but from somewhere inside the range itself. By definition, this means that prices will have to clear the barrier resistance on their path to the profit target. That does pose a certain threat to the undertaking, but when the technical signs point very much in favor of the trade's direction, this does not have to be of great concern. What's more, at times the IRB setup may even be a scalper's only chance to capture the range break at all. In other words, next to the undeniable disadvantage of being in a trade that has to crack solid resistance on the way to the target there is also the interesting advantage of being potentially positioned for an impending event that may not be tradable otherwise.

Another advantage of this supposedly riskier IRB variant is the magnet effect of the range barriers themselves. Just like the vacuum principle regarding the round numbers, a little selling or buying hiatus often precedes a barrier touch, too. After all, when the range boundaries are pretty established, traders, logically, will try to wait as long as they can before playing a turn of the market. When there are such explicit levels to trade from there is no need to front-run the market in fear of missing out—as traders often do in the case of a strong trend. The majority of smart barrier traders will either sell the very top or buy the very bottom of a range, or do nothing at all. That way their stops can be placed very close to their entries (a little outside the range). As a result, a well-chosen trade originating from somewhere inside the range may see the pleasant surprise of being literally sucked into the vacuum of low activity above or beneath the nearest barrier. Upon arrival, these barriers may very well spring to life, so to speak, even up to the point of reversing all of the current gains completely. But experience has it that when a trade has already traveled in the plus for a number of pip, it tends to eventually reach target more often than not; or else it may result in a somewhat healthier scratch. By and large, it is the trade that goes awry almost instantaneously that causes the inevitable damage control to be the most expensive.

It goes without saying that entering the market inside the range in anticipation of a barrier break should only come as a result of an IRB setup that is properly backed by a set of technical conditions that indisputably favor the trade's direction, and not as a means to front-run a barrier breach out of impatience or greed.

Just like all the other setups already discussed, the IRB requires little technical skill to be identified. After all, everything in scalping should be fairly easy to do. We do not base our trades on some magical sense of market direction, nor is there is any need to complicate matters by adding indicators, trendlines, retracement levels, multiple time frames, or whatever tools and tricks a standard charting package nowadays may come up with. Brewing over charts, calculating price levels, computing momentum and weighing forces as if constructing an architectural masterpiece may please the diehard technical analyst, the proficient scalper, on the other hand, will strip his chart to the absolute bare minimum. All he needs are the price bars in it. He may allow himself the luxury of a moving average but will only use it as a visual aid. At the end of the day, a scalper's task is all about tuning in to the beat of the market with as little information as possible. In a scalper's world, less is definitely more.

We should always bear in mind, though, that, regardless of our wonderful setups, trades do go sour all the time. No strategy could ever be devised to prevent that from happening. But once we understand that giving profits back to the market is part of the exact same process as taking profits from it, the whole idea of losing will simply become a non-issue. Losses are the costs of business in a trader's line of work, nothing more and nothing less. Just like the restaurant owner needs to pay rent, buy food and hire staff in order to run a profitable business, so does the trader need to lose in order to take profits from the market. For one can simply not exist without the other. Therefore, feeling euphoric after a winning trade and depressed after a losing one are clear signs of a trader not understanding his own business model. The sooner a trader stops deluding himself that being up or down on the day bears any significance, the sooner he will be able to see his profession for what it really is: a profession, and not a constant game of win or lose.

Now let us see how this IRB setup is best taken on in a real market environment. To summarize on its appearance, there are essentially three categories in which the setup can be classified. 1: as a barrier bounce. 2: as a midway trade (in a wider range). 3: as a breakout trade. In the more compressed ranges, the IRB could very well pose itself as a representative of all three categories. But it is important not to forget that the overall price action, at all times, should favor the direction of the trade. If not, then the setup, no matter how good-looking, is best ignored.

Figure 12.1 This chart immediately shows the power of the IRB setup when used as a means to trade a barrier bounce. The block itself should not be too hard to distinguish. The encapsulated price action (second box) is quite similar to the earlier tug-o-war within the dotted box to the left. Both boxes clearly demonstrate this range's instinct of self-preservation. We only need one look at the large number of equal tops in the chart to understand how well the defense mechanism kicked in when the bulls had a go at that particular level.

Although not absolutely necessary, it is always nice to see at least one, but preferably two or more smaller bars appear right before the block break sets itself up (in essence, a miniature squeeze). After all, it makes sense that the same general principles regarding the false break trap also apply to the boundaries of a block pattern, which is essentially a little range by itself. This means that the breakout is best preceded by some pre-breakout tension, usually in the shape of one or more little dojis (remember that for the sake of simplicity, our method regards any little bar, of usually no more than 3 pip in length, as a doji). When the block is rather compressed, however, it is not uncommon to be broken on one end by the same bar that also shows an extreme at the opposite end of the block. That is not necessarily a reason to skip the break, though, particularly when the conditions for a healthy trade look very good and the block itself is not too wide—say, not beyond 5 pip or so. In other words, it is not always necessary to see the typical two dojis reflect pre-breakout tension; the whole block itself may represent sufficient tension to warrant a trade. When it comes to the not so picture perfect entry, a scalper always has two options to choose from. 1: wait for the situation to improve, but run the risk of missing the trade. 2: take the trade but run the risk of a premature entry and a possible scratch. In general, when the technical conditions seem very supportive regarding the direction of the trade, then stepping in on a break of the block is probably the wisest thing to do. This is not to be confused with foolishly trading a textbook tease. The differences, at times, can be subtle, though.

Figure 12.2 In the range above, the first low of (1) and the subsequent high of (2) basically marked the outer barriers for the next hour of trading. Note the typical tease break (T1) and the typical false break (F) a few minutes later. It is my sincere wish that the reader, whether a complete novice to trading or already a veteran in other ways of speculation, really pays heed to these very obvious scalper traps that keep on tricking so many traders day in day out. Scalping, more than any other trading

style, is all about timing trades as smartly as possible. A trader trading a bigger time frame, and with a good feel for reading the forces in play, may easily say to himself: this market is going down and I want to be short in it. So he sets to work, picks up his contracts here and there and gets himself positioned for the ride. After having already acquired a number of contracts, say, within a range, he may even sell some more at the typical false break levels that make a scalper cringe—and be totally okay with that. His stops will probably reside somewhere on the other side of the pattern, or maybe above a former top of some kind. There is no immediate necessity for his trades to show profit, nor for the market to immediately crack. He may even decide to short some more when prices take their time to break. In case the market has other plans, this trader may suffer some serious losses, that's true, but these losses will most likely be relatively small compared to the potential profits that, on occasion, emerge out of a well-built position that is allowed to run profitably for as long as the market is kind. It is not uncommon for one good winner to offset five or more losers. But that, dear reader, is trading from a bigger time frame. The scalper, on the other hand, will not see the market being so forgiving on the part of his entering too soon or at terrible, low odds spots. His timing has to be correct almost to the very pip. His 10 pip stop is merely a safety net for a worst-case scenario. His average stop will be a manual scratch, keeping the damage as minimal as possible. Sitting it out to see how things evolve is a luxury the scalper cannot afford—not for entering and not for exiting. When dealing with a small and predefined profit target, like 10 pip, the scalper will never experience the hail-Mary ride that offsets a serious wave of earlier losses. So, obviously, the trick is to keep these inevitable losses as low in number and in pip as possible. The only way to avoid getting squashed as a scalper is to aim for the near perfect entry. When there is no pre-breakout tension visibly justifying the possibility of prices being ready to break, then the chances of seeing a tease or a false break pop up are extremely high. That does not in any way mean that proper buildup will guarantee a smooth ride from the moment of entry. But then again, a scalper has no need for guaranties, he only needs good odds.

There was another failed attempt to crack the top barrier (T2) just twenty minutes after the failed break at the other side. This one may not literally deserve the tease status since it did not surpass the level of the earlier tease (T1), but the idea of buying there, from a scalper's viewpoint, is almost just as foolhardy. Or, as a subtler way of putting it, it makes for low odds.

Ranges of about 10 to 15 pip in width, on average, show a tendency to expire much sooner than the visibly wider ones. If such a market has not been able to decide which way to force a break after about an hour of sideways action, it may really pay off to stick around and even sharpen up the focus. This one hour mark is by no means a law, not even a rule of thumb. At all times, the price action in the chart should do the talking and not the time scale below it. I believe the point has already been stressed that boredom easily sets in when a market cannot seem to make up its mind on direction. That always makes a trader more vulnerable to either see things that are not there or decide to leave his desk out of sheer chagrin. And then he may just miss a nice little IRB like the one in this chart (8).

If we look at the IRB setup in relation to its place in the range, then it could not be more neutrally positioned. In that respect, it is not that bearish a pattern. And what's more, if we look at the bottom part of the range formation, then in the course of about an hour the market put in a double bottom (1 and F) and two little higher bottoms (5 and 7), which, all in all, clearly represents strong underlying support. But that is looking at things through bullish glasses. If we also bring the bearish signs to the table, then we can see the range appear in a bit of a downtrend (beginning of the chart shows higher prices), and we can count no less than four almost equal tops (2, 3, T1 and T2) plus a lower double top to boot (4 and 6). That just about evens the score. Frankly, at this point, the bears have earned themselves a slight benefit of doubt. But even with that notion in mind, it is still advisable to not entertain a bearish view on this market for the sake of picking sides. If the bulls really wanted to, they could put pressure on the bears in just a very short amount of bars.

What makes this IRB a tradable pattern (to the downside) is maybe the very fact that the bulls did not, or could not, put pressure on the bears. Almost every bar in the box turned out to be a bearish looking doji, first touching the higher part of the box and then closing in the lower part of the bar. The fact that this setup had no more than two equal lows to show for it, does not make it any less a setup. If broken to the downside and not immediately countered, a number of bulls will definitely bail out. And that will come in handy to all those traders short of the market. And inspire others to go short also.

Should a 10 pip scalper trading that IRB be very worried about the bottom barrier of the bigger range about 6 pip below? Let us examine the situation for a moment. In case the short was initiated immediately below the IRB signal line, then the trade, upon reaching the bigger barrier, will be in a comfortable plus of about 4 pip. At that moment, anything can happen. The market may crack without a pause, prices may stall, or traders may perceive the barrier as support and start to buy prices back up. In case of the latter, what would be the level where rising prices are most likely to be halted (and possibly turned)? Technically, that would be right underneath the IRB pattern from where the short was initiated. They *may* pierce through it—why not?—but chart technically, the odds favor the bottom of the setup to rather hold up as resistance than to give way to rising prices. And even if prices were to march through that level, maybe by a pip or two, chances are still good that they will soon be pushed back out again. After all, higher prices in resistance, that spells a great opportunity to at least a number of sideline bears ready to short the market in the face of good odds. In other words, and irrespective of the ultimate outcome, the decision to trade an IRB like this is a proper call.

Figure 12.3 Traders trying to short the bottom of the market between 15:00 and 16:00 were not very successful in provoking much follow-through among fellow bears. However, up until the first twenty minutes, it is understandable that they gave it a try. Not only had the market dropped 20 pip below the round number of 1.36 in the beginning of the chart, it had done so quite aggressively, offering credit to the notion that the bears meant business, leaving prices prone to drop some more. The first real attempt of the bulls to do something about this was to try and break an earlier pullback high (F1 took out 2). If that turned out to be successful, then a retest of the round number would have made for an excellent target. But the break clearly backfired, resulting in a classic false break doji sticking out like a sore thumb (F1). Any false break, as no doubt the reader will have already gathered, is an unmistakable clue as to who is currently dominating who in the marketplace. Short-term scalpers, big and small, trapped in these breaks, can get seriously damaged if they do not immediately deploy their bail-out techniques. Each new second of hesitation may result in even more damage, which is why most of them will have no regrets dumping their newly obtained positions as if being scorched by them. This is the exact predicament the dominating party tries to instill upon the dominated: forcing them to act

not only to their own detriment, but to the benefit of their opponents to boot. It also represents the *principle of double pressure* and in essence portrays what professional scalping is all about: to find that particular spot where the beaten party is most likely to bail out and the sideliners, with similar views as the reigning party, will jump to get in. If so, then both groups will fire off their orders in the same direction, which makes for excellent double pressure; and probability has it that price will simply travel in line with that pressure more often than not.

Should a neutral scalper on the sidelines want to rise to the occasion of a sudden false break, and thus consider a trade in the opposite direction, then the closer his intended entry point in relation to the false break level, the better. In the chart above, for instance, the scare-effect of the false break of (F1) will most likely have worn off by the time prices hit the bottom of the range again (5). But, as we can tell by the chart, it proved to be quite beneficial to the alert scalper immediately shorting the lows of the triple doji pattern at (4).

In a way, the common paranoia regarding the false break is highly understandable, because the charts are full of them. But let me be quick to add that most of these breaks are quite predictable, even bordering on insult. Still, traders do get trapped in them, all the time.

Note: There is a subtle distinction to be made between a false break with-trend and a false break countertrend. The latter is often set up as a trap by big volume players, or at least it is a low odds break very much exploited by the more astute traders that know when to strike. The with-trend breakout, on the other hand, is much trickier to prove false, even by bigger players, because any moment real with-trend volume may hit the market and prove the break true. That is why follow-through is such a vital ingredient for these breaks to be successful. And why a lack of it is such a pleasing sight to the countertrend aficionado. The longer the market stays non-responsive to a break, the more likely that break is to fail; either due to countertrend traders going against it, or as a result of with-trend traders bailing out of their positions in the absence of follow-through. Not uncommonly, however, it may only take one or two bars for the market to reach that verdict.

A good example of a lack of follow-through in the chart above is depicted by the false break through the bottom barrier, when the market refused to sell off despite the fact that prices had taken out the earlier double bottom lows (5 took out 1-3, and then F2 took out 5). Whatever reasons lie hidden behind the failure of any break is of little relevance to the disciplined scalper observing the market. Seeing a break fail is simply market information.

As a whole, the battle over the 1.3580 support level (the first 20-level below the 00-level) turned out to be an interesting fight. Within the course of an hour, the bears had no less than eight shots at it, but each time they failed in cracking that support. Demand was simply stronger than supply.

When watching a lengthy clash from the sidelines, it is advised to always keep an open mind towards the ultimate conclusion. There is no sense in guessing who will win, nor in favoring one party over another. At times, a scalper, longing for a trade and slowly getting impatient, may unintentionally maneuver himself in a tricky situation should he hold preference over one direction more than the other. He may even go so far as to put his favoritism into practice by subconsciously starting to disregard signs that oppose his directional bias and welcome those in support of it. A dangerous disposition to trade in.

As long as any clash proceeds, both parties could very well come out on top. Especially in ranges, it often needs no more than a couple of bars to change an outlook completely. And besides, there is no need for favoritism to begin with, for both sides of the market can be equally played. If only the scalper remains neutral and patient.

In the chart in question, the bulls eventually succeeded to exhaust the perseverance of the bears. That is all very nice in hindsight, but was there a real-time opportunity to capitalize on this victory? To the untrained eye, the IRB setup may seem of rather dubious quality. And indeed, despite the bullish double bottom in it (6-8), the price action looked a bit nervous and it was not really that obvious where to draw the signal line of the box. The high of (7) was a result of a strong two-bar attempt to move away from the lows and at that point a scalper may have considered it a possible reference point for a potential signal line. But then again, with prices back at the lows just a few moments later (8) that upside break did not seem so evident anymore. In fact, if the market could not force itself back up again but instead built up pressure to the downside, then maybe the bears could finally create what they had been attempting to do all along: a downward break. But alas, a quick change in fortune brought prices swiftly back up and all of a sudden there appeared two lovely looking little dojis, sharing equal highs, forming a higher bottom in the 20ema (9). To the observant eye, the pieces fall immediately into place. An alert scalper, present on the scene, could now trade a full-fledged IRB setup backed up by strong chart support. He should just trade a break of the highs of the dojis (10) and not wait for the high of (7) to be taken out first. Barrier bounces, when built up properly, usually allow for a little more aggression. Since the market shows a tendency to jump away in the break, it is best to catch the ride on the bandwagon as soon as we can. Notice how prices in this particular case were immediately sucked into the vacuum of the round number above. After all that backing and filling at the bottom of the chart, there was hardly any fight once prices broke free to the upside. And that fits perfectly well with the principle of double pressure.

When it comes to tradability versus visual presentation, it will serve a trader best to accept that the perfect setup, as much as it is welcomed and referred to as such, is essentially an illusion. The overall picture, at all times, should weigh heavier on the decision-making process than the shape of the setup alone, which, in the end, is no more than a *means* to get in on the market, and not the reason to. This does not mean that a trader should go around trading all sort of tease breaks, for instance, when he perceives the overall conditions to favor a break. Regardless of the circumstances, timing will always be crucial. The point is that too many opportunities may go by unexplored if a trader entertains the perception that he should only be looking for the *perfect* trade—for his pet textbook setup may simply not surface for sessions on end. The scalper, looking for perfection, may repeatedly find himself in a knot. Either he spots the ideal setup but does not see it backed by current conditions; or he perceives the conditions to be ideal for a trade but cannot find the setups to match them. And so he constantly postpones entering on very valid trades because his box, for example, does not show him the perfect double bottom followed by a higher bottom and a nice set of triple dojis underneath an ideal signal line. But that is living and trading in a fantasy world. And not a pleasant one at that. The sooner the scalper sets aside his fear for entering the market (because that's what we're looking at here) and accepts that he also *needs to lose in order to win*, the sooner he will be able to benefit from the countless possibilities presented to him.

In this particular chart, it wasn't really that essential to think in terms of ranges. Maybe the top barrier should have been lowered to the 1.3590 mark, or there about, turning the range in a more narrow box. But that would not have altered much. The bottom barrier here, that was were the true fight was fought.

Not a day goes by without seeing a range barrier, or a very prominent level of support or resistance, being fought over for at least the biggest part of an hour. Stay with them and be patient. Instead of being bored or irritated, the smart scalper should consider it a great prerogative not having to engage in these tedious tug-o-wars but to simply join the side that's winning once the smoke clears up from the battleground.

Figure 12.4 Once again, we've got ourselves a range formation that gets resolved in about an hour's time. As we have seen already many times

before, it is not essential for the market to have prices attack a particular barrier up to the point of exhaustion. Quite often, it needs no more than a double top or double bottom to show all participants who is in charge. At times, it can make you wonder, though, why at some point the strongest walls of resistance get attacked with a relentless fervor, while elsewhere in the market a mere halfhearted expression of power remains completely undisputed. But the market is what it is and does what it does. In the end, the direction of prices is a big players game and the mortal scalper has no business asking questions. The good thing is, however, that although the tiny trader may never know the *why* behind the big player's agenda, he may just be able to tell the *when* if he pays close attention.

Up until the encapsulated IRB setup there was not much to make of this range in terms of possible direction. Prices had printed a clear double top (3-6), indicating resistance, but a series of consecutive higher bottoms betrayed unmistakable support (2, 4, 5 and 7, all higher than 1). But once again, signs of support and resistance, no matter how prevalent in the chart, are not necessarily reflecting major levels in the market that need to be conquered unambiguously in a heroic fight, with one party ultimately succumbing to the other. In fact, they could dissolve in a matter of seconds without any signs of protest. That is why it is probably not a very good strategy—at least not for the aspiring scalper—to simply sell in resistance or buy in support, not even for the sake of a brief little scalp. Overall, the safer approach is to see how the market handles these zones and *then* try to trade them.

Whenever the market is approaching a barrier, or even just a former top or bottom, basically three things can happen. 1: the level is broken as if non-existent. 2: the level is fully respected and prices bounce off of it as if hit by a hammer. 3: the level is heavily attacked as well as defended.

It is the latter situation that presents the best opportunities in sideways progressions. And the longer the fights lasts, the bigger the pain of those who eventually lose out. In order to stop it, they can only do one thing, which is to flee from the scene as fast as they can. This hurried flight to safety, a mass exodus at times, is what presents the sideline scalper with an excellent opportunity to earn some pip at the expense of those on the run.

Almost by definition, any tension in the chart represents the dreams and hopes of two opposing parties. A bull, for instance, is basically telling the bear: I am buying your contract but I am shorting your dream. And, likewise, so does the bear scorn the bull in return. Inevitably, one of these two will soon pay the price for their bravado and the bill can be a painful one. Each and every trader on the sidelines, aiming for profit, has essentially just one thing in mind: to find out who gets the bill presented and then quickly capitalize on a burst of demoralization as many hopes and dreams get crushed. It should come as no surprise that the average trader is not particularly burdened by moral inhibitions, nor does he feel the need to pledge a humane disposition towards his fellow trader in the market. After all, he knows very well he is not exactly operating in the welfare industry and that at any moment in time he himself may get trampled by another. But the game, at all times, should be played fairly, with equal chances for all involved, big or small, bull or bear, novice or experienced. It is the novice, no doubt, who will get burnt the most in his line of duty; that is why it is so important to escape that status as soon as possible through sound preparation and extensive study, and with the inevitable lessons in the market costing as little as possible.

The IRB pattern in the chart above is another great example of how to trade a top barrier bounce. Or we could say, it shows how to capitalize on the pain of demoralized bulls running for cover after their dreams of higher prices got shattered by a simple break of the pattern lows. The pattern itself shows three arches, the second and third lower than the first, colorfully named a *reversed-cup-and-two-handles* formation by those who love their classic patterns (8, 9 and 10). No less than six identical bottom touches formed an excellent signal line before prices finally gave way to the downward pressure.

It would be a misconception to think that prices, at any one time, could tank or rise more than 30 pip straight on account of such a tiny IRB setup alone. Predominantly, the markets move because of the overall technical conditions. There could be a number of other reasons for markets to rise and fall as they do, even against the current trend, for that matter. But it is highly unlikely that a little tug-o-war with a vertical span of a mere 5 pip can cause the market to move six times the width of that pattern. The setups are nothing more than tools for entering at the best possible spots. The pattern here, for instance, was put in by the market at just the right place and the break occurred at just the right time; it only provided the proverbial trigger for the bulls to get out and for the bears to get in.

Whenever one party yields to the pressure of another, bulls and bears alike, though be it for complete different reasons, will start to aggressively hit prices in the same direction. In many instances, it only needs one single pip to surpass a certain level to provoke this unanimous act. It is a scalper's task to locate that very crucial spot beforehand and trade it the moment it breaks. He may only have a split second to act before it may be too late. But a split second is all it takes to fire an order that is already set.

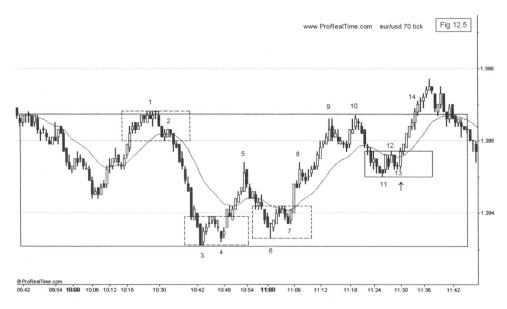

Figure 12.5 To the untrained eye, the chart above may have a somewhat chaotic feel to it. When you see action like this develop on your screen, just let the market do its thing and wait for at least a couple of highs and lows to get established. Then take your box tool out of your

toolbox and start wrapping. Sometimes, as the price action develops, it may take several tries before you capture the picture satisfactorily, but once you do, almost any chart will earn immediate clarity (remember, instead of a box, you can also place a horizontal line across the highs and another one beneath the lows).

At first glance, it looks like we are dealing here with a very speedy market, quite similar to one digesting a news release. But it is the length of the bars and the size of the moves that trick the eye. On average, a typical European and American session, when trading in their most active phases, will print about 120 of individual 70-tick bars in a span of an hour (comparable to a regular 30-second time frame chart); the chart above, recorded in the opening of the European session, showed about 160 of individual bars in two hours' worth of trading. So it was not that speedy at all. Prices did swing voluptuously back and forth, though, and even though the range did not produce a lot of tradable setups (from the perspective of our method), it did present numerous technical particulars that are definitely worth pointing out.

A look at the price scale on the vertical axis tells us the market more or less moved in a 40 pip range, with the round number level of 1.3950 running right through the center of it. Eagerly as the bears may have deployed their shorts from the top, the bulls at the other side showed even more aggression, by buying the market at higher levels on three consecutive occasions (4, 6 and 7). If we combine the four lows in this bottom area in pairs of two (3-4 and 6-7), we can see that they technically make up the bottom part of a giant W-pattern (1-9). Considering how mean the market had sold off from the top, swinging prices all the way back up was quite a technical achievement.

With the market now back at the highs (10), the most healthy way for prices to behave (should they want to travel higher up) is to first pull back to lower levels and establish a base for further advance. Since this chart seems to have the round number level as a dividing line between bearish and bullish territory, a sideline scalper will be interested to see if the bulls will be able to keep the market above it.

Usually, when bars get printed rather nervously, swinging wildly back and forth, prices tend to display less technical respect for the absolute levels of resistance and support. For example, when challenged from below, the 50-level may easily get pierced by a fair amount of pip before resistance kicks in (5 and 8). The same holds up for the extremes at the range boundaries themselves: the more eccentric the swings, the more a barrier may get pierced without truly breaking. To a scalper, it is all the same. Whatever the market does, it is just information. Let the big guys throw rocks at each other for as long as they like. Eventually something tradable will emerge on any chart. It cannot be stressed enough how important it is to remain patient, even as a scalper.

From the perspective of our method, the first tradable opportunity presented itself in the shape of the IRB setup (the non-dotted box). In a way, this is also a BB pattern, as discussed in Chapter 10 on Block Breaks. Let us take a close look at the price action within the box. It shows a well-known technical pattern which is often referred to as a *cup-and-handle* formation. Sometimes it is called a *1-2-3* formation. The pattern is made up of two u-shaped arches—a bigger one, the cup, and a smaller one next to it, the handle (11 and 13). The midpoint that attaches the cup and handle together is a high (12), and once this high gets taken out, the market may show a strong reaction in the direction of the break. It is not uncommon for the pattern to show multiple handles next to the cup, which only enhances the buildup within it. Like any other chart pattern, this one also works in reverse. Have a look at the three dotted boxes in the chart, these are also cup-and-handle patterns. Take note of what happened each time these boxes got broken.

Indeed, the cup-and-handle formation can lead to very powerful moves. They are often played in the hope of catching a market turning point, like the first and the second dotted box, but it should be noted that that kind of aggression has a tendency to backfire. Personally, I prefer to play them in a pullback situation, like the IRB setup in the non-dotted box.

No matter how attractive a particular setup, we still need to see some technical backup to grant it validity as a tradable event. Let us look at what could be derived from this chart to support the idea of the IRB trade. 1: The unmistakable W-pattern implied a possible continuation of bullish pressure. 2: The bottom of the IRB setup found technical support in two former tops (5 and 8, not spot on). 3: The round number level had been recaptured by the bulls and now offered support to the setup (11). 4: The position of the IRB pattern more or less found its footing in a 50 percent retracement of an earlier swing (7-10). 5: A possible vacuum effect below the top barrier may suck prices straight up.

Of course, we should not only concentrate on the bright side. As for the technical clues that could negatively affect the trade's potential, there is not much to be found, though. 1: The double top underneath the range barrier (9 and 10) could scare some traders off, possibly resulting in less follow-through. 2: The entry bar that broke the box was rather tall; it started from the low of the handle and ran all the way up to break the pattern in one go. This will affect our risk on the trade. Although we will take on the specifics of stop placement in another section, it will be no surprise that stops are often placed directly below or above a handle that gets broken on the other side. The more compressed the handle, the more economical the stop. A good example of such a compressed handle is the reversed one in the first dotted box (2); it stands just three pip tall. However, it is not necessarily a bad thing to have to apply a wider stop on occasion, certainly not in a market that has temporarily lost its subtlety of movement, like the chart above. Let's not forget a very simple trading fact: the smaller the stop, the bigger the chance of it getting hit in a countermove. Therefore, the problem with taking a trade like this would probably not be so much the issue of the handle being too deep, but more if a trader would truly have been ready, or deemed it safe, to fire his order at that point in time. After all, that handle bar shot up pretty fast and there was no pausing before the break.

As far as that double top is concerned (9-10), in a more subdued chart, a pattern like that may seriously put traders off scalping against it. In order to get to target, prices would have to plow through it; that is not exactly trading along the path of least resistance. But facing an element of resistance does not necessarily mean that we better skip the trade. We have to take into account the contra pressure that is attacking it. If we compare the potential for downward pressure, suggested by the double top, to the potential for upward pressure, suggested by the IRB cluster, then we could say that the forces are more or less evenly distributed. And with the overall pressure pointing very much in favor of further advance, there is no technical reason to skip the IRB on account of that double top.

All in all, the IRB venture stands a pretty good chance of working out. By no means it is the ideal trade, even the market's strong reaction after the break cannot alter that fact. The reason why a trade like this should be acted on is simply because the odds for it to work out are slightly better than those for the trade to fail. Or look at it this way: with a 5 pip handle, the trade, if it fails, will most likely be stopped out for a loss of 8 pip (to calculate the risk in pip, we have to always add 3 pip to the size of the bar, or pattern, the stop resides below or above: 1 pip on each side for the bar to be taken out, and then another pip to account for the spread). On the other hand, should the trade work out, then that will pocket us a profit of 10 pip. That's all very nice, but what are the *odds* for each of these outcomes?

If nothing else, we should ask ourselves at least the following question: do the forces supporting the position appear strong enough to sufficiently counter the forces against it in order to justify the payment of the spread. The more we can answer that affirmatively, the better the odds will be. Of course, this way of looking at probability holds up only if the assumption of having an edge is correct. But then again, that is what trading is all about, or else we might as well not bother. The good thing is that we do not necessarily need to win seven or more times out of every ten trades. Not even six. For instance, when a winning trade produces a 10 pip profit and a losing one a 7 pip loss, then having just as much winners as losers would run up any scalper's account significantly in no time.

This chart also shows a great example of how a trade taken from inside a range may see prices get sucked straight into the vacuum of the nearest barrier. In this chart, prices even spiked through it. Of course, that was a terrible way of the bulls to go about breaking that range (14). A clever sideline scalper would never consider trading such a low odds break. In fact, he would most likely have traded the IRB, and then sold out his contract for a 10 pip profit to the very same trader getting trapped in the break above.

Figure 12.6 Price action does not always have to win a beauty contest to deliver a tradable event. Granted, if the chart truly shows a mishmash of erratic movements that make no technical sense then it is best left alone until the picture clears up. But do not give up on a chart too easily. More often than not, from below the surface of non-descriptive price action clarity will emerge and before you know it the pieces of the puzzle may fall neatly into place. One more reason to always stay alert and focused, even throughout the less attractive doldrums of lunch hour ranges.

Like the proverbial ball that is pushed under water, so is the price action within a range suppressed and contained. But the equilibrium in both upward and downward forces is an artificial one and can only be of a temporary nature; eventually, like in any tug-o-war, one side will simply have to let go of the rope. When that happens, prices usually do the one logical thing: they pop. Of course, in the marketplace the pressure can escape at either side and it may not be in textbook fashion. What's more, even a classic break may turn out to be a trap. But does it really matter? Classic breaks are valid breaks and the occasional trap is just part of the game. The point is not to question the valid break but to avoid the classic trap. Regardless of his years in the market, a scalper will never be able to tell whether his break will be true or false. All he can do is follow the clues in the chart and trade any valid break that comes along.

Let us look at the chart above and see if we can detect the signs that may have inspired a scalper to trade the IRB breakout. In the beginning of the chart, prices came down from a 20-level to test the round number of 1.33. They subsequently bounced up and rose to test the former highs. Things got interesting when prices surpassed the earlier high of (1) by a mere pip (F). A classic trap. Countertrend traders, always ready to punish those less able, quickly rose to the occasion and started slamming prices as fast as they could. Just by watching this, our scalper is already offered two very technical clues that may prove to be of value later on: support in the round number zone and resistance about 20 pip above it. He may not be able to draw exemplary and workable range boundaries yet, or feel the need to, but at least he has gained an impression of what the future price action may be about. Should prices travel all the way down to support again, then the most prompting question, of course, will concern the round number defense. Will it hold up, or give in to bearish pressure?

The false break aside (F), we cannot blame the bears for shorting the market in an area of a former top (5). It is often seen that when prices initially bounce up from a round number (2), the market will attempt to revisit the level at least once not long after. It can even be defended that traders initiated new shorts when the market, a little later, cracked below the 20ema (6). At that point in time there was still plenty of room for a quick scalp into the vacuum above 1.33.

However, it soon became obvious that the market had no intention of revisiting the round number to the pip. Instead, it formed another double bottom (7-8), reinforcing the base of support put in by the earlier lows (3-4). An important clue.

Next up was about fifteen minutes of very choppy price action (8-11). Although the bears did manage to keep a lid on the upward pressure, fact is that they were not powerful enough to prevent the bulls from putting in another double bottom in support, and a higher one to boot (9-10).

Now that the price action was slowly starting to tip its hand, how hard was it to find the setup within? First of all, with prices in an area of support, there was no point in looking for a DD, FB or a SB setup, because these patterns are best played from a pullback situation in a trending market. Nor was there any need to think RB with prices slowly moving away from support. As the market moved between hope and fear within that sideways cluster, the only workable setup to contemplate was an IRB.

In this particular chart, the setup seems a little rough and one might think it was not that easy to locate. Still, if we ignore the tease break (T), the pattern showed an excellent signal line of five equal touches, the last two put in by a very familiar duo of pre-breakout dojis. Not only did the two little bars help to form and complete the breakout level, they also built up tension beneath it. On top of that, the lows of these dojis found support in the 20ema, adding one more cherry to the cake.

All in all, this chart presented numerous practical clues. The setup may have required some focus, but it was very tradable nonetheless. A good reason to really study these type of IRBs in round number support (or the reversed variety in round number resistance) is because these breakouts can be so powerful that they considerably diminish the potential of seeing a regular RB show up at the other end of the range. Remember, a little a aggression may be called for in a barrier bounce trade; the speedy nature of the breakout reduces the possibility of a pullback to the signal line and thus the opportunity for a scalper to get in on second instance.

Figure 12.7 This charts represents a typical lunch hour congestion during the U.S. session. Bear in mind, the term lunch *hour* is quite a euphemism when it comes to the American markets, because these breaks may easily surpass the two hour mark. Why anybody would need such a lengthy retreat after a mere two and a half hours of trading simply bewilders the industrious mind, particularly so since the span of the average U.S. market is already one of the shortest on the planet. The U.S. stock markets, for example, have a daily life of only six and a half hours, at least two hours less than the average market across the ocean. Anyway, since all noteworthy markets are heavily dependent on U.S. activity, it is not so strange for the eur/usd contract, too, to switch into sleeping mode at the start of that break; and even more so because at that same period all major European markets close up for the day.

There is a bright side to the typical lunch hour session, though, and that is that it tends to produce highly readable ranges in which the battle between supply and demand is quite visibly displayed. More often than not, these ranges revolve around a round number level, and just as often they show a strong tendency to break once traders come back to their screens.

Let's take a good look at the chart above. A couple of things are worth noting and rather easy to make out. First of all, the range unmistakably revolved around the round number level of 1.31. In fact, the number lay right in the center of activity. The top side of the range initially looked a little jagged; an earlier line may have been placed across the highs of (3) and (5). Eventually the market managed to put in a high equal to the most prominent highs (1-12), but by then a scalper would have already been in position on the IRB trade. The bottom part of the range showed an excellent double bottom (2-4), a strong indication of support that not much later got confirmed by a higher triple bottom (6-7-9). All in all, there was little bearish enthusiasm to be detected in the lower part of the range, enhancing the odds for the round number to hold up.

Note: If you think of it, the evaluation of a chart is very much akin to adding and subtracting numbers in a simple mathematical equation. But there is a catch. Whereas the true mathematician is not likely to entertain a preference for one outcome over another, the typical trader is not nearly as neutrally inclined. Not only may he not like his outcomes and thus ignore them or even defy them, he may even go so far as to alter his numbers so as to be ultimately presented with a more desirable result. It is amazing what a person is capable of when it comes to fooling himself on the brink of a trade. Would a restaurant owner picture himself a room full of customers when there are none inside? Probably not. Yet traders see trades all the time, even when there are none to be found; or they refuse to see them when they are very much present. Indeed, the typical trader is truly the king of all con men, for he is able to con himself every day again and not even know it.

How about that IRB setup. The double bottom in it looks solid, equaling the earlier low (hence the triple bottom). The top part shares five equal touches that together make up the signal line. It is best to just ignore the highs of (8) peeking through it. As we have seen here and there before, the signal line to a block break (BB as well as IRB) has a tendency to only get clear at the last couple of bars that get printed before the break takes effect. Up until the last three bars in this block, for example, it was still very probable to see prices travel up a pip more to equal the highs of (8), and if so, our signal line may easily have been placed a pip higher.

Note how two little dojis, once again, presented themselves right before the break (10). The break itself occurred in the heart of the range, just two pip above the round number of 1.31. If it was somehow missed, an alert scalper would have been able to participate still, by trading the one-bar pullback that tested the breakout (11).

It should be understood that when you accept an IRB trade in a compressed range, that you also accept the fact that prices may have to crack the extremes of the range to ever reach target. Therefore, this type of IRB should only be acted on when the setup meets all the requirements of validity. Whereas a scalper every now and then may get away with front-running a pullback trade in a solid trend, entering prematurely on an IRB in the midst of a tight range is not likely to be rewarded with similar forgiveness. Yet under the right circumstances, almost anything can be traded, resistance or not, as long as the pros clearly outnumber the cons in the chart.

Figure 12.8 The reader may remember the *trend-equals-trend* phenomenon discussed earlier on. It was stated that a noticeable swing leading up to a sideways formation is often followed by an almost identical swing once prices break free from that congestion in the same direction as the trend. The chart above shows a perfect example: a trend followed

by a range followed by a near identical trend.

During the sideways congestion, both top and bottom boundaries were pretty much regarded with equal respect. They both held up excellently. Of course, with a chart so bearish, it was the bottom barrier that really had to prove itself. A solid break of it could very well cause the market to rally south again, trapping every bull that bought in the range.

Take note of the words *solid break*. By now, we have already seen many examples of what is likely to happen when a break has not built itself up properly, even with the overall pressure being very much in line with the break's direction (T). The result is often a lack of follow-through, which is not likely to go unnoticed by the ever-present countertrend opportunists who thrive on exploiting every faltering break they can get their hands on. And with reason; not only are they offered a great chance to trap their opponents, if nimble they can do it with a minimum of risk to boot. After all, if his instincts serve him well—and with a touch of good fortune—the smart countertrend trader may see the market take off in line with his trade from the very moment of entry. This way, he can place his stop a few pip below his long entry or a few pip above his short, while at the same time being positioned for what could very well be the turn of the market.

To be able to buy the bottom of the market, or sell the top of it, has been, and will no doubt remain, the ultimate dream-come-true to many a novice trader entertaining the illusion that his proficiency one day may reach a level of pure foresight. It has also been the number one reason for that same type of individual to wind up on the ever expanding graveyard of nameless traders fallen in battle. It probably does not need explaining that, more often than not, strategies that aim for market turning points are simply doomed to fail. Quite ironically, these very strategies are exactly what is causing the markets *not* to turn, for those trapped in a failed turn have no option but to bail out, forcing prices to travel even further along their original intent. Still, if one was destined to design a strategy around selling tops and buying bottoms, then it is best construed around the many sideways phases of the market as a with-trend approach, and never as a countertrend tactic in trending markets, no matter how extended these trends may appear. In the case of the bearish chart in question, for example, a clever range barrier trader, in the long run, is much better off selling a top (possible turning point) like the one at (5), than to buy a bottom like the one at (4). Regardless of these specifics, the reader should understand that the scalping method explained in this guide is by no means the only way to trade the markets profitably on a consistent basis. Countless other approaches and tactics can be put to work with excellent results, even shooting freely from the hip, for that matter. The question is whether the aspiring trader wants to go the route of the rare freehand master, or the safer path of the novice following an overall with-trend approach with clear setups, targets and stops.

Seeing a with-trend break fail does not necessarily have to mean the end of the trend. In fact, it may actually trick a number of countertrend traders, too—into thinking that the market has really turned. In our chart, for example, the bulls who bought themselves into the market when prices crawled back inside the range immediately found themselves in a terrible spot. In their eagerness to join the countertrend parade they had lifted prices straight into technical resistance (6). That provided the bears with fantastic odds to deploy with-trend aggression.

Notice that when prices came down from that new lower top and touched the bottom of the range once more (7), a number of bulls still stubbornly tried to buy themselves in. This time around, though, they did not wait for the barrier to crack. They basically ignored the lower prices of the earlier break and quickly fired their orders at the level of original support. And that makes sense if you're bullish on this chart. Waiting for the level to crack to pick up contracts more economically (as in the tease) involves two immediate risks that are best avoided. The first is that it may leave a trader empty-handed on the sidelines at what could very well be the turn of the market. Because the market may not crack. The second risk is that another break below support may trigger a waterfall of orders going the other way, trapping every countertrend bull on the spot. With that in mind, it makes sense to put on a trade right *in* support. And also, any buy order in support will contribute to the solidity of it.

Question remains, though, whether it was really smart to buy at (7), regardless. Let us look at the facts that indicate why that may not be the case. First of all, the beginning of the chart showed a huge bearish downswing. Second, for over an hour the bulls could not even produce a noteworthy pullback in response to the bearish trend. Third, with four equal tops in resistance (1-2-3-5) and a lower top as a follow-up (6), what are the odds for a market to still swing up?

All in all, we can say that the bearish pressure had far from evaporated and that buying at (7) was more wishful thinking than anything else. Still, prices did travel up for a handful of pip, but a little later the bulls met their doom in yet another lower top (8).

That brings us to the forming of the IRB setup. In the face of all these equal and lower tops, the bulls will surely have realized that there was only one way out of the trap and that was to take out one of these tops and form a higher high. They never made it out.

As you can see, the entry on the IRB setup lies about two pip above the actual bottom barrier. The actual low of the tease break lies three more pip to the downside. Was it premature to act on the IRB as depicted by the arrow in the chart? With seven touches of the signal line and one more lower top (9) within the setup, I think the answer is self-explanatory. Furthermore, we could also ask ourselves if postponing the entry until the range barrier was broken as well would truly have served to alleviate risk on the trade. Then we might as well have waited until the tease break low was taken out, too. An immediate short below the IRB signal line and an acceptable stop above the pattern is a scalper's best shot in this situation.

Technical chartists may have noticed a very tiny yet tell-tale head-and-shoulders pattern within the IRB box. In fact, that pattern revealed in miniature the same message the complete range had been conveying all along. Just look at all the arches in the range; triple tops, lower tops, head-and-shoulders, cup-and-handles—whatever you like to call it, the implications are the same. In other words, if this chart was put to the stand after being sued for a lack of bullish interest, it has no option but to plead guilty and accept the penalty of falling prices.

Fig 12.9   www.ProRealTime.com   eur/usd 70 tick

Figure 12.9 Despite the earlier downward pressure in the beginning of the chart (prices well below the 20ema), the bulls managed to squeeze out a respectable rally, almost from the moment the market formed a tiny double bottom in round number support (1). In fact, the market never even reached the level to the pip, such was the eagerness of the bulls to buy prices back up. After about thirty minutes of constant buying, the bulls stepped off the gas a bit, which made some early-bird bears confident enough to try to scalp a few pip against the tide (2-3). Though courageous in their attempt, these countertrend traders, for over half an hour, could not produce anything more than a 7 or 8 pip decline after that 30 pip rally, which certainly gave rise to the notion of a market still being very much in buying mode.

But no matter how strong or weak a market, or how much a trend is expected to continue or break, when in consolidation, everything is still possible and both bull and bear, when smart and on the sidelines, have no option but to sit it out and see how things evolve. Unless one has the power and the guts to steer a particular market, a trader is best advised to take a passive stance and only become active once an indisputable signal comes his way.

Before any signal can ever reach the status of validity, a trader will first need to see some distinctive signs within the overall price action to back the suitability of his potential setup. In that respect, the tease break through support (T) was a pretty good start of things to come. Initially, the market reacted rather subdued, as well to the break as to the falseness of it, but prices do have a tendency to take their time. Frankly, the fact that they do is what causes most of our setups to display such welcome technical tension within their boundaries. Just look at the IRB in question (basically a textbook BB): no less than seven equal touches produced the top line of the box. The bottom of it was made up by the earlier false break (T).

Trading this market to the upside after a break of the box should hopefully come natural to any scalper with a sound understanding of market pressure and a sharp eye for smart entries. No doubt, this scalper will also have spotted the potential of a trend-equals-trend formation should the market be so kind as to break the consolidation to the upside. That means that after pocketing his profits on the IRB trade, he will remain very much on the alert to possibly reap some more profits on the way to 1.34. But hopefully he would not be so foolhardy as to forgo his initial 10 pip target and stay in the IRB trade in anticipation of an extended rise. That kind of plan deviation, as a result of opportunism, or plain greed, is bound to backfire sooner or later, and most likely with a vengeance.

The width of the IRB in this chart could hardly be more tiny in shape. The bulk of it stands just three pip tall. If the current pressure of the market had not pointed very much in favor of the bulls, the little pattern by itself would have had very little meaning. But that also goes for the very explicit setups that present themselves as textbook cases in a chart. Even those need to be backed by strong underlying conditions. So, in that respect, we can look upon this little IRB in the same manner as any other valid setup. After all, we only use a setup as a means to get in on a trade in technical fashion, and not because the little pattern is convincing us on the matter of market direction. As a rule, a trader should never want to be convinced on any kind of matter, not by fancy algorithmic indicators, not by other people, and not even by himself. All the information necessary is already displayed through the price bars in the chart. Why look for more or question what is there? The pressure is either up, down or neutral. If it is pushing prices more one way than another, without much resistance in sight, a trader simply sits tight until he spots a tradable setup that offers him a good entry to participate. The actual shape of the setup is quite irrelevant.

Chapter 13

Advanced Range Break (ARB)

It can be an awkward misconception on the part of an aspiring scalper to harbor the notion that a trend is more likely to produce profitable trades than its more lackluster counterpart—the range. No doubt this is instigated by countless chart examples, on the web and in trading books, in which the trend is almost invariably glorified. The trouble is, however, that this wonderful, trade producing and widely celebrated trend seldom materializes in prolonged fashion, even on a fast scalping chart like the 70-tick. Admittedly, there will always be sessions, sometimes a string of them, in which the market plays itself out so vividly that it literally reflects a trend trader's dream come true. But much more likely, and lasting much longer, there will be stretches that just cannot seem to produce any sort of meaningful follow-through, sometimes for days on end. These dreaded phases of the market can even turn the most composed and patient trend scalper into an anxious, irritated trader. And with reason; not only does the market refuse to oblige, it will often wear the treacherous cloak of a trend and then trick and trap a flock of early-birds when it's time for costume change. Of course, even the tormented trader knows deep inside that the market has no agenda of its own, let alone a desire to punish those in it. But that will not sooth the pain and anguish of those being constantly misled.

An impartial scalper, equally accustomed to playing the trending phases of the market as well as the ranging ones, is much less likely to get upset throughout his sessions, because his neutral disposition will keep him in a balanced state of mind. When the market is trending, his focus will be on playing it from a pullback perspective; when ranging, he will try to trade a break of the barriers, or scalp some pip within the span. Simply by accepting things for what they are, he will have a much more pleasurable time at the markets than his agitated fellow trader who has a constant need for something but seldom seems to get what he wants.

It goes without saying that in order to be able to display such a relaxed and neutral stance, a scalper must first find a way to become fully confident that he can truly recognize his opportunities, regardless of whether they are presented by a colorful trend or by the most boring range formations known to man.

With the trending market arguably being outnumbered at least 4 to 1 by the sideways variety, it is not for nothing that this scalping guide is paying such extensive attention to the characteristics of the latter. So far we have discussed how to trade a successful break of the range (RB) as well as how to identify and even trade a failed one (IRB). We also looked at the possibilities to scalp some pip inside of the range (BB/IRB). The Advanced Range Break setup (ARB) is the last of three on range tactics and this one could best be seen as to augment the regular RB.

As any scalper will acknowledge, ranges do not always get broken in textbook fashion. However, that does not mean these breaks cannot be traded with acceptable risk. It just requires a little more subtlety on the part of the scalper. And that's where the ARB comes in.

The setup can be classified in two distinguishable ways. The first is as a clustering number of bars stagnating around the broken barrier level, but resilient enough to not prove the initial break false. The cluster basically hangs around the barrier, either on top of it (for possible longs) or below it (for possible shorts); and sometimes the barrier level is running right through the center of it. Once this cluster of price bars, often resembling a BB setup, eventually sees its signal line broken, a scalper could enter at the market just like he would on any other trade. The main distinction between the RB and this type of ARB is that the signal line of the latter setup is not equal to the barrier; it lies outside of the range.

We often see this sort of hesitance appear when the typical range boundaries are of debatable nature; it leaves traders wondering whether the range actually broke or not; but even the clearest of barriers can get broken with similar reluctance. As always, there is no point in asking ourselves why things happen as they do. The Powers That Be are beyond comprehension and so is the volume needed to swing this market back and forth. As always in trading, it is best to not concern ourselves with the men at the helm. As much as it can be frustrating, at times, to be at the mercy of the big players' agenda, the tiny scalper should also be happy that it is not his task to provide the market with a sense of direction, whether true or false. He can freely watch from the sidelines, all day if he wants, void of obligations, and no one will ever be on his case. He is a spectator more than a participant, and a clever one at that. For he will not engage in battle in the heat of a fight. The tiny scalper will use the big players even more than be used by them, very much aware that he himself has no battle to fight. But he can join the victorious the moment they emerge, and no one will ever hold a grudge. His only concern is to catch that ride on the bandwagon and not wind up underneath it.

The second type of ARB is more of the pullback variety. Once again we see a range get broken, with the RB not being able to catch the move. In contrast with the abovementioned occasional hesitance, range breakouts can be very powerful as well, with prices simply shooting out way beyond the barriers. However, this does not have to mean the opportunity for a trade is fully lost. As we have seen many times in a trend, even in a very distinctive one, at a certain point prices habitually pull back to some significant level of support or resistance, from where they can then reverse in the original direction; this same phenomenon is not uncommon to show up in case of a range breakout, too, particularly one that initially shoots off in untradable fashion. The more the buildup to the break originates from somewhere deep inside the range (relatively speaking), the bigger the possibility that prices at some point after the breakout will need to take a breather and thus come to a halt. If they not only halt but also pull back to test the zone they just broke out of, the ARB could be an excellent tool to scalp a reversal of that pullback.

The setup starts to take shape when the pullback after the breakout is successfully capped by the broken barrier zone and a particular bar in it is setting itself up as a signal bar to a potential break. Quite similar, actually, as with our classic with-trend setups. If the bar indeed gets broken in the same direction as the earlier break, the ARB is a fact and a scalper can enter at the market just like he would with every other setup.

Since we have already discussed the characteristics of the ranges themselves quite extensively in the previous two chapters, there is no point in going over them again to shed more light on the ARB setup. The difference between the ARB and RB setup lies solely in the matter of trade entry, which is either depending on the way pressure is building up in the breakout area or on the way prices pull back after a break.

Figure 13.1 This first chart immediately shows the occasional fine line between a regular RB trade and the ARB variant. In hindsight, it is pretty easy to see how a scalper could have gone about trading this break. Of course he would not have acted on the tease (T) but simply have waited for the market to either set up a regular RB or its more subtle cousin, the ARB. The latter was presented as a tiny cluster with the top

barrier of the range running right through the heart of it (the little box). With four of the neighboring bars matching the level of the tease, a perfect signal line was formed. Shortly before the break, the 20ema caught a mini break to the downside (1), from where prices quickly shot up and then broke out. A textbook ARB.

In the actual market, however, things may not be so evident as they tend to appear from the safe distance of hindsight evaluation. In fact, in the reality of a live trading environment it is very easy, and common, to even miss the best looking setups, purely because a trader, at the time, does not expect the market to behave like it does. This is why it is important to not limit your thinking by *imagining* what is going to happen next and then *needing* to see it materialize. Particularly on the verge of exploiting a technical situation, this little mind-game of predicting how a setup will present itself, as if to prove your skills to some fictitious bystander, can have a detrimental effect on your ability to see the price action in its proper light. The moment you expect the market to behave and break in a certain way, and the market defies that, you stand to lose face in your own scheme of things and it may hurt your ego just long enough to completely miss the alternative break.

Figure 13.2 When range barriers are of dubious quality (in terms of equal highs or lows), the likelihood of a very straightforward RB is naturally somewhat diminished. At all times, the most unambiguous price action is seen when multiple time and tick frames all show the same barriers and thus the same breaks. In the absence of a clear line, many traders will resort to using their bar extremes to determine the level of a break. But what breaks on one time frame may not do so on another. As a result there may be less conviction in the break, which usually shows up on the chart as a lack of follow-through. This hesitation is very understandable. As much as traders hate to miss out on a good move, they don't want to get trapped in a false break, either. Clear and distinctive barriers, on the other hand, will have most traders witness the same breaks at the same time, resulting in more unanimous action and thus more directional pressure.

The good thing is that sloppy breakouts can be very tradable, too, provided a scalper remains calm and patient and allows the market the time to set up the trade.

Was the ARB setup as depicted in the chart the only way to trade this market according to our method? It probably wasn't. We couldn't argue with a more aggressive scalper trading an immediate break of the top barrier when that nice bullish candle stuck its head through it (2). The two-bar buildup (1) may have been a bit on the thin side, the underlying forces certainly were not, nor was the potential for a nice trend-equals-trend formation.

Within the ARB setup there appeared a similar duo of pre-breakout dojis (3). If not already in position, trading a break of these bars would make for an excellent entry. For the sake of detail: the ARB in the chart here displays a box around a handful of bars, the actual setup is made up by the last three of them (the bullish breakout bar and the two dojis next to it). In a way it is also a miniature BB setup.

Figure 13.3 Getting slammed back by the bears after making a new high (3), does not necessarily have to spell the end of bullish fun, but it doesn't look pretty on the chart and it is a round lost; however, if the bulls can still keep the pressure up by not letting prices slip through former lows (1 and 2), chances are that more and more sideliners will actually welcome these lower prices and start to buy themselves into the market again. In other words, with the top levels in the chart momentarily out of the equation, the focus will now be on the bottom levels and smart traders will watch the action there attentively.

Albeit that there was no direct need for a bottom barrier at that stage in the chart, the three equal lows in the first 30 minutes (1-2-4) certainly provided a scalper with an excellent level to draw a possible barrier beneath. Of course, in the beginning of a potential range it is not necessary to immediately start wrapping boxes. A single horizontal line beneath some lows or one across some highs will often do just fine. This also makes it a little easier to play around with the barriers individually, as opposed to erasing a complete box and then drawing a new one.

Although that first support pretty much held up, prices in the second half of the range clearly lost their bullish touch. The low of (5) actually represents a tease break below the earlier lows. About ten minutes later this tease was matched by another low (6). Reason enough to experiment with a barrier a pip to the downside (as depicted). This level was briefly perforated by a classic tease (T) and then respected again by the next two bars that came along (8).

All in all, after about an hour of backing and filling, a technical chartist, knowing his classics, will certainly have recognized a very tell-tale head-and-shoulders formation within the confines of the box. It is actually a multiple head with multiple shoulders, with an almost perfect neckline (bottom barrier) running below it. Not every low of the pattern may have touched the neckline spot on, but eight individual touches should really be enough to draw a bottom barrier with confidence.

After the tease break was bravely bought by the ever-present bottom fishers and countertrend opportunists, prices even managed to make a higher high by taking out a former top (9 took out 7). For a moment it seemed like the bulls had once again taken the initiative, a number of them now comfortably sitting on profit on whatever contracts they picked up at the lows of the pattern. The smartest ones will have had no trouble exchanging some of these paper profits for the real variety, particularly after seeing prices stall in the area. By taking profits they naturally put pressure on prices.

When it comes to head-and-shoulders formations there are multiple ways to go about them, but two well-known strategies stand out. More aggressive traders will start to initiate short positions the moment they sense the right shoulder (the last arch on the barrier) to roll over. Others will wait for the neckline to give in first and then take it from there. Traders of the first type will love their IRBs. Traders of the latter type will do well to study the characteristics of the ARB setup.

Whereas the first two charts in this chapter showed the ARB as a way to trade a hesitating break, this chart shows the ARB setup as a typical pullback trade.

The reader is prompted to study the following paragraphs with some extra attention. To cleverly trade the ARB setup, we have to address a technical concept that is often overlooked. At this point, it concerns the validity of the ARB setup, but the price action principle itself is present all over the charts. Being unaware of it could result in some nasty quick stop-outs, and quite often totally unnecessary. I am referring to what I have come to address as the *test of last support* or the *test of last resistance*. The idea is that these tests are often superior to a test of *the most obvious* support or resistance. A simple explanation would be to attribute the phenomenon to the tendency of the market to regard recent price action as being more dominant than the price action before it, even though the earlier levels may have more say in the overall picture.

Let us look at this from the prospect of a possible ARB short position in a bearish chart. First we see prices come down from the top of the right shoulder (rolling over) to the neckline below. Subsequently, the neckline, also known as the bottom barrier, is broken down by a fair amount of pip. If this feat gets accomplished in a pretty straight move, then there was no way to trade it as a regular RB, nor as an ARB of the clustering kind. With prices breaking through support quite unexpectedly (relatively speaking), it is safe to assume that such a move is missed by a large number of sideline bears. As much as they want to join in on the action, the clever ones will remain calm and not chase prices down out of fear of missing the break entirely. They will postpone entering in anticipation of what is likely to come first: a retest of former support. The idea is to deploy their short positions not only at more favorable levels, but in chart resistance as well. And this is where we get to the interesting part. After a pullback, the principle of a more favorable level usually holds up; but to regard a broken barrier as unquestionable chart resistance could at times be a costly mistake. As much as a broken range barrier stands out in a chart as the *most obvious* level of support or resistance, from a scalper's standpoint it is often inferior to a level that resides back inside the range.

To explain the concept of superior and inferior levels, it is best to take a little detour to look at things more graphically. Imagine yourself a horizontal line (neckline) with, say, three arches on it, the last of which of somewhat lower height. That spells a classic bearish pattern. The bottoms of the arches are all resting on that same neckline level. Each of these arches, naturally, has a ceiling, basically a series of bars in the top of the arch going sideways before prices roll over to the neckline again. At times, this ceiling can even be made up of one bar, creating a rather pointy arch. Any ceiling, by definition, is capped by resistance (otherwise prices would have traveled higher), but at the same time the lows of the ceilings are finding temporary support, hence the sideways progression before prices roll over. It is this ceiling support that we should keep in mind because it may play a role later on. Now, once prices break through the neckline beneath the three arches by a fair amount of pip (so chart technically it looks like a proper break) and then start to stall and pull back, what could be the typical level for this pullback to peter out and reverse into the original direction of the break? Ideally, to the hasty barrier break traders this would be no further than the very level of the neckline itself from where they initiated their shorts. Unfortunately, probably in the majority of cases prices will not stop at this neckline exactly but force themselves back into the range in search for *the ceiling of the last arch*. The most technical reason why this is, is because the market likes to move in stepwise fashion. If prices find support at point A, then break down to a lower point B, they show a strong tendency to first test point A again before turning lower to point B and beyond. Below point B there is a tendency to first test point B again, and so on. The stronger the trend, the more the market may skip the need to retest *all* of the broken levels. In case of a range break, however, the ceiling of the last arch is a level that stands a very big chance of getting tested, despite the alleged resistance of the broken barrier on the way to it. Regardless of where exactly that ceiling is situated, in a bearish formation it will be higher than the barrier itself, so in order for it to be tested prices would have to crawl back inside the range again. If so, it is not hard to imagine a fair amount of break scalpers getting stopped out in what seems to be classic false break price action. The point is that these false breaks can be extremely treacherous, for many of them are just plain old ceiling tests, so in essence they are true breaks in disguise.

The motivation behind summing up these technical specifics so explicitly is to point out the necessity of prudence when engaging in a break play that does not stem from pre-breakout tension, particularly when applying a super-tight exit technique. The safest way, at all times, is to participate at a spot where prices are technically blocked from traveling in the opposite direction, not so much by the most prominent level of resistance or support, but by the most recent price action in the chart. In that respect, we could say that pre-breakout tension is doing just that, for it blocks prices from climbing back into the range in search for the last arch's ceiling (or in search for your stop, for that matter); in fact, we could say that the cluster of pre-breakout tension is essentially representing a flat last arch itself, with the bottom of its ceiling flattened on the barrier line. Therefore, in the absence of break buildup, the best way to trade a pullback situation is not necessarily by simply shorting the barrier level. Arguably, a safer approach would be to anticipate prices climbing back inside the range in search for what could be a ceiling test, and then try to short a reversal the moment they are pushed back out again. Bear in mind, this represents the ideal scenario. If prices never make it to the ceiling or simply stall in the barrier level, then that provides us with valuable information, too. The point is to not expect a broken barrier to hold up as resistance per se, and to not immediately perceive a break false when prices climb back inside the range. Of course, all this is simply reversed when dealing with a bullish chart, with arches hanging below the barrier and prices breaking out topside.

Let us take a neutral look at the price action around the range break in Figure 13.3 again. Depending on one's strategy, it is not necessarily foolhardy to trade an immediate break of the barrier level. But in that case it would be safest to place a stop not simply a few pip inside the range but one pip above the top of the last arch (above 9). A pretty hefty stop, but it could very well safeguard a trader from getting shaken out in a possible ceiling test. Of course, it is not any of our business how other traders go about this. But when it comes to our scalping method, it is safe to say that a stop above the last arch (or below the last reversed arch in case of a long) in most instances will be too far out, which is why we smartly shun the non-buildup breakout. But that doesn't mean we could never participate in a non-buildup break.

Have a look at the chart to see how it could be done. After the break of the neckline, we simply wait for a pullback reaction. If it doesn't come, then so be it. Once prices travel back to the barrier level, we do not simply short the market like many pullback traders would, but we spot for a bar that *stalls* and is then broken to the downside again, in the original direction of the break. Any stalling bar is a potential signal bar, but remember that they need to be broken to be become the true variety. Take a good look at the signal bar in question (11). It makes a high back inside the range before being slammed down again and turning itself into a signal bar to the upcoming ARB trade. This represents the ideal ARB pullback trade because the bar not only stalls in the barrier area, the high of it managed to test the bottom of the ceiling of the last arch (10) and the low of it fell back outside the range again. With the test of last support (now resistance) out of the way, visible to all participants, the subsequent break of the signal bar's low gives off a clear signal that prices may very well have picked up their downward momentum. As a result, many scalpers, previously questioning the break's validity, will quickly cast their suspicions aside and start firing off their shorts as fast as they can.

Figure 13.4 This chart shows a less ideal, but still very tradable way to take on a range barrier break pullback situation. Never mind the range here (pretty straightforward bottom barrier), but let us look at the break and the ensuing price action for a moment. There can be no doubt about the validity of this barrier break.

Presumably, the rapid manner in which the barrier gave in must have left a lot of traders empty-handed on the sidelines. Since chasing prices after a break is never a good idea, those with bearish views on the market will now have their hopes set on the possibility of a tradable pullback.

And indeed, after prices fell down for a number of pip, the chart printed a rather typical, almost v-shaped pullback to the broken barrier (2-3). There is absolutely no way of telling whether prices will stop and reverse at that level or go on to do what they often do, which is to aim for a ceiling test, as explained in the previous example. Naturally, this leaves a scalper to solve a pressing dilemma in case a potential signal bar is already in the making, while at the same time the most ideal scenario of the ceiling test has yet to play itself out. In case this signal bar breaks, should he already act on it (as depicted by the arrow), or should he risk missing his trade by waiting for a better, deeper pullback (or at least an attempt), and then take it from there? If he opts for an immediate trade, he may get stopped out on a possible ceiling test because his tight stop will probably be placed a pip above the signal bar's high. If he chooses to wait for that ceiling test first, the market may take off without him and never look back.

Now, how does a scalper decide between these two evils: the risk of missing a trade and the one of entering prematurely. In fact, this must be by far the most classic dilemma presented to all traders in the market, regardless of their strategies, time frames and instruments of choice. It will most probably not surprise the reader that there can be no one definitive answer to this question. But in the case of an ARB setup there is something to be said on it that might just do as a typical *on average* approach. It basically depends on how the pullback relates to the price swing that contains the range break.

Let us consider the matter by comparing two hypothetical situations. Each will show prices breaking through a barrier by a fair amount of pip without much of a fight. As we have seen countless times, it is the very nature of the market to ultimately reverse a big chunk of any swing, also known as the pullback. In many cases, prices will even take back 40 to 60 percent of it. Or at least we could say that if prices do retrace that kind of percentage, they stand a good chance of reversing again. Now, let us first imagine prices swinging down from a shoulder, say, about 7 pip above a range barrier. This barrier is then cracked without any problems and prices fall down for another 7 pip before they come to a halt. That puts a 14 pip one-directional swing on the chart. If prices from that moment on start to travel up again to test the broken barrier level, they will have retraced about 50 percent of the last swing on arrival. Retracements of this length are extremely common and they offer players on the sidelines excellent odds to deploy new positions in the direction of the break. And even more so when prices collide with very visible chart resistance, like a broken range barrier, for instance. In the scenario of our 14 pip swing and the 7 pip pullback to the barrier, we can be dead certain that a vast number of pullback traders are carefully monitoring how the market handles this resistance. Of course, the smart scalper will not just enter on account of stalling prices. He needs to see a signal bar first and then see it break in the direction of the trend. That will not prevent the market from ever stopping him out, but the odds certainly favor this approach.

Next, imagine a somewhat wider range. The top of the right shoulder lies, say, 15 pip above the barrier. Prices break through it again but are now halted at, say, 4 pip below. That makes the swing about 19 pip deep. A pullback that takes prices back up to the barrier (give or take a pip) will now only have retraced about 20 percent of the last move. If a similar signal bar would set itself up, a non-aggressive scalper could now decide to pass up on the break of it. Chances are very real that this pullback is not over yet. This is quite similar, actually, to the SB setup situation, in which a first break is skipped in favor of a potential superior break (see Chapter 9, on Second Breaks).

In short, we could say that the more compressed the right shoulder, the more a typical pullback play may be worth our while. Subsequently, the further out the ceiling of the shoulder, the more we should monitor the swing/pullback relation attentively. Preferably, we would like to see at least a 40 percent retracement before considering with-trend positions on a non-ceiling test break.

In the chart in question, the market retraced about 50 percent of the last swing (3 retraces half of 1-2). Prices also halted in the barrier as well as in the resistance of the down-sloping 20ema. A small signal bar set itself up (4) and the low of it was broken by another bar (depicted by the arrow). Despite the absence of a ceiling test, this represents a very valid ARB pullback trade.

I hope all of the above has not confused the reader to the point of dreading the pullback ARB. Furthermore, the reflections above merely stem from personal observation and therefore can only offer a scalper a guideline on how to consider his options in the trading arena. The same goes for everything else that is presented in this book as a way to trade the market. There are no absolutes offered. For they don't exist in trading. Does that leave an aspiring scalper in the dark? Most certainly not. As long as he trades on moderate volume along the path of least resistance and manages to avoid the entries of the worst variety, he will stand an excellent chance to weather the unavoidable learning curve without being thrown out of the game prematurely.

Note: In case an ARB pullback trade gets stopped out when prices travel back inside the range, it does not have to mean the end of a range barrier play. The false break, though mean enough to hit a tight stop, may very well be false itself, and another ARB, maybe of the clustering kind, could still set itself up (pretty much like a SB or BB situation). Needless to say, of course, that a scalper should not go about firing off a new trade just to punish the market for stopping him out. That usually backfires pretty fast.

Figure 13.5 As much as that triple top (2-3-5) in the 20-level, and the lower double top next to it (6-8), spelled a retest of 1.32 with a capital R, early-bird bears who shorted the tease (T) were no doubt unpleasantly surprised by the complete lack of follow-through, if not by the mean reaction of the bulls. Not even a well-placed stop above the former top of (8) could have saved them from being shaken out in what is arguably one of the most painful ways to take a loss: getting stopped out on the pip (9) only to see prices immediately reverse.

What is painful to some can be quite a welcome sight to others, even when still on the sidelines. Seeing prices immediately travel lower after that false upside break will certainly have inspired a number of clever scalpers to sharpen their short pencils. A triple top, a double top, a tease out of the way, a false bullish breakout and a round number below, what more does a bear like to see.

When it comes to that false upside break (9), the reader may remember the principle of the *odd* versus the *obvious* as was explained in the chapter on Range Breaks, Figure 11.6. Since the chart above, despite the topping patterns, was slightly bullish (beginning of the chart showed lower prices), the tease break through support (T) could be regarded as a countertrend break, so technically an obvious tease. The false upside break of (9), on the other hand, since it was a with-trend break that failed, could be regarded as odd, and therefore more tell-tale. Ironically, just by looking at a chart like this, we can see how relative this basically is, because anyone with a bit of a technical heart would have rather shorted the tease than have bought the upside break. In general, however, we could say that a false break to the downside in a bullish chart is considered obvious (its falseness that is), because it is a break against the current pressure. Accordingly, a false upside break in such a chart could technically be labeled as odd (the fact that it fails), and in that respect more tell-tale.

Arguably, the actual bottom barrier as depicted in the chart could have been placed three pip lower. It would then have run beneath the low of (1) and the low of the tease (T). Personally I would not prefer to draw a barrier like that because it would have left the lows of (4) and (7), that make up the current barrier, hanging in midair, so to speak. But even if the barrier was drawn like that, thereby turning the ARB in a bit of a squeeze formation, would it have altered anything? When range barriers are of debatable quality, the focus is much less on the actual barrier break than it is on the way prices behave in the breaking area.

Actually, it was technically defensible to already fire off a short when the low of (10) broke through the bottom barrier. That would have turned the trade in a regular RB. Traders who shorted the market as depicted by the arrow engaged themselves in a classic ARB. Those who favored the barrier to be drawn beneath the tease break low could book this trade as an IRB, because it broke one pip before the barrier did (entry is the same as on the ARB trade). As you can see, it doesn't really matter what you call it. As long as you trade it.

Figure 13.6 This chart shows a typical and quite extended range formation in a calm Asian session. The fact that the foreign exchange markets
are open 24/5 does not mean we can expect them to always swing like a
monkey through the trees. When it comes to the eur/usd pair, volume,
understandably, can be quite thin during the Asian hours. At times, this
can cause huge and very trending price swings, but more often than
not, it simply delivers ranges that easily surpass the two hour mark (like
the one above). Not uncommonly, though, these ranges produce picture
perfect boundaries and if only a scalper can remain patient and alert he
will not find it too hard to trade the breaks of them, with overall good
results. To those still struggling with identifying ranges and the specifics regarding their breaks, the typical Asian session provides excellent
study material and it may pay off to analyze these sessions attentively,
even when not engaged in trading them due to the time-zone factor.

After being very much in sleeping mode for over two hours, the market first produced a classic tease break to the downside (T) and then
an equally classic false break to the upside (F). The three-bar pullback
from the top of the false break on (three black bodied candles) retraced
about 50 percent of the swing from (T) to (F). By itself that is quite insignificant; it is the subsequent price action that will determine the value

of it. Evidently, in the next coming candles the low of the pullback pretty much held its own and an alert scalper may even have recognized a typical BB block being formed by the five bars in the 20ema, which, in this situation, could be classified as a textbook IRB setup (1, just imagine yourself a little box around it).

However, it is understandable for more conservative scalpers to pass up on this slightly aggressive IRB option because the entry lies exactly in the top barrier of the bigger range. Anyway, trades get missed or skipped all the time for various reasons. Should this happen undesired, it is advised to not dwell on past reservations but to acknowledge the break for what it is and then try and find a valid opportunity to hop on the bandwagon after all.

After seeing prices shoot off for about 9 pip after the barrier breach, the anticipated setup, naturally, will be one of the pullback variety. Not much later there were basically two ways to participate, the first slightly more aggressive than the second.

Let us check out the option as depicted by the first arrow. It seems like the chart printed a pretty straightforward signal bar in the barrier zone (2). Why would trading a break of it to the upside be typified as somewhat aggressive? Basically for one reason only, which is that the signal bar had its low not fully testing the range barrier yet. It may have only differed a mere pip but especially in non-trending markets scalping is very much about these little details. Ideally, we would have seen the low two pip lower, testing not only the barrier but also the last resistance (now support) in the range (the top of the IRB setup, 1).

At first glance, the reason to skip an otherwise valid long on account of a low falling a mere two pip short of support may seem on the silly side of things. But let us consider our protective stop for moment. Most stops, according to standard exit technique, would logically reside below the signal bar's low, which, in this situation, is exactly at the range barrier's support. To a place a stop at a spot where you would sooner want to get in than get out just feels kind of awkward. But let me be quick to add that every now and then there is no way around it. A scalper could go so far as to occasionally adjust his exit technique by lowering his stop on a long to give the trade some extra room to wiggle. As much as that may serve a proficient trader's purposes, the aspiring scalper, still in the learning stages, is advised to keep things as simple as possible and not acquire the habit of altering his stops out of fear of being stopped out. The best stops are placed at a point in the chart of which it is fair to say that the technical reason to take the trade has been negated by prices hitting the stop (at least temporarily). Naturally, this point in the chart can be different for all traders and will very much depend on their time frame, if not their perception. On average, we could say that if our stop would have little technical validity—and a better stop would be too far out for comfort—then maybe it is best to skip the trade and await a setup that provides a more attractive entry/stop relation.

The second arrow points towards a breakout of a BB type of ARB, definitely a superior break at this point in time. It is superior because it is safe to say that with the passing of time (a number of bars) the market apparently lost its need to test the range break at a deeper level. Of course, at the moment of the first ARB setup (first arrow) there was no way of knowing that this second one would set itself up.

By the way, it was also valid to enter the market one bar earlier, when the signal bar (3) took out the small black doji before it, as in a regular SB trade. Still, waiting one extra pip to see the box break (as shown) could be perceived as preferable in this situation, for this extra pip provides a stronger confirmation that the bulls really mean business. Why is that? Because not only does it take out a valid signal line, it takes out a little top, too (the top in the little box), and this will print a visible new high in the chart on plenty of other scalping charts as well, which can only serve to attract more traders.

Note: If you decide to pass up on a trade, for whatever reason, then that decision stands. In the event of prices taking off anyway, it is easy to become a little upset, since the verdict of the market clearly seems to contradict your second thoughts on the venture. But that is just a hindsight illusion. The issue is not whether a trade would have worked out or not, for that is beyond your control. Just like it is pointless to analyze the outcome of a coin-flip. What is relevant, at a later stage, is to assess the reason for skipping the trade. Why at a later stage? Because live sessions are meant for trading and not for analysis.

Fig 13.7   www.ProRealTime.com   eur/usd 70 tick

Figure 13.7 Hopefully, the occasional subtleties regarding the signal bar have been sufficiently explained to make out the distinction between this excellent ARB pullback trade and the very similar but more questionable one in the previous chart (Figure 13.6, first arrow). This nice snappy pullback delivered a textbook signal bar (2) that perfectly tested the last resistance in the range (1, the little bull flag pattern to the left). The barrier here, of debatable quality, could actually have been placed two pip lower, why not, and that would have given the signal bar's low a double function: testing last resistance as well as a range barrier. The barrier test may be less significant, it is still a welcome sight. Either way, with a test of last resistance, now support, out of the way, there is no technical reason to skip a trade like this, for it presents a scalper with excellent odds.

Figure 13.8 Charts that show false breaks against the trend are strong candidates to travel further in with-trend direction. At times, when with-trend momentum is waning or not solid to begin with, a false break against the trend may be just what is needed to give the market another push. If nothing else, it will at least offer sideliners a good opportunity to pick up some contracts at more favorable levels. Fast markets will make a lot of traders short the current bottom or buy the current top out of fear of missing the trend; slow markets, on the other hand, offer the best odds on some sort of pullback reaction. The odds are good not necessarily in terms of direction, but more so in relation to the place-ment of the protective stop. Think of it this way: if you short a pullback that rolls over in the trend's direction, then you can place your stop eco-nomically and very technically above the pullback's highest point. But if you short the current bottom of the trend, where do you place your stop? Technically, above the same high of the last pullback; depending on one's strategy, that may just be too far out, either for comfort or in terms of risk control.

In hindsight, this particular chart offered a somewhat flattened trend-equals-trend opportunity, but at the onset, the price action was far from overly bearish. In fact, it is fair to assume that halfway through it the bears backed off in anticipation of the bulls' reaction to the round number support of 1.3450. Quite ironically, one party's hesitance to push on out of fear of a counterstrike is exactly what invites the bravery in the other party to produce what is dreaded. Strategic blunder or not, in a place void of loyalty and moral obligation, you will not find too many volunteers ready to sacrifice themselves for the greater good of saving a waning trend. But you will always find a small minority of eager individuals whose greed is simply stronger than their sense of self-preservation. Hence the many false breaks in any chart.

A little before 10:00, prices slowly arrived at that round number and immediately some buying pressure entered the market (1). Of course, some of the bears caused this themselves by taking profits in that zone. In terms of market pressure, a bear stepping out is synonymous to a bull stepping in. Anyway, it is fair to say that the number did not get pierced as a result of buyers being temporarily more aggressive than sellers. Still, that does not turn a chart from bearish to bullish. When a trend, even a meager one, is suffering some headwinds, with-trend traders do not just crawl up in a turtle position. We can expect at least a number of them to switch to plan B, which, in case of a bearish chart, is to lay off until the market shows sufficient pullback reaction and thus more attractive levels to initiate new shorts from.

Their first fine opportunity was presented to them when the bulls took out the tiny top of (2) at (4). Prices may have taken out that little top, they still faced chart resistance from the earlier action. Almost immediately the bears started slamming prices back, which left the bulls with a classic false break to chew on.

Quite typically, this little victory over the bulls rekindled enthusiasm in the hearts of sideline bears; but those late to the party found themselves immediately trapped. By recklessly attacking the round number lows, they forced upon themselves the same predicament that had cost the bulls dearly just moments before. The result: a textbook tease (T). That pretty much evened the score.

Seeing a break below round number support fail will not remain unnoticed by the ever-present countertrend enthusiast. Strengthened by the lack of bearish follow-through, he is now offered excellent odds to do what he loves to do best, which is to buy the market at a potential bottom and put his stop below the low of the false break. A number of bears must have smelled the rat coming and quickly got out of the way at these bottom prices. But they cleverly returned on the scene to start slamming the bulls a bit higher up, by shorting the level that equaled the earlier false break high (5 equals 4). To little avail, it turned out.

Every now and then it is nice to see how even a boring and compressed chart like the one above can still present numerous traps and tricks and classic price action subtleties. What about yet another failed break to the upside at (7).

If we zoom in on the chart at the moment of that upside break (before it got slammed back), then we can actually make out a couple of very bullish signs. Not only had the market printed a triple bottom in the support of a round number (1-3-T), the last of which even showing a false downward break to boot, it also showed a fourth bottom slightly higher (6), and not much later prices even surpassed the resistance of two former tops (7). These are all unmistakable bullish signs.

Therefore, it is not hard to imagine the rude awakening that befell the bulls after seeing their carefully crafted bottoming pattern get slammed to smithereens in a matter of minutes. Such was the nature of demoralization that the desire to defend what they had built up was almost non-existent. Prices almost dipped instantaneously below the former lows, which naturally brought some countertrend opportunists back in the game. But all they could muster was just a brief stalling of prices in the now very questionable area of support (8). A nimble scalper will be grateful for this heroic bravery, for it presents him with just enough chart hesitance to wrap himself a nice ARB box around it.

Figure 13.9 Despite the excellent quality of the range formation, top side as well as bottom side, the initial break was rather sloppy. No doubt the potential resistance of the 50-level looming a few pip above the range had made a number of bulls somewhat reluctant to step in (or we could say that the bears did not feel the need yet to get out of the way).

Well before the first barrier break, the market had shown clear signs of building up towards it: a nice double bottom (2-3) in support of an earlier bull flag top (1), a 20-level to bounce off of (1.3240), and a couple of higher bottoms as well (4, 5 and 6).

When watching this price action build up, it is important to just remain calm and composed, and above all open minded. All through the day, the chart, one way or another, will leave unmistakable clues in terms of future direction. You do not need a long range with higher bottoms in it— or a good solid trend, for that matter—to get an idea on where prices are going. Nevertheless, the path to failure is paved with traders who were right on direction, yet very wrong on timing. Whether they lacked the proper skills, the right setups, or simply the patience to time their trades is not of our concern. An aspiring scalper should realize, though, that he is just as human and susceptive to the vagaries of the mind as all those who failed before him. To think oneself above that can be a costly mistake that sooner or later may come to collect its debt. Arguably, the only way for a scalper to stand a fighting chance is to acknowledge his personal follies and not deny them. Behavioral scientists believe that the human mind is not cut out to entertain continuous rational thinking. And they may very well have a point. What's more, we do not need to look around us, or watch the six o'clock news, to find daily evidence of the constant moronic idiocies displayed by our fellow human beings, even by those deemed intelligent. One honest, introspective look will most certainly bring our own warped view on reality to light. And if we ourselves can display irrational tendencies even in the most calm and non-threatening surroundings, as we often do, then we are best advised not to picture ourselves beyond such follies when under pressure in a live market environment.

But if we look on the bright side, the inability to display rational behavior in a continuous fashion does imply the ability to do so short-term. The trick is to apply these brief spells of mental clarity at the exact moments they are needed the most. Can we really be that selective? I don't see why not. An excellent trick to counter intuitive folly is to force yourself beforehand, mentally or even verbally, to rationally defend your reasons for taking a trade, as opposed to just pulling the trigger because things look good. Rationalizing your next step will instantly demobilize a big chunk of potential irrationality. This is a crucial concept to grasp; it is also the very reason why I have been so elaborative on the specifics of price action buildup in any chart as a whole.

Depending on one's appetite for aggression, this particular range break could have been traded in three different ways. The first is to consider the squeeze before the first break as sufficient pressure to trade the breakout as a regular RB (first arrow). In case that valid trade was somehow skipped, then the re-break makes for an excellent opportunity to redeem oneself (second arrow). The third way to take on this barrier break is to trade it as an ARB pullback setup. That means waiting for a signal bar to set itself up in the barrier zone and then trade a break of it (third arrow).

Note how the last resistance in the range, now support, was offered by the squeeze formation below the barrier level. Not uncommonly, that kind of bar clustering stops any pullback right in its tracks. There is simply no technical need (relatively speaking) for the market to travel back further into the range in search for other forms of support because it is already offered at the best possible spot. Remember, the squeeze basically represents a flattened ceiling of the last arch that coincides with the barrier line (in this chart in reverse). Therefore, it makes for excellent support or resistance should prices pull back to the barrier after the break.

Despite the initial tease break and the slight hesitation back on top of the barrier line, at a certain point the bears had no alternative but to step out of the way of bullish pressure. Either take a small hit or suffer heavy losses.

Figure 13.10 If we look upon the dotted box as a small range within a bigger range, then the encapsulated price action in the top right corner of it can be classified as a textbook ARB setup (1). But since the breakout also occurred within the span of a wider range, this setup represents an IRB as well (see Chapter 12). Of course, a clever scalper, on the brink of a trade, will not concern himself too much with futile semantics; his primary task in that precious moment is to identify a level of entry and a level of protection and make sure he does not miss his trade.

If indeed in position on the first ARB option (first arrow), a 10 pip scalper would have saved himself the hassle of having to choose between skipping and trading the second ARB (second arrow). Frankly, it is probably a pretty easy skip to those conservatively inclined. Yet scalpers who entertain a more aggressive approach may find the opportunity too tempting to leave unexplored. After all, prices had come back to test the top barrier, formed a signal bar in it (2) and then broke away again. That usually makes for an excellent continuation setup. Why would it be defensible to pass up on the offer?

This addresses an issue already discussed earlier in this chapter, Figure 13.6 (skipped first arrow). The reader may remember the problem of the *awkward stop*. An awkward stop is basically a valid stop when regarded from a setup perspective, yet price technically it defies justification because the level reflects a very obvious area of support or resistance. It is awkward in the sense that when you are bullish on the market, you don't want to sell out your contract in technical support. You want to sell out below it. What's more, if the support level is truly obvious price technically, the market may even go on a typical hunt for it, quite similar to the vacuum principle concerning the round numbers.

Of course, when confronted with a fine entry but a terrible stop, one always has the option to replace the level of protection to a much safer or more technical spot. Preferably, it will be put at a level of which it is fair to say that when it gets hit, the trade has lost all validity on true technical grounds. But any scalper will acknowledge that that may not always be obtainable within the boundaries of allowable risk. In our method, when the better stop cannot be found within a 10 pip span, the only sound thing to do is to skip the trade. There is always the possibility of second instance, meaning that after skipping an inferior option, another, and most likely superior option may present itself; this very much reflects the principle of the SB setup as discussed in Chapter 9.

That superior break, of course, may never surface and the market may take off without looking back. But that is irrelevant from the standpoint of a justifiable skip. Still, having rejected what would have been a winning trade can be a painful experience, but only to those who think in terms of being right or wrong. And indeed, to many traders the verdict of the market either justifies or condemns a particular decision. But that is a terrible way to look at probability and variance. At any moment in time, the market may produce a 10 pip rally, either up or down. So why not after having skipped a trade. Whether in or out of the market, whatever prices do is just information; it should never be regarded as a compliment for being smart, nor as a reprimand for being foolish.

Of course, this is not to say that one's decisions cannot stand corrected. Even proficient traders are bound to make bad calls. They are only human. The point is to never judge a particular decision by whatever happened afterwards. It should only be judged by the available information before it.

Now how about that other ARB option (third arrow). Observant readers will certainly have noticed its striking resemblance with the SB setup. Note how the bottom of its signal bar did not test range support to the exact pip either (3). Price technically, the most preferable way to test support would have been for prices to hit and test the highs of (1), a few more pip to the downside. But what may seem preferable at one time can become completely irrelevant just a few bars down the line. Technical feats are not created equal and the appearance of a SB setup is one such achievements that incorporates the ability to erase all previous reservations.

In this example, the entry level of the second break matched the level of the skipped one to the pip. Had it been less economical, which is not uncommon, the implication attached to the double bottom features of the SB pattern would still have remained intact. In the marketplace, things are never an issue of price. The only thing that counts is how the majority of participants will likely respond to a particular event. Therefore, trading the last ARB in this chart (third arrow), essentially a SB setup, was a proper call.

Trade Management

Chapter 14

Tipping Point Technique

Now that we have gone to such great lengths to study the specifics of trade entry, it is crucial to devote equal attention to the principles of exiting As much as technical skills will contribute to a trader's survival in the markets, it is the way he handles his open positions that will ultimately determine the degree of his consistency. For it can be quite a bumpy ride to either target or stop; if not from a technical perspective, then most certainly from a psychological one. Most any trader, novice as well as experienced, will acknowledge that being in an actual trade can cause more anxiety and doubt, pain and frustration, than the whole process of trade selection itself.

Indeed, it is a mysterious type of demon that springs to life in the mind of the typical trader the moment he puts his position on. Just seconds before he may have felt calm and composed, very much in control, confident in his ability to do what needs to be done. He may have analyzed the forces in play correctly and cleverly identified the setup of his choice. If the market prints the next bar or two in such and such a manner he will gladly oblige and fire away. But the very moment he is in position, more often than not, the situation rapidly deteriorates. All of a sudden this trader's say in things is reduced to nil and he can't help himself but think that he walked straight into a trap. A sense of powerlessness erases all feelings of previous comfort. Fear and anxiety swiftly enter the scene and gone are the technical skills that got him into this trade. How did this happen, who forced this trader to throw himself at the mercy of the market? Why, he did it himself. From the king of the castle to the fool of the court in the blink of an eye. No faster can self-image disintegrate than in the heat of the trading game.

And it doesn't stop there, not by any means. On the slippery slope of a running trade things can quickly go from bad to worse. And traders realize this all too well but they just can't help themselves. Who hasn't hit the exit button in an act of desperation at the first sign of a little pullback? Who hasn't felt that sickening sense of betrayal when prices moved against him, and couldn't bear to watch it. Who hasn't conquered his fears so proudly and entered into an extended rally, only to instantly regret it? And even with a trade comfortably in the plus, who hasn't felt the instinct of flight to be so much stronger than the desire for further profit?

To the non-initiated, the woes and worries of a trader at work may seem a bit like slapstick—why can't he just do what needs to be done? Yet those who ever ventured out in a live market environment know these follies to be all too real. Particularly when still in the learning stages, it is not an easy path to rise above one's fears. However, it is far from evident to see these problems simply evaporate on account of mere technical proficiency. More likely than not, somewhere down the line, the intermediate trader will find himself at the proverbial crossroads. And this is where he has to step up to the plate and ask himself how much he is prepared to commit. Will he take himself to mastery in the next stage of his journey, or hold on to his fears and remain forever stuck in the old habit of emotional trading.

In this respect, it is fair to say that true mastery is not so much defined by a flawless understanding of price action principles but more by how much a trader is able to do what needs to be done. For the true master will not be affected by whatever happens in a chart. He will enter his positions unconcerned and exit them without any sense of discomfort. If the market stops him out, he will simply move on. He has no particular desire for consecutive winners, nor will he be affected by a string of losing trades. The true master knows that every trade is just one out of many. He knows the odds to favor his strategy, but he does not expect to win.

To ever reach this kind of mastery, the carefully crafted skills of trade selection may need to be outmatched by an even better understanding of proper trade management. For all the hard work will surely be in vain if traders do not get their bearings straight when it comes to handling their open positions. The good part is that proper trade management is rather straightforward from a technical perspective. Once in the market there are no more underlying forces to assess, no major points of resistance or support to take into consideration, no setups to figure out. A scalper only needs to keep a close watch on the next so many bars, knowing he has but two options to consider: either let the trade be on its way to the target or scratch the trade beforehand by a click of the mouse.

Naturally, the decision to do one or the other should not be based on greed, fear, gut feel, or whatever false perceptions are known to warp a trader's mind. At all times, it is a technical price level in the chart that determines what we can refer to as the *tipping point of trade validity*. If the point is surpassed by a mere pip, the trade will be scratched with no questions asked; if not, a trader will simply stay in.

In this chapter we will delve into the specifics of the tipping point. We will see how it is initially chosen and how it may be replaced by another as the trade progresses. The tipping point forms the core of our exit strategy and therefore lies at the very base of proper trade management.

The essentials are pretty easy. For example, the maximum loss on any trade will be determined before the actual trade is put on (not including occasional slippage) and will stand for as long as the position is active. This last point to get out—the ultimate tipping point—usually lies a pip above or below a signal bar or at a level above or below a top or bottom in a particular pattern. In this scalping method, the average stop will be about 6 to 7 pip. The target objective, at all times, is 10 pip. Whereas the target level should never be tampered with, the stop level, on the other hand, is free to be adjusted as the trade progresses, but only in the direction of the target and never the other way. The idea behind this, obviously, is to minimize the damage in case the market turns sour on the trade.

Using an adjustable stop is very common practice among traders all around. The general premise is to keep a trader in a favorable position for as long as possible but to at all times be protected with a tight stop. On a bigger time frame, say, a daily chart, these so-called *trailing-stops* can run for what seems like an eternity above or beneath a good trend; on a 70-tick scalping chart, however, the price action is much more volatile, which certainly enhances the likelihood of a trailing-stop getting hit in what could be a false countermove. It is often referred to as being shaken out. Those that object against the use of a trailing-stop, and many do, will often argue that the risk of getting shaken out prematurely is just too high. They certainly have a point. On the other hand, it can also be quite costly to stoically have to wait for the original stop to be taken out when the trade could have been scratched at an earlier stage for a much smaller loss, or even for a little profit. So who is right in this respect? It may depend on various things, like time frame, strategy and personal preference. But all in all, it is safe to assume that those who understand the concept of the tipping point are likely to produce better results (in the long run) than those traders who either trail their stops indiscriminately or not at all.

Before we go on, let us consider the practical side of exiting for a moment. The reader may recall the principle of the bracket-order as mentioned earlier on. If set correctly, this order springs into action the moment a trader enters the market. If the position is a short, the bracket will show a target order 10 pip below the entry and a stop order 10 pip above it. Vice versa for a long. The target order reflects the ideal exit; we do not aim for more than 10 pip. Should we be so fortunate as to see prices hit this level, the platform will automatically close out the trade. The same can not be said for the stop-loss order at the other end of the bracket. In almost any instance (bar a very speedy market), we will be out of the market by manually hitting the exit button before the automated stop-loss gets triggered. That will certainly save us a few pip, if not a whole lot more. Of course, our decision to exit is a technical one and based on a tipping point.

The reason for the 10 pip stop-loss order as part of the bracket is purely a safety measure in the event of technical trouble. If so desired, traders could even set it a few pip wider, just to avoid the possibility of a manual exit coinciding with an automated one (for those that exit their positions by firing an order in the opposite direction, as opposed to hitting a close-out button). The sole purpose of this stop-loss order is to protect the account in the event of a platform freeze or a failed internet connection. Alert scalpers with a proper understanding of trade management may trade for many months on end without this safety stop ever being hit.

In contrast with this server based stop, the tipping point stop resides in the mind of the trader. Not only does this make sense from a practical standpoint (no fumbling around with the platform), price technically it would be virtually impossible to determine the *exact* level of the stop. Remember, the chart may show the price action in increments of a full pip, the trading platform will still divide every pip into tenths, the so-called pipettes. Therefore, should a scalper recognize a particular level in his chart as a tipping point, say, 1.3924 and want to place a protective stop underneath it, he would first have to figure out how the spread circles around the price level of 1.3923 (which triggers the exit). But how can he tell? It could be 5 pipettes one way and 5 pipettes the other, but who is to say? Should he place his stop at 1.39/225, or 223, or throw in a couple of extra pipettes to be on the safe side? No matter what he does, unless he plays it very safe, chances are quite real that his physical stop may take him out of the trade while the chart itself never took out the tipping point. To avoid all this, a scalper should just hit the exit button the moment a bar in his chart *visibly* takes out the high or low of the tipping point.

Now let us consider the characteristics of an open position. In essence, there are five ways to distinguish the current price action in relation to the entry point. 1: The trade is immediately going sour. 2: The trade is reluctant to take off. 3: The trade is going well, no pullbacks yet. 4: The trade was going well but is now suffering a classic pullback. 5: The trade was going well but is now seriously stalling.

In the coming charts we will see examples of each of these stages and how to go about them in terms of management. As a general guideline, it is recommended to always expect prices, at some point, to travel against the open position. If nothing else, it will at least eliminate the element of agony. The market will always find traders ready to counter anything that comes their way and that is not likely to stop when we ourselves are in position. Prices are known to bounce up and down in any possible order. It is the perpetual battle between opposing ideas that causes the charts to look like they do. If prices go one way and then reverse, they will either leave a top or bottom in their wake. These tops and bottoms, the very footprints of supply and demand, will guide us into determining the current tipping points. But before we act on them, we will have to assess their significance first, for not all new highs and lows deserve the tipping point status of trade validity.

Before we go on to study the specifics of proper trade management, let us contemplate for a moment the most common follies regarding the subject. Although basically limitless, in essence there are only two. 1: Not exiting an invalid trade. 2: Exiting a valid one.

The first is widely regarded as the cardinal sin of trading. It has been a recurring theme in many trading anecdotes, and this one folly will no doubt continue to entertain the public for as long as there are traders around. Countless promising traders have been blown out of the business just for disrespecting the golden rule of trading only once in their careers. Needless to say, we are not talking about the trailing-stop here, but about the absolute tipping point, the initial and at the same time final stop above or below a trade. This is not to be taken lightly, or to be regarded as a folly of others. Having to exit a position that has evidently gone sour is known to cause tremendous reluctance to traders of all levels. Instead of regarding it as a means to prevent further damage, it is often seen as a shameful act of admitting defeat. The more emotional a trader's disposition, the bigger his tendency to postpone his walk of shame, no doubt fooled by a notion that everything is still possible if he just holds on a little bit longer. But that is the world upside down. Respecting a stop can never be a shameful act; disrespecting one, on the other hand, is the true disgraceful feat.

Note: As much as the finesses of trade management can be explained in fine detail, quite similar to pointing out all price action principles regarding a possible entry, there is something about the act of protection that simply cannot be taught; and that is the personal commitment to pull the plug on a trade once the level of the final stop gets perpetrated. Identifying the level itself is pretty straightforward and will shortly hereafter be clarified. And so will be the options of handling a position between target and stop. But the moment prices travel past the point of no return, all bets are off and a trader has got to pull the plug, whether automatically through a served based stop, or, as in the case of scalping, by manually hitting the exit button.

The second folly of trade management, exiting a valid trade, is almost a mirror image of the first. It will not have the disrupting effect of causing huge losses or even account wipe-out, but it can just as much obstruct a trader's path to consistency, with similar results in the end. This particular folly can be fought successfully by enhancing one's tipping point technique. We will take it on in detail.

Although basically falling in the category above, there exists a third and quite notorious slip-up in trade management: it is called the break-even stop. There is such a widespread misconception regarding this phenomenon that it deserves to be taken up on its own. The idea behind the much advocated break-even stop is to protect an account from traveling back in the minus once a position is up. Those with a strong sense of imagination may even call it the ultimate trader's dream: a free ride in the market. Yet from a technical perspective, the break-even stop is seriously flawed, if not plain unsavory. First of all, the idea of a free ride is an illusion if it does not involve a risk-free proposition. Clearly, the moment a trader puts on his trade he runs a risk of prices traveling against him. So much for no risk. It can safely be stated that those who entertain the fantasy of the free ride have little concept of probability and solely live or die by the result of their current trade. In other words, they are highly dependent on euphoria and feel the need to protect that state of mind. But that can backfire quite strongly. And it doesn't take much technical insight to see why. Imagine yourself to have entered the market at a break of some kind. It could be a break of a signal bar, a range barrier, a block, anything; but most definitely it will be a technical spot, why else enter the market. Next, imagine the trade to travel neatly in the plus, definitely clearing its starting point. You can probably tell where this is going. We all know how often these technical levels are being put to the test by a quick visit back to the breaking point. To protect a trade from ever becoming a loser by pulling the stop to break-even—the very point of entry—is simply asking for an early exit. In fact, many smart traders have built their strategies around this one simple phenomenon, that of prices pulling back. That certainly would not be the case if pullbacks were more exception than rule. Of course, a break-even exit *could* be the proper exit, but only when a tipping point, later on, coincides with the level of entry. Similarly, traders who do not opt for a break-even exit when comfortably in the plus, but, say, place the stop at 2 pip profit, are just as much guilty of the same fallacy. The point is that they do not exit according to the chart but to a non-technical idea of loss prevention. Never forget: the tighter one's stop, the smaller one's gains.

All in all, the trickiest part of trade management is not to survive the pullback attacks. They either take us out of the market or they don't. The good part is that once these pullbacks are countered themselves, they leave distinctive tops and bottoms in the chart from which to derive new tipping points. Arguably more complicated is the proper assessment of price stagnation. It can either be very telling, or completely harmless. As we have seen many times before, stagnation, also called a lack of follow-through, delivers a strong incentive to countertrend enthusiasts to step into the market. The longer prices halt at a certain level, the more a cluster is formed somewhere between entry and target. At times, these clusters even show very visible signs of impending reversals, like double bottoms and double tops. If these patterns are broken against our position, even with the trade currently in the plus, it may mean the end of trade validity. However, it is important to not misjudge the action, for stagnation may very well be harmless. Bailing out of very healthy trades at the slightest sign of counter activity, grabbing whatever tiny profit, is a surefire way to remain forever stuck in the non-profitable phase of trading. A scalper, any trader, has to rise above his fears of losing and giving back profits, or else chances are slim that what is gathered in profit will sufficiently offset what will surely be gathered in loss. A trader can be dead certain that nine times out of ten in the course of a running trade, a little moment of truth will put him to the test.

In every instance, the decision to bail out or stay in is technically derived by respecting the current tipping point in the chart. Either it lies above a particular top (when in a short position) or below a particular bottom (when in a long position). In many situations, these tipping points will be attacked and even touched to the exact pip, but may hold up nonetheless. So it is not uncommon for a trade to come dangerously close to being stopped out. Such is the nature of scalping and working with extremely tight stops. It cannot be stressed enough how important it is to not hit the exit button when confronted with these very typical counterattacks. When prices take their time, the power of demoralization can be excruciatingly strong. Fight it. Many times it is not the tipping point of trade validity that is surpassed, but merely the tipping point of what a trader can mentally bear.

The next so many charts will show numerous examples of when and when not to exit a trade. The most important technical aspect of trade management is to be able to tell the difference between a valid tipping point and its invalid counterpart. There will be plenty of examples clarifying the matter.

As has already been stated, proper trade management is relatively easy from a technical perspective. In fact, much more than the practical matter of defining one's tipping points, controlling one's emotions makes up the bulk of it. The urge to get out of a trade when it is still technically valid can be extremely powerful. And so can be the reluctance to pull the plug on a position when it is truly time to bail out. Regardless of experience, these two little quirks reside in each and everyone of us. In my opinion, they can never be defeated. But, fortunately, there is a weapon clever enough to stop these little demons right in their tracks, and that is commitment. To simply do what needs to be done, *even when it hurts*.

In the coming charts, the dotted lines represent the tipping points that are not taken out; it is not uncommon to see several of them during one particular trade. A new one invalidates a previous one. A thicker black line marks a tipping point that is taken out, at which point a trade is immediately exited. Any first arrow points towards the entry (sometimes there can be more than one arrow in the same direction, depending on one's choice of entry); on occasion, the actual point of entry is marked by a thin signal line or a box. Any arrow in the opposite direction points to a breached tipping point and thus indicates the end of the trade, marked by an X. Trades that reach target leave no specific indication in the chart. It simply means that the position closed itself out automatically for a 10 pip profit before any tipping point got breached.

Figure 14.1 After an extensive but quite harmonious pullback, scalpers watching this chart were given two opportunities to speculate on a continuation of the earlier bullish momentum. The first was presented in the shape of a DD break, a little below the 20ema (first arrow); the second came as a BB trade a few minutes later (second arrow). It is irrelevant which setup is the better one or whether the first trade actually reached target or not in this particular chart (it may have).

Let us look at the initial stop first (dotted line). It is placed below the lows of the two dojis that make up the DD setup. With no support underneath these lows to catch falling prices there is no point in giving this trade more wiggle room than this. Needless to say that prices could easily dip a pip below these lows, only to quickly shoot up again. But who is to say they will not dip a bit more. It is crucial to always take a technical stand on the matter of protection and that usually means setting the stops right where they belong: underneath a low or above a high; we do not want them dangling in midair for the sake of eventualities.

The placement of the initial stop on the BB trade is a little more subtle. Technically, it could be placed below the bar that formed a higher mini bottom within the BB setup (1). But by giving it one extra pip to the downside, equaling the dotted line, a scalper improves his chances for a successful trade considerably, because now his stop resides below the very technical level of the DD lows. Look at it this way: the mini bottom, a pip higher than the DD bottom, is visible on our scalping chart and maybe on a bunch of other very short-term charts as well. So, small as it is, it does have technical meaning. But the lows of the DD setup, obviously, will be highly visible on almost any short-term chart, and thus bear more relevance. Allowing trades this extra pip of wiggle room, a little insurance we may call it, should not be practiced indiscriminately just to stretch a stop. It should solely be based on technical grounds. In this situation it does make sense to apply it. After all, below the DD lows, that is where most bulls will dump their positions. Above it, or equal to it, they may still want to buy themselves in, providing support to our trade in the process.

In this chart both trades took off pleasantly. On their way to the next 20-level, prices made several intermediate lows, all nicely caught by the up-sloping 20ema. Trailing a stop beneath these insignificant lows would be way too aggressive. That is asking for a premature exit. We should always try to give the trade some room to breath. An important aspect of tipping point technique is to not trail the stop too eagerly. At times, it can be tempting, though, to want to lock in some profits or to minimize the maximum loss on a trade. But that will cut short almost any 10 pip run. Maybe more than half of the trades that eventually reach target, at some point will have to endure a more serious pullback. But as much as it is dreaded by those in position, it is equally welcomed by those on the sidelines. Therefore, trust the current pressure to hold up. You are not in that trade for nothing. Either exit on solid technical grounds, or stay in position and let the market run its course.

In this chart, a valid opportunity to lift the original tipping point to a more economical level was presented by the first little pullback that managed to close below the 20ema (2). Another nice characteristic of the pullback, once it is reversed, is that it often leaves an excellent tipping point level in its wake. Bear in mind, though, the tipping point can only be placed underneath a pullback low if prices indeed reverse to the upside again. Just like a signal bar needs to be taken out by an entry bar in a setup situation, so does the tipping point bar need to be taken out, too, to activate its tipping point level at the other end. Therefore, the moment the bar of (3) took out the high of (2), the protective stop was lifted to the level of the pullback low (black line).

Three bars later, this new tipping point came dangerously close to being taken out (4). It is extremely vital to not lose calm when that happens. Hitting the exit button just a pip away from a tipping point break is one of the worst things a trader can do. And not only because all he stands to gain is a measly pip in comparison with a valid exit. There is also a very strong technical reason not to give in to these dreadful premature exits. After all, did prices not bounce up from the tipping point level just a brief moment ago? What does that tell a scalper? The point to truly grasp here is that a well-chosen tipping point is not just a spot in the chart, it bears technical significance. In other words, if it represents support, then we can be sure a number of sideline bulls would love to buy themselves cheaply into the market right at that spot. And that is the reason these levels so often hold up. Exiting into the level of a tipping point before it actually breaks is very much akin to the folly of the break-even exit: bailing out at a spot just when prices are most likely to reverse. In this chart example, the right moment to exit presented itself a few minutes later, when the market dipped below the tipping point line (X). The very moment the chart prints that break, a scalper simply hits the exit button to close out his trade (with a market order). It is irrelevant whether a scratched trade books a profit still or is exited for a loss. What is relevant, is to manage all trades properly, regardless of outcome. If so, then before long a proven edge will certainly surface.

To understand the significance of a chart technical spot, have a look again at the original lows of the DD setup, the dotted line. If you extend this line to the right, then you can see how this exact level repeatedly found buyers every time prices hit upon it (5-6-7).

Notice also how cleverly the big and smarter bulls allowed the bears to eventually crack the level by a pip, only to immediately swallow up all contracts offered at that spot, and then some. A beautiful trap (8-9). Painful as these shakes can be, they are an essential part of the trading business. In fact, they keep the markets alive. Imagine a market in which you could safely buy in support and sell in resistance without ever getting stopped out. That would be a terrible thing! All traders would simply wait for that one perfect spot. Now that can be a long wait. And even if it arrived, by way of a miracle, no trader sound in the head would be so stupid as to take the other side of these contracts. And soon the market would simply cease to exist.

Figure 14.2 This chart serves to point out the occasional extra pip added to an otherwise very technical tipping point. If you look closely, you can see that the dotted line is not placed exactly above the highs of the dojis, but 1 pip further out. This one extra pip gives the stop more technical weight, because now it matches the highs of the earlier price action to the left (1). These highs, though tiny, represent resistance in the chart. And whatever proved resistance, may prove it again. Therefore, by lift-

ing the original stop a pip, we buy ourselves a chance of surviving a miniature false break above our DD highs.

Compare these DD highs to the DD lows in the previous chart, Figure 14.1. Can you see the distinction? For the price of a sole pip, a scalper is offered a chance to protect himself just a tiny bit better. It would be wise to grab it, because every now and then this little insurance may pay off handsomely. What's more, in this situation the added protection only needs to work out to a trader's advantage once every fifteen times. Why is that? Let us quickly do the math. If prices take out both the normal stop and the plus 1 variety, then the balance is minus 1 pip. If, on the other hand, the stop with the extra pip indeed manages to protect the position where the more economical stop would have failed, then, instead of incurring a 5 pip loss (more or less), the trade pockets a 10 pip winner. The balance is now plus 15 pip! Naturally, one could argue that any added pip, regardless of technical considerations, has the potential to fence off a premature stop-out; but that is not the point. Or we could say that *is* the point, for a smart scalper will never base his stops on random leeway. His decisions will always be based on technical criteria.

Figure 14.3 In rather compressed ranges, the high or low of the last arch before the break usually delivers the initial tipping point (2). Although

range breaks are known to cause a little fight before taking off, and thus should be given some room, a scalper, trading short, normally will not allow prices to go against him past the high of the last arch. Nor past the bottom of one when he is trading long.

Let us imagine for a moment that the arch before the last had its high just one pip higher (1). Should we insure ourselves with an extra pip by lifting the tipping point to that spot? Most probably not. It is not unthinkable to ever do it, but the standard approach is to stick to the original stop. In the previous chart, Figure 14.2, it really *made sense* to do it. Just like it did on the BB trade in Figure 14.1 (second arrow). Because that one extra pip really buys us a technical spot.

Logically regarded, pullback highs and lows bear more technical weight in a trend than in a sideways progression. Therefore, placing an arch tipping point a pip higher to match the top of an earlier arch feels kind of awkward. Where does it stop? Might as well give it one more pip to meet the high of another arch. When trading ranges, the most economical tipping point will usually do just fine. That is why it is so nice to see pre-breakout tension (like two little dojis or a tight squeeze) right before a break. Not only does it represent technical buildup, it also creates excellent tipping point levels.

Figure 14.4 Just to drive home the concept of the initial tipping point, here is another trade that should be protected with the tightest variety. There is no point in giving it an extra pip since the first resistance in the chart that could possibly offer some extra protection lies way above the top of the dojis (the lows of 1).

By the way, in a bearish chart, lows as well as highs can provide resistance. It just depends on what is met first. In the chart above, if prices would take out the dotted line, the first chart resistance to come upon is offered by the lows of (1). In Figure 14.2, for example, resistance was offered by former highs. Of course, in a bullish chart, this same principle works the other way around as well.

Fig 14.5   www.ProRealTime.com   eur/usd 70 tick

Figure 14.5 The first trade is a nice RB originating from a classic squeeze situation. Before the break, prices formed five equal lows (dotted line). Could a scalper not have placed his stop 1 pip lower, underneath the absolute lows of the squeeze (1)? A fair question, since this deeper low is quite distinctive here. If we compare this situation, for example, with the one in Figure 14.3, then placing the stop a pip further out makes more sense here than in the earlier chart. Still, my personal take on these range breaks is to keep the stops as tight as possible. In a way, after a solid squeeze, prices should basically take off and not look back—relatively speaking, of course. But it would be out of place to argue with a scalper that throws in the extra pip in a situation like this.

The second trade, a tiny SB, deserves to be protected, initially, with a stop below the tall doji bar (3). Why not place it more economically below the smaller doji, the signal bar that led up to the actual entry (4)? Because, technically, the deeper low stands a much better chance of holding up than the signal bar in question. It is two pip further out, that is true, but, with the chart so bullish and the pullback so harmonious (a nice 50 percent diagonal retracement), I would be more than happy to pay for that extra insurance. Note how the low of the pullback is also perfectly capped by the support of the bull flag to the left (2). One more reason why this low would probably hold up if attacked.

In most situations, the signal bar itself will serve as sufficient leeway for trade protection. If it is three pip tall (more or less the average), then a scalper has to add three pip more to calculate his total risk on the trade. A pip up and a pip down are added because the bar needs to be broken on both ends, and then one more pip to account for the spread. This one pip spread may be divided by half a pip on either side, but it could also be, for instance, one pip on the buy side and zero on the sell. It is irrelevant. If price breaks through the level of, say, 12, the chart will print 13 and the spread on the trading platform would theoretically show 12,5-13,5. If the spread somehow shows 13-14, then a market order to buy will be filled at 14. By definition, that means that a trader going short at that same moment will be filled at 13. Is this more advantageous? It really doesn't matter. Assuming both traders strive for 10 pip profit, then prices, either way, would have to travel 11 full pip from the moment of entry to reach target (remember, every trade starts out with minus 1 due to the spread). The buy scalper will ultimately be filled at a spread of 24-25, which allows his long to be sold at 24 for a 10 pip profit. Likewise, the short scalper will reach target at a spread of 2-3, which allows his short to be bought back at 3 for a 10 pip profit. So, either way, it boils down to the same distance in pip.

Applying these considerations to the chart in question, we can see that the maximum loss on the SB trade will be about 8 pip (not accounting for possible slippage) because the doji that forms the low stands 5 pip tall (3). Quite a hefty stop. But the chart looks excellent and there is still less to pay in terms of risk control than there is to gain in terms of target (10 versus 8).

In the absence of very strict guidelines, aspiring scalpers may falsely get the impression that tipping point definition is just a matter of gut feel, if not hindsight reflection, but that is certainly not the case. However, since the practice of proper trade management is beyond any kind of rule, there is a certain aptitude required in the process of tipping point selection. In the more easier chart situations, sound logic will do. When more subtlety is demanded, my advice would be to rather give the stop the extra pip than not. True, an unfortunate string of somewhat bigger losers may seriously add up, but as we have already calculated, the wider stop only needs to hold up once every so many times to compensate for earlier extra insurance.

If a trader is living too much in the moment, and thus temporarily negligent of the long-term aspect of his business model, he may feel slightly irritated when having paid for insurance and getting stopped out anyway. Or even worse, he may opt to pass up on stretching the stop to a more technical level the next time around. But the trader beware; economizing on stops, understandable as it may be, is a surefire way to get burned many times over. If the proper technical stop somehow seems too far out for comfort, then it is better to pass up on the trade than it is to cheapskate on protection by setting the stop too close.

Let us contemplate the management of the SB trade once prices nicely took off. After shooting up for about 8 pip after entry, prices pulled back and formed a higher low in the 20ema (5). To use that low as a new tipping point is cutting it rather fine. I would advise against it. It means that at that point in time, we leave the original stop as is, thereby risking a full 8 pip stop-out still. However, the *odds* for this bullish chart to pursue its upward momentum are certainly better than for it to turn sour on the trade. The three-bar SB setup (3-4), a tiny cluster by itself, may also come to the rescue should prices want to dip down. As a rule of thumb: before an item of support is tested, it is better to have a stop below its lows than anywhere else. But once this item is tested and this test forms a higher low, then, in most instances, the old level of support immediately expires in favor of the new one. This, in short, is the essence of trailing. It also points out why a long position should not be trailed indiscriminately below any higher low. The best new tipping points obtain their technical significance by first testing an area of previous support or resistance.

After prices indeed halted in support of the setup (6), the bulls quickly took control and bought the market back up. When the bar of (7) took out the high of (6), a scalper was offered to trail his original tipping point to a much more economical level (second dotted line).

Prices did have trouble clearing that resilient 20-level, though (1.3560). A few minutes later, the tipping point came close to being challenged (8), but once again the market was bought. It rose just enough to take out the high of (8) in the bar of (9), thereby allowing the scalper to once more lift his stop (black line). It is marked by a black line because not much later the level was broken and the trade had to be exited for maybe a 1 or 2 pip loss (X).

Figure 14.6 The first two tipping points are self-explanatory. The first is placed beneath the little cluster of the squeeze formation that led up to the ARB trade (1), the second beneath the low of the BB setup (2). Once the BB setup delivers its entry, the ARB scalper, already in position, can lift his original tipping point to the comfortable low of the new setup (second dotted line). If the tipping point below (2) is good enough for the BB trader, then it is good enough for the ARB trader as well.

A more interesting situation involves the third setup, the DD trade at 20:31 (third arrow). If you look closely, you can see that the black stop-out line (originally a dotted one) is not placed exactly underneath the very tiny DD setup lows, but 1 pip lower. That level matches the earlier low of (3). That one extra pip may not mean much, but it is all a scalper has in terms of technical aid and it might just do the trick. In this case it did not and so a scalper can scratch his trade immediately upon a break of the black line, simply because there is no other spot nearby that could possibly help him out. The stop-out may be a fluke, a typical shake, but who is to say. Despite the bullish chart and the potential for higher prices, a scalper is strongly advised not to entertain the folly of hope.

Just ten minutes later, the chart shows a rather textbook block pattern, quite a common occurrence when an extended pullback in an unmistakable trend flattens out. An alert scalper will not let such a great BB opportunity go by unexplored. The topside of the box can also be placed a pip lower, to allow for a somewhat more aggressive entry; after all, there are a number of equal touches at that level, too. This is at times a personal choice. In either case, the tipping point to this trade remains the same (third dotted line).

Would it have been wise to trail the tipping point below (6) when the bar of (7) took out the high of its predecessor? I really would not advise it. Just look at where our new stop would reside, right on top of the box barrier support. Remember the folly of the break-even exit? A clever bull would rather pick up a fresh contract at that spot than sell out an old one for zero loss.

But how about when the bar of (8) took out the high of (5)? That makes a lot more sense. Not only is (5) taken out, the previous high of (4) is broken also, strengthening the significance of the technical feat. In the light of this development, we do not want to see prices test the BB box again. That would look pretty ugly in the chart. Therefore, a new tipping point could be placed beneath the low of (6).

Figure 14.7 The top of the last arch in the range marks the initial tipping point on the IRB trade (dotted top of the box). Granted, this trade (first arrow) is somewhat aggressive but acceptable nonetheless. A scalper could also opt to pass up on it and then later trade the ARB setup (second arrow).

When prices dip below the range barrier, the IRB trade is comfortably in the plus. Two tiny dojis at the top of a pullback to the barrier line make up an ARB setup (1). Look closely where a scalper could best place his stop on this ARB trade (dotted line). Not exactly above the doji highs. The reader may recall the concept of the last arch's ceiling as discussed in the ARB chapter, Figure 13.3. Here that ceiling is made up of the signal line to the earlier IRB trade. And that is also where we can place a protective stop. That allows the market to briefly crawl back inside the range to test the last arch's ceiling without stopping the ARB trade out. It is two pip extra insurance, but with the ARB dojis themselves standing two pip tall, the risk on this trade is still quite acceptable (about 7 pip).

An interesting question might be whether or not the scalper in the IRB trade (with the more economical entry) should adjust his tipping point from the highs of the IRB setup to the lows of it, and thus place it at the same spot as the scalper trading the ARB. It is a matter of fact that he should. After all, an open position, from a price technical perspective, is either valid or has lost its validity. But the distinction between the two is not derived from contemplating one's point of entry. It is solely based on the price action characteristics between target and stop. In other words, from the moment the ARB scalper enters the market, both traders will manage their trades exactly the same.

Until the lows of the two dojis below the range barrier are taken out, the original tipping point on the IRB remains were it is. In all instances, prices need to deliver a technical feat first before a new stop-level takes effect. Quite similar, actually, as in waiting for an entry bar to take out a signal bar before firing off a trade.

The third setup, the DD at (4), offers a very clear tipping point above its highs. This level also matches the earlier highs from ten minutes before (2)—a great place to put a stop at. This trade would probably have been filled for a 10 pip profit not much later, but let us assume it had not. A little before 22:00, a tiny pullback forms a high below the 20ema (5). To place the tipping point above that high, after the low gets broken, is very aggressive. As a rule of thumb, but by no means a rule, we can say that the highs below the 20ema in a short, and the lows above the 20ema in a long, should be monitored carefully for their significance. Personally, I seldom exit a short below the 20ema or a long above the 20ema. However, that little high of (5) does represent chart resistance (offered by the lows of 3) and another scalper may not want to see prices travel above it again. If so, then he will exit the trade the moment that high is surpassed. He should not be surprised, though, to see the market take out his stop, only to immediately head south again. When prices are still trending (as opposed to clustering), sneaky false breaks like that are pretty common.

The next top in the chart (6) leaves little room for debate. The setup itself is not another DD. The bars are too big compared to those in the pullback. But to a trader still in position on the DD trade of (4), this new top does present an opportunity to adjust the original tipping point level to a more economical spot. He just has to wait for the bar of (8) to take out the low of (7). It would also have been defensible to wait one more pip for the more distinctive low of (6) to be taken out, too. Note that if the high of this top (6), and thus the tipping point, was broken topside, this trade would have been scratched at break-even. But not for the sake of zero loss. Purely because a tipping point exit coincided with the earlier entry.

Figure 14.8 This chart displays a very common situation. A range barrier gets broken (RB, first arrow), is briefly taken back, and then broken again (another RB, second arrow). Both trades are valid plays and share the same level of entry. The initial stop below the first RB setup is logically placed beneath the three little dojis that make up the squeeze (1, first dotted line). The stop on the second trade is placed a pip higher, below the signal bar's low (2, second dotted line). The moment the second RB takes effect, the stop on the first can be lifted a pip to match the tipping point of the new setup. This is all pretty standard stuff.

After the second break, within a 6 pip span, prices pulled back twice to the average. That left two higher lows in the chart (3 and 4). It would be very aggressive to trail a stop beneath either of these intermediate lows. You may get away with it, at times, but more often than not the trade will simply be cut short in even a minor barrier test. And that would be quite a waste because the barrier level here, 2 pip above the current tipping point, is of very fine quality and may provide excellent technical support. Also, the market has already put in a ceiling test (the signal bar's low in the second RB setup, 2) and there is even a nice 20-level to help out (1.3560). All in all, that makes for dependable support should prices decide to briefly test the barrier zone. It is best to keep the current tipping point where it belongs, back in the range, below that ceiling test's low. To put it in another way: in this chart, whatever prices do *above* the barrier, it will not affect the trade's validity much (unless an unmistakable reversal pattern gets formed); *below* the barrier, traders will seriously start to question the earlier break. But *in* the barrier zone, traders will most likely try one more time to pick up prices cheaply. Of course, not all ranges are created equal, nor are their barrier breakouts and their barrier tests. However, a rather straightforward range break like the one above is best traded in standard fashion. That means keeping a technical stop inside the range for the biggest part of the trade and only trail it higher when the chart starts to show serious signs of stagnation or even a potential reversal pattern, like a double top or a lower top.

Note: Every now and then, it may leave the reader a bit confused as to when he should prefer prudence over aggression or the other way around. What's more, the impression may have arisen that there are two complete different ways of playing this same method, and choosing between them somehow seems to hinge more on the situation at hand than on any kind of rule. However, the whole issue between prudence and aggression may be much less important than one initially might think. As much as an aspiring scalper may hope to obtain a proficiency that one day will allow him to always make the proper calls in times of subtle distinction, such mastery, if it even exists, is absolutely not essential to survive in the markets. Scalping at that kind of a level is just putting the cherries to the cake. At all times, a trader's main concern should be to acquire a sound understanding of price action principles, so as to avoid the most classic and costly mistakes. That will keep more pip in the books than any fine touch of mastery could ever hope to add.

Fig 14.9   www.ProRealTime.com   eur/usd 70 tick

Figure 14.9 After three attempts to break the barrier (hence an ARB instead of a regular RB), we want the market to just take off and not look back (first arrow). That allows for a tipping point of the tightest variety (first dotted line). Placing it one pip lower, below the bar of (1) is doable, but, from a bullish perspective, it would not look pretty to see prices once again dip below the dotted line. If this ARB gets disrespected, the bulls might very well throw in the towel. The tight stop still allows for one last little pullback below the barrier, but no more than that. Had there been less struggle to force the break, then maybe it would have been safer to opt for the extra pip, as a token of insurance. In general, only apply the bigger stop when questioning the technical significance of the more economical one.

The second dotted line, beneath the DD setup lows, is beyond question. It is placed at the most economical spot and below a prominent low in the chart. If challenged, the low will either hold up or crack, but there is no point in giving it an extra pip, at least not from a technical standpoint. The nearest level below the low that may offer some support is presented by the top of the little bull flag pattern of (2). That is way too far out to be of any help.

Just briefly before, I mentioned the rule of thumb of not scratching a long position when prices are still above the 20ema. This chart shows a nice exception. Have a look at where the third dotted line is placed. It represents a lifted tipping point in the DD trade, quite against standard procedure. Why would it be wise to put the stop underneath that low? To answer this we have to look a bit to the left and take note of the earlier, and rather distinctive, double top (3-4). These tops should not keep a scalper from trading the DD break, given the bullish credentials of the chart, but it is good to not lose sight of them. They do represent unmistakable resistance.

Let us sharpen our focus for a moment and contemplate the situation in that top area in detail. Once the tiny pullback doji of (6) gets broken topside, the market basically has only one option to keep the bullish pressure up and that is to take out the double top highs of (3) and (4). If not, and prices dip below the low of (6), then that will print a triple top pattern in the chart (3-4-5). It does not have to mean the end of this nice uptrend, but to a scalper in a long position, it would be extremely uncomfortable. The market's reaction to that technical feat may be quite hefty and therefore it is recommended to just get out of the way by exiting as soon as the tipping point low is taken out. In this chart the DD scalper got lucky because the false break above the highs of the double top took the DD trade to target just in time before prices dipped heavily south (7).

This example gives to show that the 20ema, no matter how faithful a companion, should not be looked upon as an absolute. It guides us 90 percent of the time, but every now and then it just has to be discarded on account of stronger technical development.

A question of conscience: when the bar of (5) matched the highs of the double top next to it, the DD trade may have been up over 9 pip. Is it truly wise in a situation like this to wait for the market to take out such strong resistance for the sake of a few extra pipettes? Yes and no. No, because of technical considerations. It may not be worth to risk a big part of profit in strong resistance for a few measly pipettes. But to just let the trade be may very well serve a purpose of its own. Once a scalper starts to allow himself the luxury of premature scratching in his daily routine, he may not be able to control himself in the many instances where he should just stand pat. After all, it is rare for a chart not to show *any* obstacles to a trade. Yet it is very common to ascribe more value to obstacles than necessary.

Figure 14.10 As has already been mentioned several times, there is no one way to scalp the markets, even within the range of a certain method. Scalpers can opt for aggressive entries or more conservative ones, and, similarly, they can opt for aggressive trailing or choose their tipping points more cautiously. In most instances, however, both the aggressive and conservative trader, when apt, will place their stops at the exact same spots, simply because it doesn't make sense to protect a trade any other way. But at times, it is just a matter of personal preference; it could also be the speed of the market that plays a role in the subtle choice between aggression and prudence. Speedy markets, as opposed to slow ones, are much more likely to take out stops in a sneaky false countermove, and not uncommonly by a mere pip. So a little extra insurance might come in handy. Slower markets, on balance, show more respect for technical levels, which should, theoretically, allow for tighter stops.

This chart shows a BB trade as a horizontal pullback that nicely breaks down in the 20ema (3). The trade is best protected with the wider stop, as depicted by the first dotted line. The stop could have been placed a pip lower, across the 5 equal highs in the block. But by giving it one extra pip, the tipping point not only matches the absolute high of the box, it also matches the absolute low of the earlier block pattern to the left (1).

Though very close, it looks like the low of (5) did not dip deep enough to bring the trade to target. The ensuing pullback brings prices very orderly to the 20ema (6). Once the market dips below the low of (6), resuming the trend, a scalper has a couple of options at his disposal. First of all, he may not want to relocate his tipping point yet because the pullback high is just an ordinary test of the 20ema; placing a stop directly on top of it would be kind of aggressive. On the other hand, if we compare this pullback to, for example, the pullback in Figure 14.8 (the bar of 3 that touches the 20ema), then the one in the chart above has definitely more technical weight to it than the earlier one. Also, protecting it with a tight stop will still rake in some profits, although that should not be an incentive by itself to tighten a stop. Still, it would be quite aggressive to place the tipping point directly above the high of (6); it would not be uncommon to see the stop get activated by one of these typical false breaks that love to take out these tiny intermediate tops by only a pip.

Interestingly, every now and then a scalper is presented with a nice middle way between aggression and prudence. How about placing the stop not directly on top of (6) but a pip higher (lowest dotted line), to match the lows of (2) and (4). This little extra insurance buys technical resistance for the price of a pip and could serve to put the chart to work in favor of the trade.

A third and most conservative way to manage the trade, is to place the stop even higher, to match the lows of the BB setup (middle dotted line).

The fact that in this chart none of these tipping points were even attacked, is totally irrelevant. What is relevant, though, is to know what to do when prices *do* travel up. Depending on one's appetite for risk, the second and third option seem the most appropriate. I would opt for the

extra pip above the pullback high (lowest dotted line). And be very much
on the alert to re-enter in case the stop immediately got hit and prices
dipped south again.

Figure 14.11 The original tipping point is strategically placed beneath the
double bottom in the BB setup (dotted line). Prices shot up nicely, but
once the second 20-level (since the start of the rally) was touched upon,
the trade had to endure a pullback that dipped deep enough to test the
entry on the BB trade (1). Traders silly enough to protect themselves
with a break-even stop, one of the cardinal sins of trade management,
will be taken out of the market then and there.

In a strong trending bullish chart, almost any pullback in support
will be swiftly acted on by the ever-present dip buyers. That was no
different in this chart. With the first test of support out of the way, and
prices shooting back up, a scalper will be more than happy to lift his
tipping point to the lows of that test (1, thick black line).

So far things could not be more technical and the prospect for a trade
like this to work out looks healthy in all respects. However, a few bars
higher up, the 20-level proves too strong to crack at that moment in
time. With his tipping point firmly in place, a scalper knows what to do
when the market dips below it.

Fig 14.12   www.ProRealTime.com   eur/usd 70 tick

Figure 14.12 We could not argue with a more cautious scalper placing the first tipping point beneath the IRB setup low (1). On the other hand, inside the ranges, the tightest technical level will usually suffice (first dotted line).

Take a good look at the three-bar sideways cluster straight in the top barrier of the bigger box (2). It represents a little barrier fight. Some may even call it a bull flag; we could look upon it as a tiny ARB in the making. When that cluster gets broken topside by the tall white bar of (3), an aggressive scalper could place his tipping point below the lows of the cluster. However, if somehow prices are slammed back down again for a quick test of the IRB signal line (top of the small box), the trade will be stopped out in support. True, that would mean a false range breakout, but the range barrier here is not exactly of the most exemplary kind. In other words, a little more fighting over the level is not unlikely, despite the very bullish bar that took prices up. A smarter way to protect the trade is to lift the tipping point to the level of the signal line (top of the IRB box). If prices are not capped by that support, then it is best to exit the trade and look for something else.

A little later, the market pulls back to the top of the bigger range and is halted exactly at the level of the earlier cluster lows to the left (4). A sideline bull will now sharpen his focus because the market may offer him a chance to get in at any moment. He could enter as the market ticks above the high of that tiny doji (the one between 4 and 5), or he could opt to wait for one more tick to the upside and see the bar of 4 get taken out as well. Both entries will take place within the bar of (5). In either case, a tipping point can be placed below the low of the new setup (second dotted line). The IRB scalper, if not already on target in the earlier top, should lift his current tipping point to that same level. As has already been stated, if a tipping point is valid in one trade, it is also valid in another. Entries do not determine the tipping points. Chart levels do.

Another pullback, not much later, takes prices back to the range barrier again, this time halting a pip higher than the earlier low to the left (6). Once the bar of the new low gets taken out topside, the tipping point can be lifted with another pip to match the level of the top barrier of the range (6, not depicted as a dotted line here).

It soon becomes obvious that prices have trouble clearing the 1.3730 area. Fortunately, a new higher low gets formed in the 20ema at (7) and a smart scalper will not hesitate to place his tipping point underneath it, tightening his stop with another comfortable 2 pip (black line); but only after prices take out the high of that bar. By the way, this is not aggressive trailing, it is smart management. After all, the range's top barrier has already been tested twice. It is time for the market to move on. Should prices dip below this new higher low, then the selling may get a little more aggressive (black line). The IRB scalper books a little profit on his trade; his fellow trader that took his entry in the bar of (5) has to give a couple of pip back to the market.

Figure 14.13 Both setups in this chart, the first an IRB, the second a BB beneath the extension of the range barrier, have their tipping points residing inside the boxes at very technical levels. It is the IRB trade that requires active management.

The most crucial bar in the course of the IRB trade is the one that pulls back to test the top barrier of the range (2). At the low of the bar, prices bounce up in barrier support. At the high of it, prices halt in resistance of the very distinctive top to the left (1). Once that resistance gets cleared by a pip a few bars later (a technical feat), a scalper is given a new tipping point to manage (black line, equal to the range barrier). With prices now above resistance, he does not want to see them below the low of (2) again. But that is the end of his trailing possibilities and not much later the trade has to be stopped out for what looks like a 1 pip loss.

Figure 14.14 The four equal lows of the SB setup provide enough technical weight to put the tipping point right underneath them (2). It is also
a plus to see these lows coincide with the support of the earlier high, a
little to the left (1). Not much later a double top ruins the trade. Since
there was no way of trailing the tipping point to a more economical level
before the original one got hit, a scalper accepts the maximum loss of
about 5 pip and moves on.

The second trade (6) is almost the mirror image of the first. Now it is
a double bottom that blocks the path to target (5-7). The original tipping
point is best set above the high of the BB setup (dotted line). Placing it
higher still, to match the high of (4), is stretching it a bit since the level
is already lifted a pip from the most economical protection.

A pullback from the low of (7) brings prices up and even back inside
the range of the BB box pattern (8). As is often seen, sideline bears grab
their chance in resistance and start shorting the market at these more
favorable levels, forcing prices down again and below the low of (8). A
scalper quickly lowers his tipping point to the high of the pullback (black
line). That is sound management because if this level is taken out, the
chart will show not only a double bottom but also a higher one next to it,
which will not look good from a bearish perspective. If we take the low of

(3) into the equation also, then a technical chartist may even recognize a kind of head-and-shoulders reversal pattern in the making (3-5-7). A scalper, understanding the implication of the information offered, will simply pull the plug on his short on a break of the high of (8). It may be too early to reverse the position from short to long (although optional at 9), but with such a strong bottoming pattern beneath him, there is no point in hoping for lower prices at that moment in time.

Fig 14.15   www.ProRealTime.com   eur/usd 70 tick

Figure 14.15 It is always nice to find a good looking DD setup in a strong trending market. Unfortunately, that does not always mean these trades will bloom to fruition the moment they are put on. The placement of the tipping point here is self-explanatory. More importantly, was there a way to have lifted up the level during the course of the trade? Technically seen, there was not. The chart was way too bullish to aggressively trail the stop beneath the low of the pullback bar, the first to hit the 20ema after entry (1). That is asking for a premature stop-out. As a consequence, a scalper, long on the DD trade, had no option but to watch bravely how his original stop got taken out. The width of the DD pattern being 3 pip, the loss on the trade will be around 6.

Figure 14.16 To save the best for last, this chart serves to show a sporadic deviation of standard tipping point technique. It concerns the protection on the IRB trade (first arrow). The entry below the signal line of the box is well chosen and the trade takes off nicely. But where exactly should a scalper place his initial stop? Preferably, he would want to place it all the way above the highs in the chart; after all, that is where any short would certainly lose all validity. For our purposes, though, that would be way too far out. So, if we want to engage in this IRB trade, we have to pick a top below these highs. Let us look at the possibilities. Within the span of the IRB setup, from the last top on, there are three intermediate highs to be counted before prices break down. The first one, a pip below the absolute highs of the range (1), is still too far out. And it would be rather odd to pick that spot for protection; might as well throw in an extra pip and put the stop above the range barrier. The second top is formed two pip lower (first dotted line) and seems certainly more reasonable; but we cannot say it marks a very specific point in the current price action. The third possibility is depicted by the second dotted line. It shows us a very tiny arch right before the break. We could say this little top has earned itself the most credentials as a tipping point level, but more by want of a better alternative than anything else. In other

words, it remains to be seen how well that little arch would hold up if attacked. Would a friendly sideline bear short the high of it and save us from being stopped out? Naturally, we could simply opt to forgo the setup altogether, but that would be an opportunity lost. This is where a scalper needs to throw in some logical tactics to solve this conundrum. He could use a combination of both tipping points.

For starters, right after the IRB break, he places his initial tipping point at the higher dotted line. That spot would probably fence off the majority of bulls in case of a counterattack and it even allows for a 1 pip false break above the tiny arch. If it gets taken out anyway, then so be it. After prices break down nicely and reach the bottom barrier below, the tipping point could then be lowered to the level of the second dotted line. This is where we deviate from standard procedure, because the price action itself does not warrant tipping point adjustment. The decision to lower the stop-out level is solely based on the situation at hand. Or look at it this way: if the lower tipping point was already optional to begin with, then it certainly couldn't be foolhardy to make use of it at a later stage, with the trade well on its way to target.

Once prices break the range barrier, too, things are starting to look up for this particular trade. However, there is always the possibility of a barrier fight and even of a mean spike back inside the range. In that respect, the two-bar pullback to the broken barrier showed very little bullish interest (3). This invites the first sideline bears to start shorting the barrier level. The moment fellow-bears take out the bottom of (3), a scalper can opt to lower his tipping point once more, this time to the bottom level of his IRB box (not depicted by a dotted line). He can also opt to keep it where it is and watch the price action a bit more. It certainly would not be smart to lower the tipping point all the way to the bottom barrier of the range, above the high of (3). That really is asking for a premature stop-out (remember the ceiling test principle).

And indeed, the next bar is a bullish spike back inside the range, eating back all of the current profit (4). A scalper may not like it, but from a technical perspective this kind of price action in the barrier zone is perfectly natural (ceiling test attempt). This also shows the pointlessness of counting current profit while in position. Keeping an eye on the profit and loss window on the trading platform is a surefire way to lose mental stability. A trader shouldn't bother and just keep his eyes on the chart. If he manages his trades correctly, then the platform will take care of the rest.

But this trade isn't over yet. For the duration of one tiny doji bar, prices are halting on top of the range barrier (5). So much for bullish interest. Next, the bears take prices below the barrier again in what turns out to be quite a bearish bar (6). But it would be rather aggressive to immediately lower the tipping point to the new highs (third dotted line). It would be sound management, though, to lower the tipping point to the IRB setup bottom, if not already done so. However, the moment prices dip a bit further, below the earlier low of (2), just a few seconds later, the tipping point could immediately be lowered to the level of the third dotted line. Why now and not before? Because the chart now prints a new low, which is a technical feat of significance and it basically should invite bearish follow-through. Should prices stall or travel up, that's fine, but a scalper does not want to see them travel past the last high again, or he will scratch the trade then and there (third dotted line).

I realize I am being painfully elaborative on this particular trade (and it hasn't even reached target yet), but for good reason. Admittedly, the chart may only reflect a snapshot impression of possible price action and chances are next to none that the market will ever present itself in the exact same way. So why bother explaining the specifics of managing this one trade in such detail? Because it very much reflects the reality of trading. How easy it would be to show nothing but textbook setups and textbook tipping point management. But what purpose would that serve? Somewhere on the road to mastery, a scalper has got to come to terms with the fact that he occasionally needs to make delicate calls or even deviate from standard procedure. Most of the times, however, things are extremely straightforward and he could enter and exit his trades without even blinking. Other times, he just has to throw in a big chunk of logic and not be afraid of it.

Let's get back to the trade. With the tipping point now technically at the break-even level (third dotted line) and prices well below the range barrier, the IRB trade looks very healthy. Another bullish attempt to bring prices back inside the range fails right in the barrier (7). It even sets up a nice ARB pattern (two tiny dojis in the barrier level) that could be acted on by a sideline scalper not yet in position (second arrow). The initial tipping point to the ARB trade is placed at the same level of the IRB trade's current tipping point, the third dotted line. It makes sense to pay for that extra pip and not place the stop-out level directly on top of the ARB dojis. A few minutes later, the IRB trade finally reaches target.

Are all these tipping point adjustments very cumbersome to pull off? Not at all, because it is all mentally done. A scalper only needs to look at his chart, with his cursor on the exit button. And what's more, he doesn't even need to pick the absolute best tipping points. For there are no absolutes in trading. But he has to make sure he does not pick the obvious inferior levels, which may take him out of his trades unnecessarily.

The ARB scalper is still in position. A little after 21:00, a pullback brings prices back up somewhat more aggressively (9), but the bulls are given very little time to enjoy that feat. It left the scalper with a great new tipping point to place his mental stop above, shaving 4 pip off of his original risk (fourth dotted line).

The most interesting part in this chart is actually the bottoming pattern that ultimately led to the trade's validity breach. I am referring to the action below the black horizontal line. The three highs of the pattern form the signal line to the exit (10-11-12). But the high of (10) was not a tipping point by itself, that would have been very aggressive trailing. But once that second high appeared and got slammed back (11), a scalper could then lower his tipping point to the level of the black line. Because he doesn't want to be in the trade anymore if these double tops are taken out (due to the bottoming action at the level of 8). It took a few minutes, and even another matching high (12), but ultimately the tipping point was cracked (X).

It is quite common for a bottoming or topping pattern to ruin a trade. That makes sense, because it takes guts to counter the current trend and a good solid reversal pattern may be just what is needed to muster the necessary bravery to have a go at it.

Speaking of reversal patterns, if we look closely, we can see that the bottoming pattern below the signal line of (10-11-12) is actually a smaller mirror image of the earlier IRB setup. Just visually wrap a box around it. Take a good look at them both. If a scalper can see the logic in trading a break of a topping pattern (the IRB), then he will also understand why he has to exit his short on a topside break of the bottoming pattern.

As a final note: There was no way of telling that the alleged reversal implications here would turn out to be a total fluke (13-14). In fact, there is no way of knowing anything at all. Nor is there any need to. The true scalper can only have but two things in mind: where to enter and where to exit. The same cannot be said of the less proficient individual. This trader's mind is mostly filled with fear, hope, pain, greed, stress, impatience, disappointment, expectation, vengeance, regret, animosity, doubt, betrayal, depression, euphoria, misery, desperation, and that is just touching lightly on the possible list of his follies. Navigating safely through this minefield of emotions when looking to trade or looking to exit is quite a daunting task, if not plain impossible. It has already been advocated many times over in this guide, but let's say it one more time: the moment a trader stops caring about the outcome of his current trade, all the baggage and weight will simply slide of his shoulders and he will obtain the calm state of mind necessary to follow his plan. If an open position is still an issue, then lower your volume until you just don't care. And start to think about your trading as executing a carefully crafted business plan that has no need for immediate profit.

Trade Selection

Chapter 15

Unfavorable Conditions

As has already been stated numerous times throughout these pages, the scalping tactics presented should only be applied in a favorable market. That way we stand to reap most benefit from our splendid little setups. Applying them indiscriminately in any kind of market may not only cause to undo all the hard work of finding and exploiting a particular edge, it may very well destroy a scalper's primary objective, which is to become a consistently profitable trader.

The mere existence of a favorable market implies the existence of its natural counterpart, the unfavorable one. But how exactly can we define it, and detect it in practice? So far, most of the setups shown in the charts presented themselves in favorable conditions, and trading them, at times, seemed no more than a formality. The reality of trading, however, is much less inclined to show us nothing but textbook setups throughout our daily sessions. More often than not, these setups show up in obvious chart resistance and acting on them with little or no regard for the overall picture may do more harm than good.

To scalp wisely, we may have to take an observational stance 90 percent of the time and only become active once we have assessed the current forces in play to be favorable towards our trades. It not only means that our setups should comply with the overall price action (in terms of buildup and directional pressure), but also that there should not be any visible chart resistance blocking the way to the target. Ideally, we want to see a clear path at least 10 pip out. But alas, since the market most of the time tends to back and fill all over the chart, particularly on a short-term frame like the 70-tick, chances are that a free path to target is more a rarity than it is common. The occasional strong trend is a good exception, but then again, it is not an exception for nothing.

The good news is that we do not necessarily need to venture out in uncharted territory to stand a chance of reaching target. Far from it. But what we do not like to see is either immediate clustering price action to the left of our entry blocking the way, or a stronger wall of resistance a little further back in time that may spell trouble on our 10 pip quest (still on the screen, though).

One could argue that whatever resistance lies in the way, sooner or later it will be cracked, or else prices would never go anywhere. That is very true. But remember that we do not want to do any of the dirty work ourselves, even with all of the underlying forces backing us up. The trick is to watch from the sidelines while other participants force themselves upon the barricades. The charts evidently show us that there will always be a number of courageous volunteers ready to sacrifice themselves by dipping into any pool of sharks head first. At times it makes you wonder, though, what kind of charts these traders are watching. Notwithstanding, these actions of bravery do thin out resistance, whether overhead or underfoot, which is why it is important to always watch attentively how these battles play themselves out. Ultimately, every path gets cleared, either up or down, and if so, then we will aim to join the winning party as smartly as we can. This, in short, forms the foundation of our method and it has stood the test of time quite well.

Most of the charts, so far, have shown the path already cleared or safe enough to venture out on and so we mostly concentrated on the setups to get us into position in these favorable markets. The next so many charts will aim to do more or less the opposite. They will show us when and why to stay out of the market, even though the setups themselves may look tradable in any other respect. After skipping a trade, prices may still proceed in the break's direction, and much further than that. But that, of course, is irrelevant. Individual outcomes never bear any relevance in a probability play. The sole purpose of these charts is to understand the concept of an unfavorable venture.

Figure 15.1 This chart shows a classic example of round number support. In the first half of the chart, the 50-level was diligently defended by the bulls on four consecutive occasions within the space of an hour (the three ellipses). The most tell-tale event was the false break below double bottom support (3); prices came straight down from the top of the chart all the way to the 50-level and even dipped a few pip below the earlier lows of (1) and (2). That was a terrible way to break support. The bulls knew it, and, not much later, so did the bears.

The rectangle here, a midway between a larger block and a smaller range, represents an interesting stand-off between both sides of the market. Although the bulls had grabbed control again in the round number zone, the bears were not so impressed as to immediately give up on defending the next round number in line, the 20-level of 1.4160. They even dealt the technically stronger bulls a nice false break to chew on (the tease through the top barrier, T).

The lesson to be learned from this chart is to never guess which party will win a particular fight. The bears had definitely something going for them, but the bulls deserved some credit of their own. From a mere technical standpoint, the latter party had shown undeniable demand in round number support. Chances are, they will not easily give up on what they had built up if once again attacked. This is not to say that the bears would not be able to vindicate their opponents next time around. But the question is: do we really want to take that leap of faith and join them on their quest by shorting the break of the box? Just look at the three ellipses and imagine what they represent. If nothing else, they surely imply strong vested interest, and not just that of tiny scalpers. And all of these players need to be cleaned out for our 10 pip target to ever get hit. A clever scalper will decline the RB trade (4).

Figure 15.2 At times, round number defense is very much akin to strategic warfare. To the bigger and smarter players, it is not a game of bluntly selling or buying into the level itself. They gallantly leave that to those who prefer bravery over vision. Take a look at the range box to see how cleverly the bears went about fencing off the bulls in this particular chart. They didn't just whack them at the 1.42 level. Instead, they treacherously allowed them to enter into the lion's den, inviting new bulls to the scene. No doubt a number of these newcomers thought they were in for a nice treat of stop-loss implosion above the technical

high of (1), the first top to be taken out above the round number. But as we have seen so many times before, it is a thin line between a victory march and trip to the firing squad. It didn't take long for the bulls to realize they had walked into a classic trap. And indeed, after the market printed a lower top at (2) and then another one at (3), the shape of things to come looked pretty imminent. Even so, a clever scalper on the sidelines will not recklessly join the bear party. He will patiently wait for the situation to become unbearable for the majority of scalping bulls. It wasn't hard to find a proper barrier to mark the dividing line between bullish hope and fear: the bottom of the box. Therefore, the RB setup made for a pretty good trade to the short side of the market (first arrow).

But is that really true? Before stepping in, a scalper not only has to assess the technical necessities of a favorable market, he has to carefully scrutinize the chart for unfavorable conditions as well. In other words, is it technically defensible to take this trade in terms of a 10 pip target. What about the level of the dotted line here? Let us not write the bulls off yet. This level represents earlier resistance and therefore could now very well hold up as support. Since it is about 6 pip below the RB short entry, we cannot discard it just like that.

In order to make the proper call of trade-or-skip, let us speculate a bit further. If prices make it to the level of the dotted line and bounce up once more, where can we technically imagine new bears to come in to save us from having our stop taken out above the RB high (the last arch)? It's hard to answer this without a touch of wishful thinking, but I would say that the bottom barrier of the range makes for an excellent pullback short. The unmistakable reversal pattern within the box will not have gone unnoticed. All in all, despite some potential trouble on the way to target, trading this RB is a proper call.

Is there similar justification to be found in trading the second trade, the DD at (4)? If we were to judge the picture by the outcome of that trade, we could say that the bears definitely made the right choice in selling the market aggressively down. But do outcomes have any say in things? From a pure technical perspective, shorting that DD is certainly not advisable. If we want the overall conditions to align with our trades, then it is best not to pick a spot where we can imagine our opponents to eagerly come in. For that reason alone, we should not want to short into obvious support and certainly not when it is presented by the current bottom of the market. That is simply asking for a good whack.

Figure 15.3 Despite the reasonable uptrend, the first arrow points towards a DD trade of the weaker variety (2). Prices may very well travel higher in the near future, but will they immediately do so after such a non-distinctive pullback that not only shows clustering price action, but multiple tops to boot (ellipse)?

Although most clear trends show a tendency to rather continue than reverse, it is strongly recommended to not just jump in on any kind of stalling. Ideally, we like to see a crisp diagonal pullback towards the 20ema before deploying our with-trend tactics. Horizontal pullbacks can be traded also, provided they are not of the clustering kind but more of the thinner variety; they can be clustering as well, but then we better long them from the top or short them from the bottom, instead of the other way around (think BB). The pullback within the ellipse looks tricky in all respects. That makes the DD trade an easy skip.

Note: When opting to engage in a potential resumption of the trend, a scalper should make a distinction between a DD, a SB and a BB setup.

All three aim to exploit a waning pullback, but not every situation gives these patterns equal weight. The DD setup, for example, especially when made up of just two dojis, shows much less tension than the cluster of bars within a proper BB setup. Therefore, as much as the DD setup is a splendid little pattern to pick up a trend after a pullback, it is best acted on when that pullback is either substantial or at least diagonal. Pullbacks of the scribbling or clustering kind demand a more cautious approach because the dojis that hit the 20ema usually bear little significance in relation to the neighboring bars. The SB setup is already more telling because its double break characteristic shows more conviction in terms of possible trend resumption. The BB setup, on the other hand, really builds up pressure within its boundaries, if only because there are usually a lot more bars involved. But this pattern, too, should not be traded indiscriminately. The stronger the resistance above or below it, the more pressure buildup is needed within it. The setup often does possess the power, though, to crack what's left of already faltering resistance.

The second DD setup (3), although better positioned in the chart, is still facing the same overhead resistance. True, it has a bottom in support of an earlier low (1), which betrays some technical significance, but I would still feel uncomfortable longing straight into overhead resistance. With the setup standing just 2 pip tall, the odds are quite reasonable, though (about 5 pip risk against a 10 pip gain). However, with resistance *above* the setup and the magnet effect of the round number of 1.45 *beneath* it, chances are this trade may easily get stopped out, maybe more than two thirds of the time. In this case, the vacuum effect could be quite strong due to the fact that the round number level had been breached earlier on but not yet tested back for support. Of course, it is not an absolute necessity for the market to test back a broken 00-level, but in a questionable environment, when considering a trade, it does add some weight on the con side of the scale. The absence of the test will keep at least a number of the bulls on the sidelines until more clarity comes along. And that usually means less follow-through on our trade. All in all, it just adds up and therefore it may be too soon to accept the entry on the DD break at this point in time.

Out of the three setups, the BB pattern (4), though tiny, stands the best chance to deliver the anticipated bullish reaction on a break of its highs. Now the bottom of the market is already successfully holding up three times in a row without the bears being able to get a grip on things. Technically, that should attract more bulls to the action. Never lose sight of the fact that you want other players to follow in your footsteps. After all, that is the only way to ever reach target and also the very reason why these so-called secret indicators, which are sold for big bucks to the ignorant and the foolish, are such terrible scams. What point is there in trading spots that others can't see.

With this BB pattern so tiny, the conditions are far from exquisite; but then again, after blocking two earlier breakout attempts without seeing the bulls back off, the bears may just call it a day on third instance. The bulls certainly had the overall trend still going for them. We can say this represents a classic situation of a favorable market, a favorable setup (though not very powerful), and a condition slowly turning favorable. This BB trade is certainly worth the shot (third arrow). But it would be wise to trail the trade attentively should prices find trouble in clearing the current highs (the tops within the ellipse). Lifting the tipping point to the low of (5), after this bar was taken out topside, would certainly have been a good idea. Take a moment to compare this situation with the example discussed in the previous chapter, Figure 14.9. A multiple top against a long position is best not taken lightly.

Figure 15.4 This chart shows a perfect example of how an otherwise very valid setup at times may have to be discarded on account of an unfavorable chart. If we would block the price action from before 12:00 from our view, then trading the FB to the long side seems reasonable in every respect (true, the pullback, though brisk and diagonal, could have dipped a bit lower to at least retrace about 40 percent of the rally). The unfavorable condition is presented by the origin of the bullish spike in relation to the price action before it. It started off from the low of the chart and then ran up to surpass all previous resistance (2-3). Shock effect or not, this FB entry would have to be taken straight into the earlier topping level of (1), which may be stretching it a bit. This chart may easily proceed on its bullish path, but chances are a number of aggressive bears will try their luck first. That would render a long highly prone to a quick stop-out. Shock effects, as much as they can rip a chart apart, are often fully countered by big and clever players, even up to the point of standing the price action completely on its head. Of course, we have no crystal ball to tell us when this will be the case. In terms of probability, a mean reversal of a sudden move is more likely to happen when the overall price action is not very supportive (yet) of the spike's directional pressure.

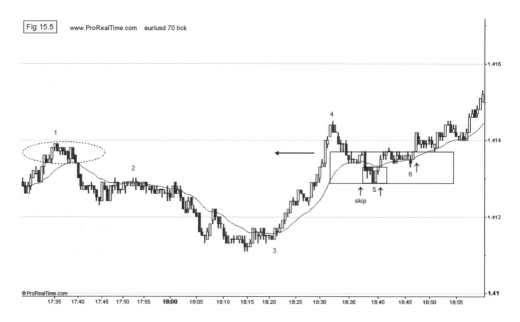

Figure 15.5 This example doesn't really differ that much from the previous one, Figure 15.4. In a similar way, the bullish attack (3-4) surpassed all previous chart resistance and only came to a hold once the earlier top of (1) was taken out. We are basically dealing here with a classic false range break trap. And we have seen already so many examples of how these non-buildup breaks are happily countered by clever traders who have mastered the art of defying the tide. Therefore, trading the DD setup (first arrow) makes for a low probability trade and thus an easy skip. That is not to say that the bullish spike has no technical meaning. Quite on the contrary. But we have to wait for the overall market action to visibly support the current directional pressure before we put our treasured capital at risk.

In that respect, things looked already a lot better about five minutes later when prices had retraced about 40 percent of the bullish spike (5) and simultaneously found support in the earlier cluster of (2). Trading that BB would still be kind of aggressive, but defensible nonetheless (second arrow).

The best opportunity was presented ten minutes later (third arrow). No less than 9 equal highs formed an excellent signal line of a much bigger BB (box). The bottom of the squeeze that led up to the break found support in the highs of the earlier BB setup. Inside the box, right before the break, prices briefly dipped below the low of the squeeze (6), but were immediately bought back up: a nice false break on a miniature level. It also allowed for a solid technical level to put a protective stop beneath.

Figure 15.6 Subtle as the difference may be, in this chart the origin of the bullish move of (2-3) started out on a better footing than those of the spikes in the two previous charts, Figures 15.4 and 15.5: a higher bottom below round number support. On top of that, the distance to the earlier top of (1) was not so extensive either. Still, was trading that SB (first arrow) a clever choice price technically? That is not so easy to answer by looking at this chart alone. The pullback neatly halted in the support of the earlier top, but it was rather tiny compared to the bullish move, and it did present itself as a bit of a double top (3). If somehow the earlier price action on the screen (not visible here) showed a strong bullish tendency, then maybe an aggressive scalper could step in and trade. But we cannot blame another trader for taking a more conservative stance and skip this offer. This is very much the reality of trading. From a probability standpoint, it is not necessarily required to only take the best possible trades in the book. After all, even slightly favorable

odds should theoretically pay off in the long run. But we do have to avoid taking the obvious lesser trades, of which there are plenty during any given session.

A good example of such a low probability trade would be the second SB situation about ten minutes later (second arrow). The dotted ellipse to the left of it surrounds the obvious dangers looming above the entry level: clustering price action and a double top to boot.

Nevertheless, prices did manage to take out these tops, negating their initial significance in the process. From that point on, a typical bull/bear tug-o-war kept prices confined in a tight range for a number of minutes. An alert scalper would surely have been able to wrap a nice BB box around it (4). Out of the three setups, this is the one that should be acted on without reservations (third arrow). The justification is found in the favorable odds presented by the strong buildup of pressure below the 20-level of 1.4420. If prices break through to the upside, we can imagine resistance to sooner give in to rising prices than to halt them and force them back.

Note: Compare this chart with Figure 15.3 for a moment. Both represent similar topping action and a buildup to a continuation of the current trend. Both saw two early attempts to push on being fenced off by the bears and a third one succeed. Still, the action in the chart above is much more impressive. In miniature, the differences are also portrayed by the BB setups in each chart. They are very similar in structure and they imply the same tension, but the BB setup in Figure 15.3 is definitely less impressive in terms of buildup. It means that the reaction to its break may be of a weaker kind. The conditions in the chart, and the chart as a whole, will determine whether these weaker setups still earn a validity status. As a rule of thumb: The more we can imagine overhead resistance to still play a role, the more a weaker setup beneath it should be shunned. Granted, there is no avoiding a touch of subjectivity in these cases; that is all part and parcel of technical assessment. All the more reason to always keep a neutral stance, because the slightest presence of bias may already disrupt a trader's ability to make a correct assessment of the finer price action subtleties.

Fig 15.7   www.ProRealTime.com   eur/usd 70 tick

Figure 15.7 Another low odds DD setup (1), right in the bottom of what could be regarded as a range formation. Prices came all the way down from the highs of the chart to the lows of it. Why would anyone want to short the bottom of this range? Taking a short in the market at a level where a serious number of bears will take profit and a number of bulls will be happy to get in is openly inviting double pressure to ruin the trade. A clever scalper simply declines the offer. But should we block the price action from before 16:00 from our view, then this setup would have been of acceptable quality, because it shows up in a bearish rally and at the possible end of a diagonal pullback in the 20ema. True, the pullback is a bit small compared to the length of the trend it is counter-ing, but that is not the issue of the lesson here. The point is that in case of an otherwise valid setup, the overall price action, when unfavorable, could still provide a valid reason to decline the trade.

Figure 15.8 A favorable chart and a textbook setup do not necessarily imply a valid trade. The condition ruining the option is presented by the price action within the ellipse to the left of the SB entry: clustering price action, indicating support. The chart is definitely bearish and prices may very well travel further down. Still, one has to pick the moment of participation as smartly as possible. If you want to short the market, it is best to do it at a spot where you can expect a large number of sidelines bears to join you and a large number of bulls to get out of your way. That way, you've got the principle of double pressure working in favor of your trade. Conversely, if you short into a potential bottom, like you would be doing in the chart above, then double pressure will work the other way around—to your detriment, that is; because you are shorting in an area where most of your fellow bears will be getting out (taking profit) and a large number of bulls will try to get in (bottom fishers). With both of these forces working against the trade, a tight stop is usually taken out pretty fast.

Figure 15.9 There is no denying the bullish eagerness to pick up all contracts offered within the boundaries of this textbook range. To those with bullish views on a market, a slightly bearish chart can be a joy to the eye because it offers excellent opportunities to deploy all sorts of bottom fishing techniques; after all, there is usually no shortage of bears ready to push prices lower, generously helping all contrarians to trade from more economical levels.

But at some point, of course, the bulls do have to turn the tables around. In the example above, creating that higher low at (3) was almost a mandatory feat. The chart may have printed a double bottom earlier on (1-2) but the bears had kept the pressure up pretty good. Unless the bulls brought something more significant to the scene, it would not have taken long for the bears to become a little more aggressive at the lower levels in order to try and force a downward break.

In that respect, this higher low in the range was a good start, but the subsequent spike through the top barrier may have been a bit over the top at that point in time (3-4). Clever bears, understanding the folly of an overly eager break, happily responded by ruthlessly whacking prices back into the range. That put a so-called v-shaped pullback on the chart (4-5), which actually represented a picture perfect ceiling test (reversed). And that immediately left a sideline scalper to solve a pressing dilemma with very little time to think things over. Should he trade the pullback ARB in this situation (arrow), or should he safely stay on the sidelines and let the market do the dirty work of either clearing out all bearish resistance or shaking out all bulls in return. My take on this situation would be to skip the trade. There is just too much resistance to the left of this chart (within the ellipse) to risk precious capital at this moment in time.

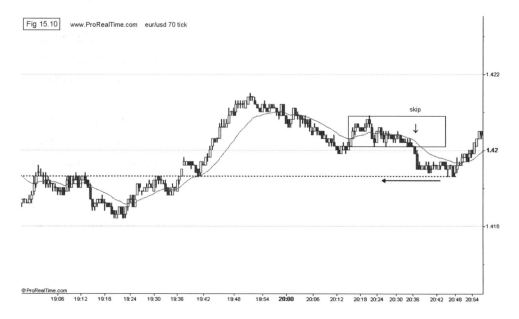

Figure 15.10 When opting to engage in a trade, whether textbook or questionable, always ask yourself if somewhere on the path to your target a level needs to be surpassed that would offer your opponents excellent odds to counter your position. For example, the level of the dotted line in the chart above bears unmistakable technical significance. Chances are, it will certainly inspire a number of sideline bulls to step into the market, and a number of bears to exit their shorts. That is double pressure indeed, but against your position. It is a nice trade, though, for those able scalpers who only strive to take a quick 5 pip out of the market. For our purposes, however, this trade is best left alone. If we compare this chart with Figure 15.2, then both ventures show simi-

lar resistance a few pip out. In the earlier chart, the setup was tradable, though, simply because of the very strong bearish pattern (the range) above the entry. In that respect, the chart above shows a weaker bearish pattern above the entry, and some stronger resistance below it as well. On top of that, the 00-level may pull prices back up. When resistance and support are battling it out in the vicinity of a round number, it often leads to choppy price action and thus less follow-through. Novice traders, in their very understandable anxiety, often harbor an urge to get into the market. Yet most of the time, the very best position in the trading arena is the one on the sidelines. That is a place of virtue and reflection, a sanctuary, a personal safe-haven and it is respected by all participants as if holy ground. It will not be trespassed on. It will never be attacked and there will be no moral judgment cast on those who seek refuge in it.

Note: A clever way to assess the significance of potential levels of resistance and support in the chart is to already scan for them when there are no trades in sight. Not only does this keep you up to date with what is going on in the chart at all times, lessening the need for surprise decisions, it will also enhance your neutral view on the price action, diminishing the likelihood of false perceptions in the decision-making process as well.

Figure 15.11 Strong bullish moves that start out from a lower low and then run all the way up to attack a distinctive high are excellent candidates to get aggressively shorted by clever sideline bears waiting for the rally to run out of steam. And vice versa, of course. Not seldom do we see the contrarians come in after prices peek through a former high or low by a mere pip (3 barely takes out 1). Even when the market is not displaying very visible evidence of ranging price action, the principle of the false break potential holds up nonetheless: at all times, the best breaks stem from proper buildup situations.

Look at the shape and size of the pullback in which the first DD trade (5) set itself up. That is just too meager if we consider the length of the rally before it (2-3); in fact, prices hardly came down. We can even spot a tiny double top within the ellipse just a few pip above the DD entry (3-4). An easy skip.

The second trade, we could call it a SB (second arrow), is still suffering the same overhead resistance since nothing really changed in terms of price. However, it is a stronger setup than the one before it because now there is a little more evidence that prices may hold up in the area; we could say that the second low of the SB forms a tiny double bottom with the low of the DD. But is that enough to put capital at risk for a 10 pip trade to the long side? I would advise against it; despite the bullish perseverance (or the lack of bearish enthusiasm to force prices down), initiating new long positions at these levels just doesn't make for smart scalping. Fact is, though, that the bears kept a surprisingly low profile and prices did march on to higher levels.

With prices now in the last ellipse there is no denying that the resistance level of (1-3-4-6) is truly taken out. We could even say that the price action from (3 to 7) represented a nice squeeze that in many other circumstances may have been a welcome sight to those bullish on the market. However, in relation to the strong rally from low to high (2-3), which by itself was a non-buildup counter rally defying the earlier trend of (1-2), this squeeze progression is on the meager side of things and it may be advisable to not entertain bullish views just yet. As much as all bears who went short in the (1-2) rally got shaken out one after the other as prices retraced every pip back up, and then some, chances are this market needs a respectable pullback first before enough new bulls will pop up on the scene to carry prices even further. With that in mind, conservative scalpers would probably decline the third trade as well (third arrow). And not just because the price action within the last ellipse forms a little sideways cluster that might block the potential of the DD trade below it. In fact, this possible resistance is most likely outmatched by the pressure within the current support of the squeeze (at the level of 8). What's more, the round number level of 1.42 may even suck prices straight up. No, a better reason to decline this trade is the fact that the counter rally of (2-3) remains an awkward move until, one way or another, a deeper pullback has found its way on the chart. If we want the principle of double pressure to work in our favor, then we need those on the sidelines to join us in battle. In other words, if *we* assess the current situation as less favorable, then, no doubt, a large number of sideliners will think of it in a similar way. And that will keep them where they are, out of the market.

Should a very aggressive scalper want to engage in these sort of trades anyway, then aggressive trailing is certainly recommended (tipping point at the low of 9).

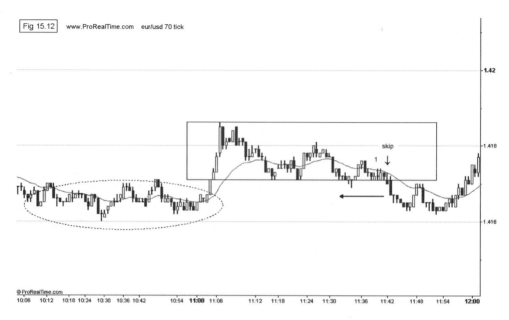

Fig 15.12   www.ProRealTime.com   eur/usd 70 tick

Figure 15.12 This is just a stand-off between bullish and bearish forces. The first half of the chart is controlled by the bulls (ellipse, representing support), the second half by the bears (box, representing resistance). Just because the bears at (1) are currently winning (forcing prices out of the range, but into support) does not mean the bulls will run for cover and not defend what they had built up within the ellipse earlier on. They could flee, of course, but that is irrelevant. It is best not to get ourselves involved in these lengthy clashes in which all pressures and forces are more or less evenly distributed.

Figure 15.13 There certainly is something to be said for trading this market from the long side, either by taking the miniature IRB trade (first arrow), or the RB trade a few minutes later (second arrow). The market had been engaged in an unmistakable bottoming process for over an hour, forming a textbook range formation below the round number of 1.43. It is obvious that the bulls were very keen on recapturing what was taken from them. Therefore, the bears had a task of their own: shorting the 1.43 level as aggressively as they could to exhaust all bullish defense below it. That can make for an interesting fight.

Take a look at the bottoms of (1-2-3-4); if that does not spell support then what does. And how about the squeeze of (5-6). But even though the bulls started to get the upper hand they still faced the task of clearing out the earlier highs a little above 1.43 (both ellipses). In a major level like this, as long as these highs hold up, prices run a pretty good chance of getting slammed back down again. Numerous times if need be. In a tight chart like the one above, it is best not to engage and just let the round number titans do their thing.

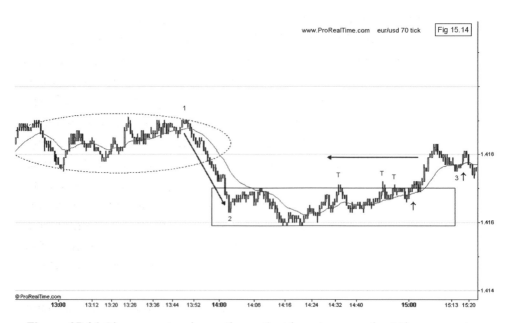

Figure 15.14 Clever contrarians, those that love to go against the current pressure of the market and who are pretty good at it, will not be seen firing off their trades into obvious resistance. They carefully await their chance and preferably like to see as little resistance on their path as possible before they give it a shot. What will certainly inspire them is to see a solid one-directional move totally flatten out on account of faltering follow-through. It is fair to say that strong one-directional moves, like the one of (1-2), once they peter out and eventually get countered, are likely to offer much less resistance than anything previously going sideways. Or think of it this way: if you were a sideline bear, ready to short, and you saw prices climb back up an earlier one-directional bearish move, where would you start deploying your shorts? And even if you had vision on these matters, would other sideline bears follow in your footsteps? On balance, you stand a much better chance of finding companions when shorting from a clustering phase.

As a rule of thumb: the more a sudden one-directional move is lacking proper follow-through, the more it stands to be retraced completely back to its origin, simply because the straight nature of the move does not offer sideline players a pullback level that coincides with resistance or support. And so the market often keeps on pulling back until all those who traded the earlier move are fully shaken out.

If we take this principle to the chart at hand, then we can tell by the range in the box that the sharp bearish move of (1-2) certainly lacked follow-through. It is not that the bears did not try, though. It took the bulls the biggest part of an hour to fence off all bearish attacks, but eventually (and after no less than three tease breaks, Ts) they managed to squeeze prices out of the range in textbook RB fashion. Note how easily prices spiked out once the bears gave in. And that makes sense because there simply was no overhead resistance blocking the advance. Prices basically could have retraced all the way up to the ceiling of (1), the last support in the chart (now resistance), without it being an odd move, really. In this case, the market halted in the resistance of the 20-level, which coincided with former support of the ellipse lows. Good enough for a quick 10 pip profit on the RB trade.

But that hands us an interesting situation. When prices pulled back from the top of the spike, do we step in again and also trade the DD setup at (3), or would that be stretching our luck? If the principle of a possible 100 percent retracement holds up, then prices may just make it to ceiling of (1) about a dozen pip above. On the other hand, let us not discard the potential resistance presented by whatever went on in the ellipse earlier on. If the trade works out, then that pockets 10 pip of profit. If not, it will cause a 5 pip loss if you manage to get filled without slippage (the setup stands 2 pip tall). It's hard to say. Not having seen a test of the range breakout and with prices now in possible resistance, the odds certainly favor the tiny stop to be taken out first before the target is reached (if at all); but by what degree? The answer to that is an easy one: there is no telling. An aggressive scalper could justifiably theorize that if a 5 pip stops gets taken out twice for every time a 10 pip target is reached, he would still break even on the venture. Depending on his assessment of the technical situation, he may opt to accept the trade. A more conservative scalper, on the other hand, could simply decline the trade because he does not perceive the conditions favorable enough to put capital at risk—without ever feeling the need to figure out his odds in such a dubious environment. Why? Because he will never be able to tell anyway. The conservative scalper most likely prefers a calm state of mind over the possible long-term benefits of more aggressive scalping.

Note: Throughout most of the examples in each and every chapter, whether dealing with trade entries or trade exits, we repeatedly stumbled on situations that allowed for both aggression and prudence, which may suggest that there are two approaches to this particular scalping method, or even to trading in general: a gung-ho attitude of taking every trade in sight, and a more conservative stance that only allows for textbook trades. I will not state that this is merely an illusion, but the differences between the two throughout any scalping session may surface much less often than one might think. After all, from a technical perspective, it makes sense that in most situations both type of traders, when apt and able, will make very similar decisions, simply because there is no technical justification to do anything else. However, bear in mind that the technical edge in trading, as much as it is the key to survival in the markets, is quite a dubious phenomenon as well. In contrast, the edge in a game of roulette, just to name one, is evident. It *will* surface. In trading, however, the edge is much more a personal perception than it is a statistical certainty. And it could be totally off. In the face of such ambivalence, how could a trader ever trust his own perception and back it up with capital to boot? Quite simple: he studies, rehearses and experiences. And then he studies, rehearses and experiences some more. There is no way around it. The committed trader who is truly determined to turn his scalping ventures into a proper business will find his edge, and his own way of trading it, eventually.

Account Management

Chapter 16

Trade Volume

With the technical side of the business now behind him, the reader has but one last element to study to end his journey into the realm of professional scalping: proper account management. It is an absolutely vital ingredient to successful trading and most certainly to those who aim to turn their scalping ventures into their main source of income. Slipping up in this department can keep an otherwise promising trader stuck in the startup phase of trading for ages, if not forever, and maybe totally unnecessary.

In this chapter we will take on the interesting phenomenon of how two traders doing the exact same thing, trading the exact same method with equal funds, and taking the exact same profits out of the market, can still show mind-boggling differences in account balances after, say, a year's trading. In fact, it is not uncommon for a trader to fully negate all the hard work of profitable scalping through the mere act of sloppy accounting.

But why would that be? Isn't taking profits from the market on a consistent basis synonymous to building up an account and earning a respectable income? It depends. If the trader in question is well-capitalized and profitable to the extent that even poor accounting could not mess things up, then maybe so. However, when starting out in trading, in the majority of cases, the line between a winning operation and its non-profitable counterpart is not drawn on the safety of a flat surface

that one can easily cross back and forth; it is more like a tightrope sus-
pended in midair that demands excellent balancing skills on the part of
the novice in order to not slide down into the deep from where a fallen
trader may never return. If the average novice trader already suffers
the disadvantage of having limited resources available to him to survive
even the slope of the technical learning curve, he will most certainly
perish before his time if he has insufficient understanding of proper
accounting as well. Therefore, all of the following principles regarding
account management, though useful to traders of all kinds, are especially geared towards those scalpers who are at risk of having to quit
prematurely due to a quick depletion of already limited funds. This does
not have to be synonymous to account blowup. The simple fact that a
trader can no longer support himself may be reason enough to throw
in the towel. To avoid all that, it is recommended to get this accounting
thing down pat from the very beginning.

The good part is that the principles of proper account management
are fairly simple from a practical perspective. In essence, it just boils
down to assigning the right amount of units, also called *trade volume*, to
each and every position. That's it. There is little more you can do.

But if this indeed is such a crucial element on the road to success, and
not even hard to administer, why then is the importance of it so often
overlooked, even by those who have diligently educated themselves in
every other aspect of the field? A good question. The most logical answer
to this is that most novice and even intermediate traders are simply not
aware of the devastating effect bad accounting can have on their per-
formances. Chances are, they are too preoccupied with trying to extract
profits from the markets and avoiding the dreaded losses that they just
pay too little attention to building up their accounts gradually and cleverly. Instead, they focus more on their current daily gains and losses,
and how this relates to their immediate need for income, than on the
long-term aspect of their business.

Before we continue, it should be understood that there can never be
one absolute way of handling an account, just like there can never be
one ultimate superior method of trading the markets. Even when trading similar methods, on their path all traders will encounter different

obstacles for sure. It could be the mere limitation of available funds, a brittle comfort zone regarding risk, a non-supportive social back-up causing pressure, confidence issues, time limitations, or what have you. Therefore, the only sound thing to do when trying to bring across the principles of proper accounting to such a diverse audience is to offer a general guideline that will most probably accommodate the majority of novice and intermediate scalpers. Of course, a trader is free to go about his business in the way that he sees fit and all that is offered within the coming pages should simply be discarded if it does not suit one's needs or purposes.

Many trading manuals and particularly those dealing with trading stocks and futures, whether from an intraday or bigger frame perspective, will discourage the novice taking up the business of professional speculation when not in possession of a startup capital of at least a $100,000. Apart from the question whether it is wise to enter the market with that kind of capital as a novice, how realistic is this, really? I think it is fair to assume that not too many aspiring traders will meet this requirement, not even if we cut it in half. Of course, the benefits of being properly capitalized and the disadvantages of being undercapitalized speak for themselves. And indeed, making a 50 percent return on investment in the first year of profitable trading on a $100,000 account will most probably keep a trader alive and kicking to go at it another round. Whereas a trader working a $5,000 account, producing a similar return, would not even be able to generate enough income to cough up the rent. These are major differences in circumstances that cannot be denied. However, this is not to say that starting out small is a futile endeavor. The Forex market, like no other, can serve the smaller trader just as well as those well-funded.

Before we delve into the specifics, allow me to entertain the following comforting prospect. When risking no more than 2 percent of capital on a 10 pip stop and adhering to the upcoming accounting suggestions, it is possible to run up any account tenfold in less than a year, scoring just 5 pip per day. In fact, under ideal circumstances it would take 232 days. Copy this exact same feat for another 232 days, and the initial balance will have gone up a hundredfold. These are just mathematical facts and we will discuss them shortly hereafter.

The most important concept to grasp in proper accounting is that of the so-called *compounding factor*. In essence, it means that all new gains are to be set to work to the benefit of account buildup. The moment a relatively undercapitalized trader (say, holding an account of less than $10,000) starts to take out his weekly or monthly earnings in order to provide for himself, he will severely impair his potential to effectively build up his account. Of course, he may be fully okay with this. Yet traders who desire a larger capital to work with are strongly recommended to not take anything out until their account, at some point, has been sufficiently run up.

This does imply the necessity of having funds on the side to cover the cost of living. But that goes for all other business endeavors as well. Just ask any entrepreneur, who just opened up a little shop, for example, about his required startup capital and not to mention his monthly overhead. We can safely say that starting out in the negative is an almost obligatory handicap to the majority of new enterprises. Still, people start businesses every day. How one goes about this is a personal matter. Naturally, a solid business plan geared towards the longer term in which the inevitable expenses and startup costs are incorporated is an absolute must.

In similar fashion, as has been professed from the very onset of this book, scalping for a living is a business, too, and not an easy way out for the meek and lazy. So, likewise, a scalper needs to invest in himself and his business, like all entrepreneurs. Before he ever seriously sets foot in the trading arena, he has got to come fully prepared and with sufficient funds *on the side* to give himself plenty of room to build up his leverage. His actual account size, in a way, is of less significance. Profitable scalpers can basically run up any amount to any desirable height. Indeed, the trick is not to start out big but to become a consistently profitable scalper.

All throughout this guide the point of proper education has been thoroughly stressed and likewise it has been advocated to start out small until one manages to rake in profits on a regularly basis. This chapter is taken up to address those who have accomplished that feat, though small their consistent profits yet may be. Anyone still struggling in the learning stages of the technical side is advised to trade very, very small until finally things start to look up. Risking 2 percent of capital on a trade when not yet capable of confidently exploiting a particular edge is a surefire way to account break-down. That would be a terrible waste.

One of the major advantages of scalping is the potential for explosive account growth. Whereas most fund managers and their customers will already celebrate a solid 20 percent return on investment on a yearly basis, this simply will not do for the nimble scalper, especially when he is doing it full-time and short of capital to boot. He has to cleverly accumulate all proceeds from his trading ventures and then immediately set them to work on the next so many trades. He has got to build up volume per trade.

Risking no more than 2 percent of capital on any one venture is quite commonplace to consistently profitable traders all around. They seldom go above it. Many seasoned traders trade well below it. Whatever percentage one holds preference to, it makes sense to respect it in two ways. Not only should one not violate the chosen percentage of capital at risk, one should also apply it to each and every trade. That means putting the maximum amount of units at work that fit within that chosen percentage. When this is applied to a maximum loss of 2 percent on a 10 pip stop, we can refer to it as the *2 percent model*.

One of the ways to go about this, and the one we will explore in detail, is to do some very simple accounting on a daily basis at the end of one's session. There is no need to be busy with it while in the act of trading. At the end of the session, the volume per trade will be set to reflect the current account size in relation to one's chosen percentage of risk per trade. A scalper just types the new unit number into the preset order ticket on the trading platform, safes the setting, and the job is done.

When computing the amount of units to apply to a trade, it will not suffice to just have a 10 pip stop represent 2 percent of capital. In order to see if that is allowed, we have to take into account the leverage granted by the broker as well as the exchange rate between the euro and the dollar. Here is a quick rule of thumb: with an exchange rate below 2.000 (1 euro equaling 2 dollars), a leverage of 40:1 will always allow us to set a 10 pip stop to represent 2 percent of capital.

Let us look at the contract specifications of the eur/usd to see how this is derived. The eur/usd contract is made up of a base currency (eur) and a quote currency (usd). A full contract of 100,000 units represents a value of $100,000 x current exchange rate. So if the rate stands at 1.5000, a full contract has a value of $150,000 which equals €100,000. To calculate the value of 1 pip on a full contract of the eur/usd, have a look at the following example. If the rate stands at 1.2500, it means that €100,000 equal $125,000. If the rate goes up a 100 pip, it will stand at 1.2600. This means that €100,000 now equal $126,000, a $1000 increase due to a 100 pip rise. That means that on a full contract, 1 pip always equals $10, regardless of the current rate.

Let us now look at a practical example of a trader running a $5,000 account. On his trades, he wants a stop to represent 2 percent of capital, which would be $100 on a $5,000 account. On a 10 pip stop this allows each pip to have a value of $10. On a full contract of 100,000 units, as explained above, a pip also equals $10. That means this trader would like to buy a full contract. But is he allowed? It depends on his broker and the current exchange rate. Let us say the current rate stands at 1.5000. A full contract now represents $150,000. Since there is only $5,000 in the account, a minimum leverage of 30:1 is needed in order to purchase it. Likewise, with a rate standing at 2,000 (at the time of writing this has yet to occur), a trader needs a leverage of 40:1. Fortunately, since most brokers grant a leverage of at least 50:1, in most instances the 2 percent model on a 10 pip stop can be applied without any broker margin problems.

Of course, there is no necessity to apply a 2 percent model. If this kind of risk surpasses either a trader's comfort zone or his current state of proficiency, then lowering it would be a good idea. Many traders adhere to the more conservative 1 percent model, or anything in between.

Let us now incorporate the compounding factor into the example above. At the start of the day, our trader's $5,000 account bought him 100,000 units per trade. Assuming he only took one trade and closed it out for a profit of 10 pip, then at the close of his session his account balance will now show $5,100. In order to use 2 percent of capital on a 10 pip stop the following session, he now has to raise his volume a certain amount of units to correspond with the risen account balance. This is extremely easy. All he needs to do is take out his calculator, type in his account balance and multiply by the factor of his risk model times 10. (The factor 10 in this equation is derived from dividing 100 by the number of pip in the stop; theoretically, a 1 pip stop requires a factor 100; a 12,5 pip stop, for example, requires a factor 8, and so on.) So initially this trader started out at 5000 x 2 x 10 = 100,000 units. The following day he will start out with 5100 x 2 x 10 = 102,000 units, which is 2,000 units more than the day before. A trader using a 1 percent risk model will start out with 5000 x 1 x 10 = 50,000 units. A 10 pip gain for the day results in a $50 profit. The next day he starts out with 5050 x 1 x 10 = 50,500 units, which is 500 units more than the day before.

From the standpoint of calculating units, it is irrelevant whether our trader actually made a profit or loss that day. Whatever the account size, just multiply by the factor of the risk model times 10. If the account has fallen in value, less units will be set to work the next day. As we can see, the marvel of the compounding factor has a double function. It not only allows for exponential account growth in the event of consistently profitable results, it also safeguards a trader from exceeding his allowable risk by immediately cutting down on his volume per trade.

Note: All of the above is based on an account denominated in U.S dollars. Should a scalper hold an account in, for example, euros, then he also has to apply a conversion factor. The most simple way to do this is to calculate his unit size as if holding an account in U.S dollars and then multiply the amount of units by whatever the current rate between the two currencies is. If it stands at 1.4200, then he just multiplies the new amount of units by 1.42. Naturally, this is just to get close, because during any session the rate will fluctuate. That's all part and parcel of the currency game. With that in mind, it would probably make more sense to calculate the new volume right before a new session than at the end of one, since the rate may fluctuate in between.

Should this juggling of numbers initially appear to be somewhat cumbersome, with a little practice it is actually one of the easiest tasks in the field of professional scalping. It takes no more than a moment to compute, but the benefits are enormous. This way, in the Forex market, a trader can gradually build up his volume per trade (and his account balance in the process) almost without noticing the psychological pressure that may accompany the application of bigger volume.

Next to adjusting the amount of units based on the daily profit or loss, when profitable on the whole, a trader can also slowly raise his chosen risk level. For example, he can start out on a 1 percent model and then raise it to 1,1 in the next week and then to 1,2 and so on, until he hits the 2 percent mark. It is all about gradually building up volume until one really feels confident enough to apply the 2 percent model.

Although at first glance it may not seem to make that much of a difference to raise volume on a daily basis, the effect it can have on one's account can be quite extensive. Let us compare two hypothetical and highly theoretical situations to look at this more closely. Trader A, oblivious to the marvel of compounding, runs a $10,000 account, scores 5 pip per day for 200 consecutive days. Trader B, also runs a $10,000 account and takes 5 pip out of the market for 200 days on end. But he will apply the compounding factor at the end of each session.

Trader A consistently takes out $100 each day (5 pip on the 2 percent model on a $10,000 account) which will result in $20,000 of profit after 200 days, bringing his account up to $30,000.

If you deem that respectable, take a look at what Trader B would have accomplished in the same period of time, taking a similar 5 pip per day out of the market. His balance will show a whopping $73,160. Bear in mind, both traders did exactly the same. In fact, we could even suggest that trader A and B are the same person, theoretically unawares of their volume per trade; they just hired different accountants.

Of course, in all fairness, we could argue that it is highly unlikely for Trader A not to have raised his volume somewhere down the line. Surely his growing account will have not gone unnoticed and this will have led him to put more volume towards his trades. That is all very true, but when exactly would he have applied this? After a week, a month? After three winning days? It remains to be seen whether this trader would have had a sound view on these matters, particularly so when already ignorant to the benefits of compounding.

If you think it is quite unlikely for a winning trader to remain stuck on the same volume for ages, consider the following. Imagine yourself someone trading one contract in the E-mini futures, for example. At some point this trader will have to face the psychological hurdle of having to raise his volume with no less than a hundred percent when going from one to two contracts. Because there lies nothing in between. That can be quite hefty on one's comfort zone. And it may not even be justifiable from the standpoint of allowable or preferable risk per trade.

The Forex market, on the other hand, allows a trader unlimited flexibility. Traders are free to use whatever volume they like. They do not have to start out on a full contract of 100,000 units, nor are they forced to raise their volume to 200,000 in case they want to move up a notch. They could start out as small as 1 unit if they so desire and adjust it whenever it suits them. When such flexibility is offered, it is best to accept! It allows a scalper to meticulously build up his volume, and so his account, without disrespecting his model by either having to trade too light or too heavy.

Naturally, there is a mathematical formula regarding the compounding factor to compute one's growth projections into the future. It is best not to bother with it. A smarter way is to find a *Compound Interest Calculator* on the web. There are many of them freely available. Find a simple one that only compounds interest annually (not quarterly). Since these calculators are designed for annual calculations, you have to discard the Years-to-Grow box and read it as if it says Days-to-Grow. You only have to type in three entries: Current Principal (your account balance), Days-to-Grow (the amount of days you want to project) and Interest Rate (fill in 1 percent when projecting 5 pip per day on a 2 percent model; to project, say, 10 pip of daily profit into the future, type in 2 percent). If it asks you for an Annual Addition, just set it to 0. Some calculators do not allow you to type in more than 40 days (years, basically). Just find another one that does. If you got it right then a random example should look like this: Current principal ($5,000); Days-to-Grow (200); Interest rate (1); Future Value ($36,580.09). The Future value is the compounded amount after 200 consecutive days of winning 5 pip, risking 2 percent of capital on a 10 pip stop (2 percent model).

To fully understand the double function of the compounding factor, and a good reason to immediately start applying it, is to project 200 consecutive days of *losing* 5 pip on a 2 percent model on a $5,000 account, so in essence the exact opposite of the above. That will leave a trader with a capital of $669.90. To compute this, type in –1 in the Interest Rate box. What's more, if we double this unfortunate trader's misery by letting him lose 10 pip a day for 200 consecutive trading days using the same model and the same original balance of $5,000, then his account, though fully decimated, would still show a positive figure of $87.94. Now all of this is not about numbers. It just serves to point out the necessity of smart accounting. For winning as well as losing in the market.

It should be stressed that these *exact* calculations, derived from a Compound Interest Calculator, will differ from reality, even if one scores a certain amount of pip per day on average. This is due to fluctuations between winning and losing trades. To put it in another way, if you make 5 pip on a day, raise volume as discussed and then lose 5 pip in the next session, the account will show a tiny loss. Because the 5 pip of the losing day was lost on bigger volume. Similarly, if one loses 5 pip on a first day, lowers volume and then wins 5 pip on the next, the account will show a tiny loss as well. Because the winnings from the second day were obtained with less volume. There is no way around it. But is it really that relevant? To a consistently profitable trader these fluctuations are quite insignificant, although they can add up in the long run. The most important issue is being consistent in both one's trading and accounting.

This does raise an interesting question, though. Why not adjust volume on each and every trade? Would that not make even more sense. Theoretically yes, practically no. A scalper is best advised to focus on his trading during his sessions and not busy himself with computing units, monitoring the level of his balance or any other accounting activity. Should a trader work on a high-tech platform that automatically adjusts his volume in correspondence with a certain percentage model, then, by all means, apply it. Also, in the event of a bad streak within a particular session, a scalper starting out with volume that represents a chosen percentage of risk per trade will be exceeding this percentage during the session. The more his account loses in value, the more his *volume of the day* runs out of line with his allowable risk. A scalper can do two things: just accept it for the day, or draw the line somewhere intraday and adjust. The idea of smart accounting is not necessarily to reap every possible penny out of a particular play, nor to protect the account to the point of paranoia. It is just an approach to serve a trader's best interests over the longer term. Without the least amount of effort, we may add.

Note: When playing around with the Compound Interest Calculator, it is very tempting to project your numbers unrealistically. Depending on your daily imagined objective, the calculator may come up with astronomical figures. For example, 10 pip a day compounded will take a paltry $2,000 account to surpass the magical mark of a million in just 314 trading days. Do take heed, though. The moment a scalper enters into the realm of unrealistic fantasies, he will be setting himself up for disappointment and unnecessary stress. The sole purpose of incorporating the compounding factor into one's volume is to cleverly run up an account and to be protected from excessive loss in case of a bad streak.

What is doable and undoable in terms of pip per day and future projections is a pointless discussion. At all times, this depends on the trader and not on mathematics. Fact remains that at some point we have no option but to assume that taking profits from the market on a regularly basis is feasible and thus an acceptable goal to pursue. Or else we might as well not bother. Taking an average of 2 pip per day out of the market—just 10 pip per week—will already double any account in about 35 weeks using the 2 percent model and the compounding factor. To a nimble and well-educated scalper this should not be too hard to accomplish. It also goes to show that once a trader succeeds in building up his account to a reasonable level, the necessity to score a lot of pip on a daily basis becomes less and less essential. It is more a matter of volume.

Whatever a scalper's goals, whether he strives for astronomical returns or just wants to make a living as an independent trader, he would be seriously depriving himself when not applying the compounding factor to his volume per trade. This does raise the question, though, of when to start taking profits from an account; after all, surely a scalper would like to see some of his hard earned profits materialize in his personal bank account, too. Furthermore, somewhere down the line, a scalper may even have to switch brokers in the fortunate event of explosive growth, because the more his account blooms to pleasurable height, so will his volume per trade and not all retail brokers could handle such volume. These are indeed some luxury problems a profitable scalper will have to solve for himself in due time. They are nice problems to have, though.

Chapter 17

Words of Caution

Whether just touching on the basics or delving into the core of the matter, to the novice there will be educational value in almost each and every trading guide. A reader should bear in mind, though, that whatever is professed, stated and sometimes even presented as fundamental facts, it merely represents an author's view on things, and quite a personal one at that. Unlike many other professions, in the field of trading the rules of the road tend to be quite elusive, if not already shady to begin with. There is no scientific evidence to back them up, nor can there ever be one definitive way to apply them. Methods and strategies are as plentiful as there are traders around and who is to say what works and what not. Just one glance at any chart will lay bare the enormous diversity in opinion and perception. No matter how sound a particular approach and regardless its wonderful statistical record, in the bigger scheme of things it is nothing other than a snapshot of personal observation. Whatever seemed evident in the past, the future may and probably will defy it.

Fortunately, in contrast with the transitory nature of strategy and tactics, the universal law of supply and demand has proven way more resilient. It has been the foundation beneath all sound trading methods, and, no doubt, so will it continue to support all those yet to be designed. For a trader to understand its concept there is no need for a degree in economics. He just needs a chart. And in it, he needs no indicators that could ever reveal what his eyes would not be able to see for themselves. Although the chart may not tell him where to buy and sell, it will clearly show him when to stay out. The path of most resistance is paved with pain and hardship of all those who ventured out against the tide. To not follow in their footsteps, an aspiring trader has no option but to educate himself to the point of exhaustion. Every chart in this guide will hopefully have contributed to the reader's understanding of price action principles; and all of the entry and exit techniques discussed will surely have served to enhance his idea on how to tell a favorable proposition from its unfavorable counterpart. But even so, that is not enough. Because a trader's education never stops.

Even when taking a serious liking to the method offered in this work, the necessity of countless hours of studying, testing and verifying on historical as well as *current* charts should be taken to heart. And when it's finally time to hit the markets, reality may soon point out that it may not be time yet. Tread lightly in all of your real-time endeavors until you truly feel confident to take your volume up. Study carefully all your mistakes and take note of your mental state as well. Some scalping days are like a walk in the park, others may drag you through an emotional hell. If you are still affected by the inevitable losses, lower your volume to the point of indifference. Trade only these setups that you can truly justify with heart and soul. If you are uncertain whether to display aggression or prudence, simply opt for a more conservative mode. As time goes by, your skills *will* sharpen. Until then, study diligently and then study some more. In times of adversity, tell yourself that you can do it. Great traders are not born and they are not created, either. They create themselves.

enjoy your trading,

Bob Volman, Sept. 2011

About the Author

Bob Volman (1961) is an independent trader, working solely for his own account. Highly skilled in reading and playing the faster chart, he has now bundled all his knowledge and craftsmanship in this extensive guide on intraday tactics. The book is written to accommodate all aspiring traders who aim to go professional and who want to prepare themselves as thoroughly as possible for the task ahead. *Forex Price Action Scalping* opens up a wealth of information and shares insights and techniques that can only be offered by someone who actually operates in the heart of the trading arena: a professional scalper.

Mr. Volman can be reached at the address below.

infoFPAS@gmail.com

Free *excerpts* of the book can be downloaded from:

www.infoFPAS.wordpress.com

Glossary

Absolute Extreme In the top barrier of a range, it is a high a little higher than the majority of highs; in the bottom barrier, a low a little lower than the majority of lows.

Advanced Range Break Setup One of the seven setups discussed in this work and one of three on range break tactics. Creates entries in the barrier area of a broken range.

Aggressive Scalping This style makes little distinction between textbook setups and slightly questionable entries. Can be very profitable in the long run if consistently executed. Not for the faint of heart.

Aggressive Trailing Trailing a stop very close to the current price at the risk of a premature exit.

Always-on-top *See* Order Ticket.

American Session One of the three sessions that make up the 24-hour market in the foreign exchange. The others being the Asian and European sessions.

ARB *See* Advanced Range Break Setup.

Arch Arch-like formation of price bars. Also called a shoulder, as in a head-and-shoulders formation. If the arch is formed upside down, it is referred to as a cup or handle, as in a cup-and-handle formation.

Asian Session One of the three sessions that make up the 24-hour market in the foreign exchange. The others being the American and European Sessions.

Automated Order A preset order to be automatically executed by the platform.

Average *See* Moving Average.

Awkward Stop A protective stop put in at a level that does not technically invalidate the open position.

Backing and Filling Aimless price action in the chart, offering little opportunities.

Bailing out Exiting an open position.

Bar Price Bar. A graphic representation of prices moving vertically within a particular setting. Its duration can be constructed based on a trader's personal preference. It contains the opening and closing price, as well as the absolute high and low reached within the duration of the setting. Also called a candle.

Barrier A horizontal line drawn across a number of equal highs or lows.

Barrier Bounce Prices bouncing off of horizontal support or resistance.

Base Currency First currency in a currency pair. The second one is called the Quote Currency. On the eur/usd, the value of the pair in the denomination of the base currency (euro) is equal to the amount of units. A full contract of 100,000 units represents €100,000. The value of the pair in the denomination of the quote currency is the determined by multiplying the number of units with the actual rate. For example, a eur/usd rate of 1.4500 means that 1 euro buys 1,45 dollar. Therefore, a full contract of 100,000 units would represent a value of 100,000 x 1,45, so $145,000.

BB *See* Block Break Setup.

Bear Trader with a bearish view on the market. Playing his positions to profit from falling prices.

Bear Market Chart that shows more supply than demand, overall resulting in falling prices.

Bear Trap Professional bulls trapping amateur bears. By showing no enthusiasm to defend a particular support level, allowing it to crack, bulls trick bears into shorting the market. Once the bears get filled, powerful bulls immediately start to buy prices back up.

Big Players All professional parties that actually move the market with their buying and selling in large quantities. These could be banks, central banks, hedge funds, institutions and the such.

Bid-Ask Spread Difference between the price to buy at and the price to sell at. Works to the benefit of the broker.

Block A cluster or group of bars printed close together without price changing much. At least one side of the block will show some equal extremes that define a clear level of resistance or support.

Block Break Setup One of the seven setups discussed in this work. It can be found in almost any market environment and is used to anticipate a break of a block formation.

Body A term used in candlestick charting. The body of a candle (bar) shows all prices between the open and close of the bar. A bearish candle has a close lower than the open; a bullish candle has a close higher than the open. It would depend on a chartist's personal preference how these bodies are colored in the chart to tell a bearish bar from a bullish one. Among many chartists it is common practice to paint the bearish bars darker than the bullish bars. Next to a body, a bar can also have one or two tails. *See* Tail.

Boomerang Effect Tendency of prices to bounce back and forth between very clear levels of resistance and support.

Bottom A spot from which falling prices bounced up.

Bottom Fishing The act of picking up prices at a perceived bottom or at the level of the last prominent bottom.

Bottoming Market After a substantial decline, the chart starts to show a series of more or less equal bottoms, suggesting demand.

Bottoming Pattern A series of bars forming a bottom or multiple bottoms, suggesting demand.

Bounce Prices bouncing up in a level of support, or bouncing down in a level of resistance.

Boundary *See* Barrier.

Box Rectangle drawn in the chart around a block of prices, or wrapped around a bigger range formation.

Bracket Order Automated order, preset with a target order on one side and a stop order on the other. Is automatically attached to the level of entry. If one side of the bracket gets filled, the other is immediately canceled. Also referred to as OCO (one-cancels-the-other).

Break Prices breaking above a significant level of resistance or below a significant level of support. Could also be the simple break of an earlier bar's extreme.

Break-even Stop A typical amateur folly. A stop set at the level of entry to protect a profitable position from ever turning into a loss. In most cases, the level of this stop is technically not defensible.

Breakout Prices breaking away from a particular pattern in which they were contained.

Breakout Strategy A style of trading that aims to play breakouts.

Broker A company that provides traders access to the markets.

Buildup A cluster of bars or a narrow sideways formation underneath a resistance level or on top of a support level. Often leads to a breakout.

Bull Trader with a bullish view on the market. Playing his positions to profit from rising prices.

Bull/Bear Fight Visible clash in the chart between bulls and bears.

Bull Flag A classic technical chart pattern in an uptrend. The flagpole in this pattern is represented by the climbing trend, the flag is portrayed by a small number of sideways drifting bars, starting from the top of the pole, slowly angling down. Is commonly looked upon as a continuation pattern, meaning that the trend is expected to revive when the flag formation gets broken to the upside.

Bull Market Chart showing more demand than supply, overall resulting in higher prices.

Bull Trap Professional bears trapping amateur bulls. By showing no enthusiasm to defend a particular resistance level, allowing it to crack, bears trick bulls into buying the market. Once the bulls get filled, powerful bears immediately start to short prices back down.

Burnt-finger Anxiety Reluctance to act on a valid situation due to a recent loss.

Buy back a Short The act of closing out a short position by buying back what was sold earlier on.

Buy Order An order that will initiate a long position or close out a short.

Buy Signal A signal, according to one's strategy, that indicates a good spot to take a long position or to buy back a short.

Candle *See* Bar.

Candlestick Charting Style of trading that derives signals from the mere shape of a price bar (candle) or a small group of price bars.

Ceiling Test Prices testing the ceiling of an arch from below, or testing the floor of a reversed arch (cup) from above. The test often marks the final point of a correction.

Charting The process of using a technical chart for price evaluation.

Charting Software Provider Company that provides traders with the technical tools to translate incoming data into customizable charts.

Chart Resistance A perceived level of resistance in the chart which may block prices from traveling higher.

Chart Support A perceived level of support in the chart which may block prices from traveling lower.

Cherry-picking To pick and choose between valid entries.

Choppy Market Prices moving aimlessly back and forth in a narrow vertical span, sending out very few clues as to the possible future direction of the market.

Clues Technical feats displayed in the chart that may aid a trader in assessing the current environment.

Close/ Closing Price The last price in a particular bar before a new bar opens.

Cluster A group of neighboring bars contained in a narrow vertical span.

Commission Fee to be paid to a broker for executing a trade.

Commission Type Broker A broker that charges a fee for order execution.

Compounding Gradually building up volume by raising the unit size each new day with the same percentage as the account has moved up in value the previous day. Works the other way as well (taking off volume if the previous day showed a loss).

Compounding Factor Formally: a formula to work out compound interest. By replacing the percentage of interest in the formula with an average expected percentage of profit, to be compounded, a trader could theoretically work out his future account balance. *See also* Compounding and Compound Interest Calculator.

Compound Interest Calculator Calculator normally used to calculate the accumulation of interest on a certain amount of capital over time. Can also be used to project one's future account balance based on an average profit per time unit in combination with compounding volume.

Congestion *See* Consolidation.

Conservative Scalping This style takes a more conservative stance when confronted with opportunities that do not present themselves in textbook fashion.

Consistency The ability to produce consistent results.

Consolidation Prices contained within a narrow band, typical for a non-trending market.

Continuation Pattern Often a somewhat sideways formation in an established trend and anticipated to be eventually broken in with-trend direction.

Contract A measurement of a certain amount of volume.

Contrarian *See* Countertrend Trader.

Correction *See* Pullback.

Countertrend A price swing against the prevailing trend.

Countertrend Trader Trader that operates against the most dominant pressure in the chart.

Covering The act of flattening an existing position. The term is mostly used in relation to the covering of shorts.

Cup-and-Handle Pattern (Cup-with-Handle) A classic technical chart pattern made up of two reversed arches, the first (cup) usually bigger than the second (handle). When broken topside, a strong reaction may follow in the direction of the break.

Currency Pair Two currencies traded against each other.

Daily Chart Very popular chart in which each price bar displays the high and low and the open and close of that particular day. Of little relevance to scalpers.

Data Feed Provider Company supplying transaction data, either as a stand-alone package, or in combination with a charting software package.

DD *See* Double Doji Setup.

Dealing Quote Current price of an instrument. Consists of a bid price to sell at, and an ask price to buy at.

Demand Willingness of participants to buy themselves into the market or cover existing short positions. Causes upward pressure on prices.

Distribution of Outcomes The random order in which losing and winning trades alternate. To be examined over a longer period of time.

Doji A price bar with an opening price equal or similar to its closing price.

Dominant Bottom/ Top Bottom or top in a chart that stands out as more significant when compared to other bottoms and tops in that same chart.

Double Bottom A pattern made up of two bottoms with their lows equal or very close to each other.

Double Doji Setup One of the seven setups discussed in this work. It is made up of two or more neighboring dojis at the end of a possible pullback to a trend. When broken in the direction of the trend, a trader may play the market in that same direction. It is therefore called a with-trend setup.

Double Pressure When bulls enter and bears exit, both parties do the same: they buy. Similarly, when bears enter and bulls exit, both parties do the same as well: they sell. In either case, this unanimous behavior creates double pressure on prices. At crucial spots this can lead to fresh one-directional moves.

Double Top A pattern made up of two tops with their highs equal or very close to each other.

Downtrend Prices trending down.

Downward Break Prices breaking support.

Early-Bird A trader who anticipates a certain movement but acts before a valid signal comes along.

Edge A perceived technical advantage based on a trader's ability to read the markets. In essence, a trader's only weapon in playing the markets for profit. In probability theory, a particular edge can be mathematically derived and statistically justified. In trading, having an edge is highly controversial and often a false assumption. Hence the failure of most methods.

EMA *See* Exponential Moving Average.

Entry The price at which a position gets filled.

Entry Bar The bar in which a position gets filled.

European Session One of the three sessions that make up the 24-hour market of the foreign exchange. The others being the Asian and American sessions.

Eur/usd Pair Currency pair made up of the euro and the U.S. dollar.

Exit Level at which an open position gets closed.

Exponential Moving Average A technical indicator that calculates the average price of a chosen number of closing prices; in computing the average, a little more weight is assigned to the most recent changes in price.

False Break After initially putting in a break, the market quickly travels in the opposite direction again.

False Break Trap A spot where traders with little understanding of proper break buildup often get trapped by clever traders countering the break. Very often seen in the barrier areas of a range.

False Perceptions Typical human follies that tend to surface on the brink of having to take a trade or while in position, causing traders to make the wrong decisions.

Favorable Conditions The underlying price action of the overall market supporting a potential setup.

FB *See* First break Setup.

50-level/ 50 Round Number Half cent level, one of the two most actively anticipated levels in the chart. The other one being the full cent level. *See* 00 Round Number.

50 Percent Retracement A correction in the chart taking back about half of the length of an earlier trend or swing.

Fill An executed order.

First Break Setup One of the seven setups discussed in this work. It sets itself up in the possible end of a pullback to a very abrupt trend. The moment a price bar in the pullback gets broken in the direction of the trend, a trader anticipates a possible trend resumption by immediately entering in that same direction. A with-trend setup.

First Test of Support/ Resistance Prices pulling back to a broken support or resistance level for the first time after the break. Often used as an entry level by those who missed the break or by those who want to add to open positions.

Fishhook Pattern A strong move followed by a sharp diagonal pullback.

Flattening a Position To buy back a short or to sell out a long in order to have no position in the market (being flat).

Follow-through Sideline traders stepping into the market in reaction to a particular market event (like that of a break, for example).

Foreign Exchange A non-centralized global market system in which currencies are exchanged (traded) against one another.

Forex Short for Foreign Exchange.

Formation A somewhat larger number of price bars that together form a technical pattern.

Front-running Trading prematurely without waiting for a proper signal.

Full Contract In the foreign exchange, this equals a position of 100,000 units. On the eur/usd it represents a €100,000. The value in dollar denomination depends on the exchange rate of the moment. As the number of units always remain the same during a trade, their tradable value will fluctuate depending on the actual exchange rate. *See* Base Currency for an example.

Fundamental Analysis The process of evaluating a market based on macro-economical information or on specific information regarding the underlying instrument.

Gap The difference between the closing price of one bar and the opening price of the next.

Going Long Taking a position in the market that will prosper when price travels up.

Going Short Taking a position in the market that will prosper when price travels down.

Handle A reversed arch formation as part of a cup-and-handle pattern. Usually somewhat smaller than the cup formation that precedes it.

Head-and-Shoulders Pattern A classic technical chart pattern made up of three arches, the middle one standing taller than the arches on either side. Perceived to be a strong indication of a topping market about to reverse.

Hesitance Reluctance of prices to act on a break without the break immediately being countered and proven false.

High A spot in the chart from which price moved down.

Higher Bottom A low in the chart at a higher level than a previous low.

Higher High A high in the chart at a higher level than a previous high.

Higher Low *See* Higher Bottom.

Higher Top *See* Higher High.

Horizontal Barrier *See* Barrier.

Indicators Technical tools found within a charting package to assist a trader in his technical trading decisions. Usually based on algorithmic computing of the last so many prices. Their practical usefulness is highly controversial.

Inside Range Break Setup One of the seven setups discussed in this work and one of three on range break tactics. Is used to play breaks inside a range.

Instrument A market to trade.

Intraday Moves Price moves in a chart between open and close of a particular day. The shorter the time or tick frame, the more explicit these moves show up in a chart.

Invalid Trade An open position that needs to be scratched due to a technical development that negates its validity.

IRB *See* Inside Range Break Setup.

Jumping-the-gun *See* Front-running.

Last Arch Last in a series of arches that share the same support. Is often used to set a protective stop above. In case the arches are reversed, the stop will be placed below the last reversed arch.

Leeway *See* Wiggle Room.

Leverage Next to using one's own capital, extra funds can be borrowed from the broker in order to trade bigger volume. A leverage of 100:1 means the broker allows the trader to work with a capital 100 times as big as his personal funds. The leverage factor depends on the broker in question. In Forex, a minimum leverage of 50:1 is quite commonplace.

Limit Order An order set to be filled at a specified price.

Long/ Long Position/ Long Trade A position initiated to profit from rising prices.

Long-term Chart Chart representing the bigger picture. Often a daily or weekly time frame chart.

Loss A failed trade exited for a loss.

Low A spot in the chart from which price moved up.

Lower Bottom A low in the chart at a lower level than a previous low.

Lower High A high in the chart at a lower level than a previous high.

Lower Low *See* Lower Bottom.

Lower Top *See* Lower high.

Lunch-hour Doldrums Non-active market phases, usually resulting in choppy price action contained in a narrow range.

Magnet Effect *See* Vacuum Effect.

Manual Order An order initiated by a click of the mouse.

Margin Required capital to initiate a new position with a certain amount of volume; or the funds necessary to maintain an already existing position that loses in value. Determined by broker regulations.

Market A tradable instrument. The total of buyers and sellers active on an instrument.

Market order An order to enter or exit at the current price in the market (as opposed to a limit order that needs to be filled at a specified price). Prone to be filled with slippage in a relatively fast market. On the good side, this order is always filled.

Mark-up Artificial widening of the spread between the bid and ask. Common practice among retail brokers during very active markets. Could seriously hurt scalpers who depend on ultra-tight spreads.

Method A carefully constructed plan of attack to trade the market.

Mini Contract A tenth of a full contract. Equals a position of 10,000 units. On the eur/usd pair it represents a value of €10,000. In the denomination of dollars it represents 10,000 multiplied by the current exchange rate. *See* Base Currency for more detailed information.

Missed Entry A valid entry missed by a trader. A common occurrence for various reasons.

Momentum Strong sign of directional pressure visible in the chart.

Moving Average An indicator that computes the average closing price of a certain amount of price bars. The current price in relation to the average price (the indicator above or below it) may provide a trader with information on the presence or absence of market pressure or direction. Can be set to compute the average of any desirable number of closing prices.

M-pattern A distinctive topping formation represented by two tops that together form the letter M. Can be rather sharp with the tops close together, but also more elongated across a wider horizontal span. Is perceived to be a reversal pattern (bearish).

Multiple Bottoms A series of more or less equal bottoms.

Multiple-Head-and-Shoulders Formation A head-and-shoulders formation that deviates from the original by showing more tops (arches) than the classic three.

Multiple Tops A series of more or less equal tops.

Neckline Horizontal barrier running below a head-and-shoulders formation or a series of arches. Clearly indicates support. When broken, a sharp reaction may follow.

Non-buildup Break A breakout with little or no buildup preceding it. Highly prone to be countered.

No-commission Broker Broker that charges no fees for executing orders. Makes profit through spread mark-up.

Obvious Event A price technical event that complies with a trader's current view on the market.

OCO One-Cancels-the-Other. *See* Bracket Order.

Odd Event A price technical event that does not comply with a trader's current view on the market. Can sometimes be more telling than the obvious event.

One-directional Move A firm price swing that finds little or no countertrend activity on its path.

1-percent Model A risk-model that allows for a loss of 1 percent of capital on any one trade.

1-2-3 Formation *See* Cup-and-Handle formation.

Online Broker Broker that allows traders to trade independently through an online platform with no broker intervention.

Open The opening price of a new bar.

Open Position An active position in the market that has not yet been closed out.

Order A means to get in or out of the market. Can be personalized to reflect a certain volume and a number of other settings as well. In this scalping method we only use the standard Market Order to get in or out manually, a Limit Order solely for exiting on target automatically, and a Bracket Order that automatically attaches the stop and target orders to any open position. The stop as part of the bracket is also a Market Order, but it only serves the purpose of a safety net. Almost any faltering trade will be exited manually before this stop order gets hit.

Order Ticket A detachable window on the trading platform to buy and sell a pre-set amount of units through. A good platform will allow a trader to run this ticket *always-on-top*, meaning it can be placed as a little window on top of the chart without ever disappearing behind it. Can be used to enter as well as exit a trade.

Overbought Extended bullish rally, ready for a bearish correction.

Oversold Extended bearish rally, ready for a bullish correction.

Papertrade Account Virtual account that allows a novice trader to get a feel for the game and learn the specifics of order execution and the such. Order fills do not reflect market reality. Once accustomed to the basics, it is recommended to use a real account and trade very low volume.

Path-of-least-resistance Prices traveling in a certain direction with little chart resistance in sight.

Path-of-most-resistance Prices heading into chart resistance.

Pattern A recognizable order in which a number of price bars are being displayed. Extensive study has shown the nature of the market to be highly repetitive. Patterns are commonly known to hand a trader specific clues about the market's intentions.

Perceptual Folly A trader's misguided view on reality based on all sort of emotions.

Usually detrimental to the decision-making process.

Pip Price Interest Point (also plural). A unit for measuring the movement in price within a currency pair. Displayed as the fourth decimal in a dealing quote of the eur/usd. 100 pip make up a full cent. One pip is divided by 10 pipettes.

Pipettes A tenth of a pip. Displayed as the fifth and final decimal in a dealing quote of the eur/usd. The smallest increment in price change.

Play A certain strategy or tactic.

Positive Expectancy A concept of importance in a probability play that is to be evaluated over a longer period of time. When the total loss is subtracted from the total gain and the outcome is a positive number, then the play in question is said to have a positive expectancy. Of course, all has to comply with certain strategy rules and requirements.

Pre-breakout Tension *See* Buildup.

Premature Break A break set without the underlying conditions being totally in favor of the break's direction, or with very little buildup preceding the break.

Pressure Underlying forces supporting a particular direction, either with prices on the move or building up towards a break.

Price Action The total of price moves on a technical chart from which to derive trading decisions. Traders who solely trade price action will have their charts stripped to the absolute bare minimum. They just watch price bars.

Price Action Principles All technical aspects concerning the repetitive nature of price behavior.

Price Bar *See* Bar.

Probability Play A betting venture that is participated in on the grounds of favorable odds.

Probability Principle If one perceives the odds in a particular wager to be favorable (having an edge), then placing the bet is the right thing to do, regardless of the outcome. This is a very simplified way of approaching the complex matter of probability. Bear in mind that in trading, the idea of having an edge may very well be a false assumption. Quite unlike the casino owner's edge in a game of roulette, for instance. However, from a trader's perspective, the edge is best regarded as a statistical fact for as long as it takes to make a proper assessment on its validity.

Profit-and-Loss Window A window in which the results of all closed out trades and/ or the current status of any open positions are displayed. In the act of trading it is best to hide it from view.

Protective Stop An order, either pending physically or mentally, to close out an open position that fails to deliver.

Pullback A price swing that travels against the prevailing trend. Usually somewhat diagonal in shape, but can also manifest itself more horizontally.

Quote *See* Dealing Quote.

Quote Currency Second currency in a currency pair. *See* Base Currency for a more detailed explanation.

Rally A firm move with little or no pullbacks in it, or showing pullbacks of very short duration.

Range Prices swinging up and down between a horizontal level of support and a horizontal level of resistance.

Range Barrier/ Boundary *See* Barrier.

Range Break Setup One of the seven setups discussed in this work and one of three on range break tactics. This one deals with barriers that are technically very well respected and then ultimately broken in orderly fashion.

Range Breakout Prices breaking away from a range by cracking a barrier.

RB *See* Range Break Setup.

Reaction Traders reacting to a certain event. Either to protect themselves or to profit from the new situation.

Rectangle *See* Box.

Resistance becomes Support A former resistance level now offering support when touched from above.

Resistance A level or area from which prices previously bounced down (new chart resistance). Also, a level or area, yet to be touched, from which prices may bounce down (former chart support).

Retail Broker Company that facilitates the trading ventures of the smaller trader. Usually on a no-commission model and with little demands as to a trader's required startup capital. Makes profit through spread mark-up.

Retail Trader Term for a trader trading from his home through an online platform, usually that of a retail broker.

Retracement *See* Pullback.

Retracement Level The actual size of the pullback in relation to the trend it is countering. Retracement levels of 40, 50 and 60 percent are often welcomed in a solid trend and used for with-trend plays.

Reversal Pattern A pattern that forebodes a possible reversal of the current directional pressure. Head-and-shoulders formations, cup-and-handle patterns, double tops and double bottoms are all classic examples of impending reversal. They do not always live up to their reputation, though.

Reversed-Cup-and-Handle Pattern A cup-and-handle pattern upside-down. A break to the downside may cause a sharp reaction (lower prices).

Reversed-Head-and-Shoulders Pattern A head-and-shoulders pattern upside-down. A break to the upside may cause a sharp reaction (higher prices).

Risk Model A chosen percentage of capital to be risked on each venture.

Round Number Level In the currency charts several round number levels can be detected. The 50-level and the 00-level being the most prominent. These levels often curb further advance or decline, if only temporarily. They can be heavily attacked as well as defended and we often see many ranges built around them. Somewhat inferior round number levels, but definitely worth monitoring, are the so-called 20-levels (20, 40, 60 and 80). Many strategies are designed to exploit the repetitive way in which prices tend to bounce off of round number levels, or on the way they are sucked towards them. *See* Vacuum Effect.

Round-turn A position opened and closed again.

Running Trade An open position.

Scalper A very technically oriented trader trading a very short-term chart.

SB *See* Second Break Setup.

Scratch A manually exited trade.

Second Break Setup One of the seven setups discussed in this work. Displays itself as a with-trend setup in either a newborn or an already established trend. It is based on the premise that a first break at the possible end of a pullback is often countered, and therefore skipped, but that a second break is likely to find follow-through in the direction of the trend, and therefore acted on.

Sell Order An order that will initiate a short position or close out a long.

Sell Out a Long The act of selling an open long position back to the market.

Sell Short Taking a position in the market that will profit from falling prices.

Sell Signal A signal, according to one's strategy, that will indicate a good spot to go short or to close out a long.

Session A trader's personal time span devoted to the market. More officially, a session points to either the Asian, European or American session that together make up the 24-hour market of the foreign exchange.

Setup A particular pattern that, under favorable circumstances, may lead to a valid trade. Could be made up of any number of price bars. A trader's edge in the market is a function of how well he can detect his personal setups in a live market environment.

70-tick Chart A chart in which each price bar represents 70 transactions (ticks) in the underlying market. The amount of contracts changing hands within each transaction is irrelevant.

Shakeout Prices taking out a number of protective stops, only to quickly reverse in the other direction again.

Shock Effect Something hitting the market from outside. Could be a macro-economical news release, a speech, an interest rate decision, political unease, terrorist attacks, basically anything. For as long as traders try to digest the shock, the charts may show extremely volatile movements that sometimes make very little technical sense.

Shooting-from-the-hip The act of trading without a sound plan of attack, usually resulting in numerous trades randomly entered and exited.

Short-term Chart A fast chart set up to accommodate a scalper's plan of attack. The price bars are usually set to last no more than a couple of minutes each, and not seldom much shorter than that. From a scalper's perspective, the short-term chart creates many swings, rallies and ranges, and thus opportunities, all through the day.

Short/ Short Position/ Short Trade A position initiated to profit from falling prices.

Shoulder *See* Arch.

Sideline Bear A trader with a bearish view on the market intending to take a position to profit from falling prices. A sideline bear's participation will benefit all bears already in the market, because the pressure of his selling may push prices further down.

Sideline Bull A trader with a bullish view on the market intending to take a position to profit from rising prices. A sideline bull's participation will benefit all bulls already in the market, because the pressure of his buying may push prices further up.

Sideways Progression *See* Consolidation.

Signal Bar A price bar to signal an entry on a break of one of its extremes. It usually shows up as part of a group of bars that make up a particular setup.

Signal Line A line across a number of bars sharing equal extremes within a setup. If it gets broken, it may indicate a valid reason to enter a trade in the direction of the break.

Simple Moving Average An indicator computing the exact average price of the last so many closing prices.

Skip The act of rejecting an otherwise valid trade on account of unfavorable conditions.

Slippage Getting filled on a market order at a less favorable price than intended. The reason could be a fast market, a slow platform or a trader not reacting alert enough.

SMA *See* Simple Moving Average.

Solid Break A well-built break that has definitely cleared the area it broke away from.

Spike A sudden sharp move ripping through the chart.

Spread *See* Bid-Ask Spread.

Spread Mark-up A no-commission broker's way to earn income. Since no fees are collected for execution, traders have to pay the difference between the bid and ask, which is artificially widened to their disadvantage.

Squeeze A gradual buildup of pressure below a level of resistance or on top of a level of support. A vital ingredient to a successful break; it is often seen in range break situations. Not only does the squeeze build up pressure to make prices break the range's protective shield, it may also block prices from crawling back in after a break is set.

Stagnation Prices unable to move further along their original intent, but not pulling back much, either. Could be totally harmless to an open position, or a first sign of trouble. If it develops into a possible reversal pattern, a trader in position should be on the alert to bail out.

Stop/ Stop-loss *See* Protective Stop.

Stop-out A position exited at the point of the protective stop.

Strategy *See* Method.

Supply Willingness of participants to sell short, or dump existing long positions. Causes downward pressure on prices.

Support becoming Resistance A former support level now offering resistance when touched from below.

Support A level or area from which prices previously bounced up (new chart support). Also, a level or area, yet to be touched, from which prices may bounce up (former chart resistance).

Swing A firm price move or trend.

Tail In candlestick charting, a typical bar is made up of a body and two tails. The body shows the prices between the open and close, the tails, when present, portray the extremes on either side of the body. Should a bar open on its high and close at its low, or vice versa, then no tails are formed because the extremes are caught within the body itself. A bar can also have one tail. To the candlestick aficionado, the size of the body and tails of any bar, and certainly of those at crucial spots, can be very telling. *See also* Body.

Target A projected spot in the chart at which profit will be taken.

Target Order A pending order to close out a profitable trade at a specified spot that has yet to be reached.

Tease A premature range break that stems from a situation that shows insufficient buildup.

Tease Break Trap A spot at which traders act on a range break that has shown insufficient buildup. This break runs a high chance of failure, but is usually not so violently countered as can be the False Break Trap.

Technical Analysis The process of assessing the possible future direction of prices based on technical criteria derived from a chart. The technical analyst differs strongly from his lifelong antagonist, the fundamental analyst, who shuns the chart and solely derives his clues from macro-economical or instrument related evidence. Naturally, a combination of both approaches makes sense, particularly when investing. To the scalper, however, the chart is the sole source of information.

Tell-tale Sign A particular market event showing up in the chart that offers a technical clue.

Technical Stop A protective stop placed at a level that makes sense technically and still complies with a trader's chosen risk-model. If the technical stop would incur a loss that perforates a chosen risk per trade boundary, and a tighter stop could not be justified, then it is best to let the trade pass by.

Test of Breakout Prices traveling back to a spot from where they broke out not long before.

Test of High Prices traveling up to reach the level of a former high.

Test of Last Resistance Prices traveling down to the last level that offered resistance before they broke up. This level may now offer support. It does not necessarily reflect the most obvious support level in the chart.

Test of Last Support Prices traveling up to the last level that offered support before they broke down. This level may now offer resistance. It does not necessarily reflect the most obvious resistance level in the chart.

Test of Low Prices traveling down to reach the level of a former low.

30-second Chart A chart in which each price bar represents the movement of prices within a 30 second frame. A one hour frame will contain 120 of these bars. Under normal conditions, this is quite similar to a 70-tick chart, yet the differences can be very visible in setup situations, and most certainly when the activity speeds up.

Tick A transaction between two parties. Also the minimum distance price can move from one spot to the next. In the foreign exchange, a tick equals a pipette (tenth of a pip). On a stock, for instance, a tick would represent the movement of one cent.

Tick Chart A chart in which each price bar represents a certain amount of transactions (ticks) that took place in the underlying market.

Tick Counter A counter, usually displayed on the vertical axis of the chart, that counts down the number of ticks to go in a tick bar before a new bar gets printed.

Time Frame Chart A chart in which each bar represents the movement of prices within a specified duration of time.

Tipping Point The dividing line between a running trade's validity and invalidity. If the level is breached, the trade needs to be scratched. Can be adjusted along the way, but in the direction of the target only. *See also* Trailing a Stop.

Top A level in the chart from which prices moved down.

Topping Market After a substantial rise, the chart starts to show a series of more or less equal tops, suggesting supply.

Topping Pattern/ Formation A series of bars forming a top or multiple tops, suggesting resistance in the chart.

Touch A bar hitting a level of technical significance.

Trade A position in the market.

Trade Invalidity A situation in which an open position has lost its validity due to a technical level being breached. Invalid trades need to be exited.

Trade Management The process of managing an open position on its way to either target or stop.

Trade-or-Skip The decision to either take or reject a trade. To be made in a setup situation that does not present itself in textbook fashion or in one that shows up under slightly unfavorable conditions.

Trade Validity A situation in which an open position is technically valid. Valid trades need to be left alone until they either reach target or lose validity.

Trading Plan A trader's complete set of specified guidelines on how to trade his method.

Trailing a Stop The stepwise process of moving a stop beneath or above an open position to reduce risk exposure on the trade, or to protect paper profits from being fully taken back.

Transaction A buyer and a seller doing business with each other in the marketplace.

Trend A prolonged move, either up or down, following the path of least resistance. Can contain many countertrend moves. But overall, the direction of the trending move will prevail until the countermoves get too powerful for the trend to continue.

Trend-equals-trend A three-step technical phenomenon that shows a trend followed by a sideways consolidation or pullback and then followed by a move that shows strong similarity to the earlier trend. The third move is often anticipated.

Trending Market A market that shows strong signs of one-directional pressure, regardless of the pullbacks in it. Is best played with-trend.

Trendline A line, horizontal or angular, connecting the highs or lows of a particular pattern or trend.

Trigger An event in the chart that causes a strong reaction among participants.

Triple Bottom Bottoming formation showing three more or less equal bottoms.

Triple Top Topping formation showing three more or less equal tops.

Tug-o-war *See* Bull/Bear fight.

20-bar Exponential Moving Average Exponential moving average that computes the average closing price of the last 20 bars; the computation is tweaked to put a little more weight to the most recent closing prices.

20ema *See* 20-bar Exponential Moving Average.

20-level Another round number level. Could be 20, 40, 60 and 80. Though slightly inferior to the major round number levels of 00 and 50, the vacuum effect, as well as the market's tendency to bounce, can also be spotted around the 20-levels.

2-percent Model A risk-model that allows for a maximum loss of 2 percent of capital on any failed trade. By applying the model on a daily basis, the volume per trade needs to be adjusted each new day in correspondence with the actual account balance.

Ultimate Tipping Point Initial stop-out level on a new trade. This stop can only be adjusted in the direction of the target and never the other way. Therefore, from the moment of entry a trader knows his maximum loss on the trade. If the tipping point gets hit, a trader immediately exits his position. This point usually lies at a more economical spot than the automated stop order as part of the preset bracket. That one merely serves as a safety net.

Unfavorable Conditions The underlying price action of the overall market not supporting a potential setup.

Units A measurement of volume in the foreign exchange.

Uptrend Prices trending up.

Vacuum Effect Tendency of prices to be sucked towards a specific resistance or support level due to the reluctance of traders to counter the move before these levels are reached. Often seen in front of the major round number levels.

Valid Setup A setup that should be acted on when broken.

Valid Trade An open position that has not yet met a technical development that forces it to be scratched.

Variance A term used in probability theory. Basically an outcome that departs from the mean. Most any trader will understand that even the best looking trades may fail miserably. However, the inevitable losing streak, when quite extended, tends to worry many traders to the point of questioning the validity of an otherwise sound approach. Chances are, it is just variance and thus part of the game.

Volatile Market A market showing relatively wild moves going both ways.

Volume In the foreign exchange, volume is determined by the amount of units assigned to a particular position.

Volume of the Day The amount of units to assign to one's trades, adjusted every new day, in order to allow a chosen risk model to comply with the actual account balance. *See also* Compounding.

Wiggle Room The space a struggling trade is allowed to find its way into positive territory.

Winner A trade exited for profit.

W-pattern A distinctive bottoming formation represented by two bottoms that together form the letter W. Can be rather sharp with the lows close together, but also more elongated across a wider horizontal span. Is perceived to be a reversal pattern (bullish).

00 Round Number/ 00-level Full cent level. The most prominent round number level in the chart.

Zone Area around a level of importance.

Index

Z

00 Round Number/ 00-level, 57, 143, 151, 155, 187, 289, 299, *see* Round Number Level

Printed in Great Britain
by Amazon.co.uk, Ltd.,
Marston Gate.